# ALTERNATIVES TO INDEPENDENCE

*When you want to see if a picture of someone or something is distorted or not, hold it up against a mirror. The flaws will become more obvious than they would be to the naked eye.*
Common wisdom in drawing classes

*Revolutionary rhetoric is all geared in one direction, and it's hard to make yourself understood if you're trying to go the other way.*
Westlake, 1972: 121 (on the Anguilla revolution, 1969).

*How strange is the one who dreams in truth of a beautiful reality, and then when he endeavours to fashion it into form but cannot succeed, doubts the dream and blasphemes the reality and distrusts the beauty!*
Gibran, 1991: 148.

# Alternatives to Independence

## Explorations in Post-Colonial Relations

HELEN M. HINTJENS
*Centre for Development Studies*
*University of Wales Swansea*

# Dartmouth

**Aldershot • Brookfield USA • Singapore • Sydney**

Published by
Dartmouth Publishing Company Limited
Gower House
Croft Road
Aldershot
Hants GU11 3HR
England

Dartmouth Publishing Company
Old Post Road
Brookfield
Vermont 05036
USA

**British Library Cataloguing in Publication Data**
Hintjens, Helen M.
  Alternatives to Independence:
  Explorations in Post-Colonial Relations
  I. Title
  325.3144

**Library of Congress Cataloging-in-Publication Data**
Hintjens, Helen M.
    Alternatives to independence : explorations in post-colonial
  relations / Helen M. Hintjens.
      p.    cm.
  Includes bibliographical references and index.
    ISBN 1-85521-069-X
    1. Decolonization. I. Title.
  JV151.H55   1995
  325'.3144'09045–dc20                                    94-19402
                                                              CIP

ISBN 1 85521 069 X

Printed and bound in Great Britain by Antony Rowe Ltd,
Chippenham, Wiltshire

# Contents

# Acknowledgements

First of all, I would like to acknowledge my continuing debt to my former doctoral supervisor, Jean Houbert. Secondly, I thank the Nuffield Foundation who funded research work in the French Overseas Departments in 1989-90 (Reunion in the Indian Ocean, and Guadeloupe and Martinique in the Caribbean). They also provided a second grant that permitted me to work in the immigration and asylum field, in several activist organisations. Sue Shutter from JCWI (Joint Council for the Welfare of Immigrants) in London organised a three-week placement for me there. She and her colleagues were extremely helpful. Claire Rodier and Patrick Mony in GISTI (Groupe d'Information et de Soutien aux Travailleurs Immigrés) in Paris also arranged a three week placement for me in their offices. Many people agreed to be interviewed, including numerous immigration lawyers and advice workers. There are many others I should thank for their stimulating comments and suggestions, including Robin Cohen, Dario Castiglioni and James MacDonald. I would also like to thank Mark for his chivvying and meals, Hamid for his encouragement; Nedira, Khadiga and Theresa for their friendship. Without the enormous solidarity and practical help of Michael Jovic, who helped produce the camera-ready copy, this book would have remained eternally in draft form.

Finally I thank my siblings and parents, and my young son Ben, for all their support and love.

I will be grateful for comments and responses from readers on all or part of this volume. Please write to me at the Centre for Development Studies, University of Wales Swansea, Singleton Park, Swansea SA2 8PP, Wales.

# Introduction – Alternatives to Independence

*...that there still exists this automatic assumption about the overlap between the boundaries of the state's citizens and 'the nation' is one expression of the naturalising effect of the hegemony of one collectivity and its access to ideological apparatuses of both state and civil society.*
Anthias, F. & N. Yuval-Davis, 1992: 21-2.

*It has been the main function of national cultures, which are systems of representation, to represent what is in fact the ethnic hotchpotch of modern nationality as the primordial unity of 'one people'.*
Hall, S., 1992: 6.

In 1956, with the introduction of apartheid, new race laws split up 'mixed' families, concentrated in Cape Province. Mothers, husbands, sons, sisters, were divided by colour; some became white; some Asian; some black, to be retribalised. Others, who did not fit any of these categories, became coloureds, a classification that belied the very idea of racial separation advocated by apartheid. The colour of love[1] was thus defined in terms of pigmentation and external physical features, and not even in terms of kinship or 'blood'.

The British Nationality Act of 1981 created several new categories of British nationals. The inhabitants of the remaining colonies were no longer citizens of the United Kingdom-and-Colonies (CUKC). As well as British Citizens, there were Citizens of the British Dependent Territories, with each territory establishing its own immigration and nationality laws. Any former CUKCs "left over from these two categories would become British Overseas Citizens, with no right of abode anywhere" (Dummett & Nicol, 1990: 242-3). At the time, these changes caused such alarm that a South African style apartheid was feared. "Rumours spread that black people's citizenship was going to be taken away from them, as a prelude to repatriation" (ibid: 245).

In Rumania it has been reported that the post-communist government has been directing its energies towards excluding and persecuting the Hungarian minority of two and a half million people (*Guardian*, 13.4.1992). Meanwhile the Rumanian opposition parties, preferring an expansionist rather than an exclusionary policy, demanded that the government take over the former Soviet Republic of Moldavia, a former province of 'Greater Rumania'.

These three examples show the Janus faces of nationalism expressed in their most dangerous form as the impulse to cut out, or excise, and the impulse to absorb and draw in. The process of unravelling of the federal state of Yugoslavia; of British nationality; of South Africa; of "the complex weave of interlocking and inter-mingled communities" has in each case resulted in a type of collective self-disembowelling. The reintegration of the bantustans into the Republic of South Africa prior to the first general elections in April 1994 suggests, perhaps more clearly than any other recent event, the retrogressive nature of segregation as a solution to the colonial problem, and the liberatory power of the simple, apparently reformist language of equal rights.

As these examples suggest, individuals form part of a minority or a majority, depending on where they are located, and how state boundaries are drawn and redrawn (Eriksen, 1993). This inclusion and exclusion of different groups is the stuff of which war, international relations and decolonisation have been made since the creation of the first states. In the present international system, the state's boundary defines the inside and outside of citizenship. The boundary represented in nationality law is physically, but also legally and politically, defined; it is subject to policy changes which may have nothing to do with 'objective' factors such as territory, place of birth, language or religion. In the present international system, the national collectivity is given prior legitimacy in claims to statehood; the claim to rights of self-determination is normally grounded in a recognised national identity among a particular group of people. Possibly the only exception to this in the post-war period has been the legitimacy of claims for separate statehood from colonial territories, grounded in an anti-colonial identity. In either case, there is no simple formula that will allow the disentangling of the national, or post-colonial, entity from the complexity of multiple identities and shared spaces. As Eve Sedgewick suggests,

> Even a simple exercise like attempting to compare the 'nationality' of a Gypsy in Germany...that of a Turkish guest-worker in France, and that of a person who works in Johannesburg, lives in Soweto and has an official assignment to a 'homeland' s/he may never have seen, suggests how ragged and unrationalised may be not only the rights and entailments, but also the definitional relations of the habitation/nation system of the modern world. (Sedgewick, 1992: 240)

Citizenship is generally regarded as a sign of a person's national identity, and as Benedict Anderson points out, in the contemporary international system everyone is supposed to have a nationality from birth (Anderson, 1983: 14). In practice, the stateless people created by apartheid, by British nationality law and by the war in former Yugoslavia are a living testimony to the illegitimate redrawing of boundaries for the purposes of ethnic exclusion.

One of the abiding features of the present international system is the primacy of national over individual self-determination. This has been sharply accentuated by the recent break-up of the former Soviet Union, the last of the large (neo-)imperial empires. According to international law, while states cannot prevent people from leaving, no state has a reciprocal duty to admit the people thus allowed to leave. This is taken a step further in recent moves to 'voluntarily' repatriate refugees and asylum seekers. Such expulsions have been carried out, for example, by the UK in the case of Vietnamese refugees in Hong Kong and in the US refusal to allow Haitians to apply for asylum.

International law recognises the individual as a belonging of the state of which they carry the citizenship; as such they are its responsibility alone. An injury to an individual national is an affront to that person's home country (Akehurst, 1984: 87). In practice, the probability that a state will intervene to defend the rights of its citizens abroad will depend on conditions at home, and on the diplomatic and economic power of the home state.

Boundaries, and our idea of boundaries, are hardened by bounded language. 'Ethnic cleansing' is one particularly divisive and destructive political euphemism. It reinforces the implication that inter-ethnic mixing of people in families and community life involves the creation of human waste (multi-cultural community organisations and mixed offspring). In the face of this quasi-eugenic form of nationalism, it is well to point out the geo-political and power considerations that lead to stirring up of group identities, the hardening of perceived boundaries and distrust between groups.

> ...social and cultural facts do not present themselves in units in which social space and geographical space coincide, and in which constituent groups are arranged and stratified in the tiers of a common, all-embracing architecture. On the contrary, we see various activities cross-cutting one another...yielding pluralistic patchworks, rather than a bounded homogeneity of social warp and woof. (Wolf, 1988: 757)

This point is similar to that made in the quotation from Stuart Hall at the start of this chapter.  Attempting to unravel what is fused and mingled, ethnic cleansing is bound to fail in its project of creating one homogeneous people.

It is interesting how frequently a gendered form of boundary emerges in hardened nationalist thinking; a double standard usually operates concerning personal and collective morality, depending on the sex of the person.  At the level of popular and symbolic political expression, the  mixing of one's 'own' women  with 'other' men constitutes a national shame, and brings moral degradation to the nation as a whole.  For men, the reverse is true; for 'our' men to have sexual relations, and reproduce, with 'other' women involves no defilement of the nation, ethnic group or culture, but rather its aggrandisement. If this logic can be extended to the political level, then ethnic separatism implies a one-way segregation and conquest in another sense.  In short this represents "the working out of patriarchal assumptions in space" (Women and Geography Study Group, 1984: 134).  The implications of the gendered discourse of nationalism for post-colonial relations will be explored later.

The scope of this book is less ambitious than this opening suggests.  First, it will explore the wider meaning of decolonisation by presenting some very atypical, highly original examples of post-colonial relations.  These examples defy the equation usually made between decolonisation and the break-up of former empires into nationally distinct sovereign states.  On the basis of these special cases, it will be suggested (though, in the nature of things, never proved) that decolonisation is possible without the creation of separate, independent statehood for the former colonies.  Self-determination resulting in separate statehood can be equated with a move towards decolonised relations only if it results in a more, and not less, equal relationship between the inhabitants of the former colonial powers and those of the formerly colonised territories.

Historically, decolonisation of overseas colonies through absorption has been relatively rare.  However, starting in 1946, this is what has taken place in the four French Overseas Departments: Reunion in the Indian Ocean; Martinique and Guadeloupe in the East Caribbean and Guyane on the Atlantic coast of South America. All four DOM (*départements d'outre-mer*), and to a lesser extent the associated TOM (*territoires d'outre-mer*) are examples of the incorporation into the North of former colonial peoples and countries located in the South. As they straddle the borders of two 'worlds', careful study of the French DOM may permit us to say something more generally about the nature of the relationship between North and South in a post-colonial era (Robinson, 1954). Many assumptions of the post-colonial era appear to be contradicted by the very existence of such territories. As integral parts of the French state and of the European Community located in the Caribbean and the South-West Indian Ocean, their position contrasts sharply with that of the few remaining British colonies in various parts of the world. In the latter, the present inhabitants' status is virtually analogous to that of the so-called citizens of South Africa's former bantustans. As Simon Winchester put it in his book *Outposts*, when a British Dependent Territory Citizen, a category of person created by the 1981 Nationality Act: "arrives at the immigration counter at Southampton docks [or at Heathrow] he might for all his loyalty and distant patriotism, be a Mongolian, a Uruguayan or a Turk" (Winchester, 1985: 87).

The poignancy of this is all the greater when it is recalled how strong pro-British sentiment has been in some of the remaining colonial territories. In the British Caribbean colony of Anguilla, as Donald Westlake observed, the 'Revolution' of 1967-9 against statehood with St Kitts and Nevis was misunderstood by Britain. The aim "wasn't really independence at all, but was simply an effort to switch sovereignties from the poor and hated St Kitts to wealthy and well-liked Great Britain" (Westlake, 1972: 76). British soldiers invaded the island only to find Union-Jack-waving Anguillans lining the streets. The seriousness of the lessons to be drawn from this episode in Anguilla's relations with Britain should not be obscured by the small size of the island. Similarly, the importance of the issues dealt with in this volume should not be obscured by the specialised and very particular nature of the case studies used.

After reviewing the main themes in Chapter 1, Chapter 2 compares the relations of Britain and France with their non-sovereign Caribbean territories. Perhaps the least known of the French overseas departments, the island of Reunion in the South-West Indian Ocean, is the focus of Chapter 3. Chapter 4 looks at the equally unusual case of French Guyane, where decolonisation is complicated by the unfinished nature of the colonisation process itself. A heavy focus on the Caribbean can be defended on methodological grounds, since the region is rich in comparative material. As Philip Mason has pointed out, for students of comparative social change, the Caribbean seems to be:

...a natural laboratory, illustrating in immense variety the problems which men (*sic*) face in their social, political and economic life; it is a microcosm, or rather a constellation of microcosms, better adapted perhaps than any other part of the globe to the study of ideas about race and their consequences. (Mason, 1970: 275)

In particular, in this book we will be considering French and British ideas about 'race' and national identity as they are translated into two field of policy: in the Caribbean non-sovereign territories, and in immigration and nationality policies.

Voluntary and involuntary mass movements of people are a feature of the contemporary world that appears to defy the idea of hard and fast state boundaries built on the exercise of national sovereignty. Of course, this movement is not new; and has continued over hundreds of years, mainly out of Western Europe and Africa, around the colonial Empires. It is only since independence in the 1960s that population movements have sharply acce-lerated from the South to the North (Castles & Miller, 1993). In particular, large-scale migrations have been associated with wars of independence and the rigours of post-colonial reconstruction.

One example considered in this book is the case of Algerian immigration into France, mainly from the 1960s to the present. This is the subject matter of Chapter 5, where we attempt to construct a model that relates inter-state negotiations and conflict to different outcomes for individual freedom of movement. Chapter 6 discusses and attempts to dismantle some common mis-perceptions which seem to (dis)colour much discussion of immigration and asylum policy in the present period. Ten common arguments against immi-gration, asylum and acquisition of citizenship are critically examined and some alternative explanations and logics are proposed. In the final chapter, a syn-cretic, feminist-humanist perspective is brought to bear on key notions such as self-determination, autonomy and liberation. This last chapter represents an attempt to clarify what post-colonial relations might mean when detached from notions of national self-determination and other collective versions of liber-ation. We also discuss the relative positions of women and men in relation to nationalist and post-colonial forms of politics. It is hoped that the final result will be to produce some alternatives to the rather black and white dichotomies so prevalent in the literature on post-colonial relations: dependence and independence; collective and individual rights; indigenous versus alien institutions, and integration versus separation.

By focusing on some exceptional forms of North-South post-colonial relations, it is hoped that the present study will highlight some crucial aspects of contemporary post-colonial relationships more generally. It seeks to do this by inversion - a technique suggested by the mirror-image formula presented at the start of this book. Instances and places where national, collective self-determination has apparently not had priority over the individual self-determination and the guaranteeing of social and economic as well as political rights to individual citizens are rare. We hope that by exploring some alternatives to formal political independence, which tends to collapse collective and individual rights, it may be possible, in some modest way, to shed some light on what 'decolonised' post-colonial relations between people might look like.

## Notes

1. This is the title of a recent book by Yasmin Alibhai-Brown and Anne Montague (1992), *The Colour of Love: Mixed Race Relationships*, Virago, London. This book formed the basis of a television programme with the same name transmitted on BBC2 on Monday 19 July 1993, produced by Salim Salam.

# 1 The Context: What are Post-Colonial Relations?

*Suppose that...the 'underdeveloped' and underprivileged population had not conceptualised their discontent in terms of nationalism, but had simply concentrated on a struggle to achieve full citizenship within the existing political units...*
Gellner, 1964: 177.

*...ultimately it is a question of how the great wealth created by hundreds of years of Empire should be divided up. The numbers who stake their claims are many. Those whose claims are recognised are few, and that essentially is the function of immigration law.*
MacDonald, 1983: 20.

## Introduction

These two quotations encapsulate the main concerns of this book. One is to consider the examples of the French overseas departments, where it appears that what Gellner describes did indeed take place. Another concern is to explore under what circumstances immigration and the acquisition of a new citizenship might be regarded as a type of 'decolonisation' at the individual level.[1] Colonial relationships are usually exclusionary, hierarchical and unequal, and may involve apartheid, expulsion or even extermination, as well as paternalist dominance and forced assimilation (Mason, 1970; Memmi, 1990; Fanon, 1963).[2]  Would genuinely post-colonial relations not be marked by greater equality in access to power, resources and information?  Can this not be seen as the outcome of immigration and full citizenship of the former colonial power?  From this perspective, the extent to which immigration and nationality laws of the former colonial powers are inclusive and non-discriminatory may be regarded as an indication of the comparative degree of openness of these states to post-colonial demands for equality, full citizenship rights and freedom of movement.

Immigration and assimilation are ambiguous terms that nonetheless are central to this study; their use cannot be avoided.  As the *Economist* magazine commented a decade ago, immigration in particular is "a muddled, emotive codeword...All too readily people lump together refugees, migrant workers and citizens who are Asian or black as immigrants" (*Economist*, 2.11.1985). As Colin Holmes has observed, the use of the term has been stretched over recent decades to include children born in the UK (Holmes, 1988: 4).

These are not mere semantic points: popular (mis)perceptions have been consolidated by legislative changes which have, in fact, retrospectively deprived certain categories of citizens of their former citizenship rights. Immigrants have been created through legal distinctions between patrial and non-patrial people born in the UK (the key to nationality becomes the nationality of one's grandparents, not one's own place of birth, according to the principle of *jus sanguinis*).  Changes in nationality and immigration law have a practical function for the state, as Ian MacDonald's quotation suggests.  The law defines which individuals may be incorporated and which excluded from the 'national' collectivity, as represented by the state.

The notion of assimilation is much less in vogue today than it was even twenty years ago.  'Assimilation' may be defined as the process by which previously distinct cultures come to form a new whole.  In practice, the term has usually been associated with a colonial policy that sought to obliterate cultural difference by forcing the colonised to take on the language, thought modes and behaviour of the coloniser (Eriksen, 1993: 123).  It was analogous to the European powers' notion of a civilising mission (Aron, 1966: 224).  In France, since the war of Algerian independence, assimilation has lost most of its positive and left-wing connotations, to be replaced by the term 'integration', which is much more neutral.  Integration can be defined as "a situation of cohesion, deriving from consent rather than coercion", and more specifically as the "process whereby a minority group...adapts itself to a majority society and is accorded by the latter equality of rights and treatment" (Bullock &

Stallybrass, 1977: 314). Though lacking the emotional overtones, the term can be used to mean almost the same thing as assimilation.

Even integration sometimes seems incomprehensible to British comment-ators, so used are they to the segregationist assumptions that underpin the Anglo-Saxon view of inter-group relations. A recent reviewer of a major study on racism in France asked "why a book dedicated to attacking racism should concentrate so heavily on the integration of minorities" (O'Shaugnessy, 1993: 59). With the recent experience of South Africa in mind, this would seem rather obvious; the question is itself surprising. The same review also acknowledges the possibility, even today, of appealing to a "potentially hegemonic 'mainstream' anti-racism" within the French context (ibid.: 55). It is unlikely that this was ever possible in the British context, where there has long been an officially sanctioned antipathy to any notion of assimilation of non-European colonised people.

What David Lowenthal observed of the Caribbean has been equally true of post-colonial Britain, namely that "Emulation by non-whites, as whites saw it, ought to stop short of such goals as social equality and high status" (Lowenthal, 1972: 74). Inclusive equal rights, however, are the very essence of integration, and of any acceptable form of assimilation. It is hard to see any other approaches to human relations that can provide an antithesis to segregationist theories of irreconcilable (and even desirable) ethnic hierarchies based on supposedly immutable differences.

**The Apparent Impossibility of Assimilation**

During the colonial period, the assimilation doctrine, generally closely associated with Latin rather than Anglo-Saxon political philosophies, was honoured more in the breach than in the observance. The two differing traditions may have been rooted in the historical needs and circumstances of the British and the French, Portuguese and Spanish colonies rather than in purely ideological differences (Thornton, 1978: 39-41, Betts, 1961). Colonial ideologies of assimilation affected the outlooks and expectations of the colonisers, and of the intellectual and political elites that emerged among the colonised. Since at least 1789 the end-point of French colonial rule has been viewed by many as full equality of legal rights and duties within the Republic (Aron, 1960: 159). The assimilationist doctrine is thus deeply rooted in the Jacobinism of the French Revolution. As a universalist doctrine, it seeks to break down distinctions and boundaries between the internal and external rather than reinforce them (Brunschwig, 1964; Eriksen, 1993: 109). Lamine Guèye, a Senegalese lawyer, described the francophone African elite as:

> brave and farsighted men...who found themselves engaged in the struggle to translate into concrete reality, transcending frontiers and racial differences, those principles of liberty and equality which in Africa were disowned by the very people who had proclaimed them most solemnly, even having them engraved on the frontage of all their public buildings. (Cited in Hargreaves, 1969: 245)

Unless the powerful hold of these ideas is appreciated, it is impossible to understand the request in 1946 by the French Communist Party sections in the former *vieilles colonies* of Reunion, Martinique, Guadeloupe and French Guyane for full French citizenship and departmental status. This came at a time when local leaders in the British colonies were beginning to assert that equality within the British Empire was simply impossible (Davidson, 1993).

Even before the end of the Second World War, after the experience of occupation under Vichy, the principle of a single French Empire without internal boundaries was reasserted at the Brazzaville Conference in 1944. Again, the reality did not match the principle. The *Union Française* remained subordinate to the French National Assembly, and only a tiny minority of the inhabitants of the larger African colonies were entitled to vote in national elections. Thus, the rest of the population remained "neither French nor free" (Smith, 1978: 74; see also Grosser, 1984: 44-5). Moreover, as French colonial subjects, they did not possess the right of separate self-determination.

It is worth remembering that until at least 1960 assimilation was a doctrine associated with the French Left rather than the Right. As Herbert Lüthy observed of the situation in Algeria: "...autonomy was even more inconceivable to the 'revolutionary' colonial reformers of the French Left, than to the hard boiled colonialists of the Right" (Lüthy, 1955: 219). Indeed, supporters of integration and full citizenship for colonial subjects, in the form of *départementalisation*, were sometimes regarded as subversives, and branded communists. "[A]ny political group which sought to secure for the natives of the French colonies the substance of [social and political]...rights" was stigmatised (Robinson, 1984: 26). In 1936, for example, one group campaigning for departmental status for Madagascar was banished to an outlying area of the colony (Deschamps, 1968: 47). The Algerian war of independence discredited the assimilation doctrine in the eyes of the colonised elite. It also destroyed any hopes that the benefits of French citizenship would be extended to the Algerian departments of 'overseas France' on the same terms as in the metropolis. Not considering himself a citizen, the colonised likewise loses all hope of seeing his son achieve citizenship. Before long, renouncing citizenship himself, he no longer includes it in his plans, eliminates it from his paternal ambitions, and allows no place for it in his teachings. (Memmi, 1990: 163)

In a challenging recent study, Basil Davidson sees a similar process at work in nineteenth century British West Africa. Many recaptives and other (usually forcibly) assimilated Africans believed strongly in the value of achieving British standards of education and public morality. Yet Anglophone West Africans faced growing hostility from the imperial power, which sought to impose its ideology of racial segregation (Davidson, 1992: 25-47). Albert Memmi also observes that colonial subjects who emulate the coloniser do not gain acceptance as equals, and may also lay themselves open to ridicule (Memmi, 1990: 190). "It is the colonised who is the first to desire assimilation, and it is the coloniser who refuses him" (Memmi, 1990: 191).

That Davidson and Memmi come to similar conclusions regarding colonial relations may seem surprising, for it is often asserted that the French assimilated and absorbed, while the British kept themselves apart (Mason, 1970: 24, 90-91). One study noted that the British lack of enthusiasm for direct representation in the Parliament for colonial people may have been due to the fear that 'colonial members' might "exercise a decisive voice in purely UK affairs" (Robinson, 1984: 37). It is certainly difficult for colonisers to insulate their home affairs from the colonised, and probably impossible. For state policy, distinctions between British and French approaches to colonial relations are very clear, and have tangible consequences in the present period for the former colonial subjects. There are many parallels between the two former Empires, however, in terms of the impact of colonialism on relations between the colonised and the coloniser.

## Colonialism is Not a One-way Street

No matter how it may try, a colonising society cannot insulate itself completely from the mutual, and unequal, interaction that is colonialism. However segregationist the colonisers' policies may be, they cannot prevent a certain blurring of categories of the colonised and coloniser, of what is internal and external. This may take place through marriage, mixing through concubinage, immigration from the former colonies to the metropolis, dependence on armed divisions of the colonised, or through the servant-master relationship. Cultural mixing, interpenetration and overlap are not peculiarly post-modern or contemporary; they were integral to the colonial relationship from the very start, however enormous the power differentials in material and military terms between the parties involved.

Efforts to insulate the home country from the 'imperial chickens coming home to roost' have a long history in Britain, and have mostly proved futile. When exclusion takes place, it may be explained as necessary to protect those vulnerable to assimilation by others. In a recent study, a revealing example is given of the English colonisers' dread of being affected and corrupted by the Irish whom they sought to lord it over unilaterally. Unfortunately for them, the English also depended on the Irish for child care, for soldiers, and even for clothing appropriate to the Irish weather (Jones & Stallybrass, 1992: 162-6).

In 1786 the British government organised the compulsory deportation of twenty thousand free blacks from London to Sierra Leone. Again, one of the reasons given for this decision was the frequency of sexual relations with English working-class women, who were thought to need protecting from this danger (Dummett & Nicol, 1990: 79). The blacks were also seen as a danger because of their good relations with the working-class 'mob' (ibid.: 80). In the context of empire, therefore, divide-and-rule policies were implemented in the metropolis as well as in the colonies. Even so, they could not work completely. For example, some working-class women no doubt gave birth to children whose fathers were now exiled to Sierra Leone. Free blacks could not be completely segregated from the national body politic without the more painful excision of children of mixed parentage.

The fear of confusion, of being 'contaminated' and transformed by that which one seeks to control, is common to all forms of domination, inter-personal and collective. That which is despised as inferior is also, paradoxically, attributed with extraordinary, and sometimes super-human, capacities for disruption and creativity (Ram, 1991). Paul Gilroy observes that the so-called new racism in Britain makes use of military metaphors to stress the vulnerability of the nation to attack from outside and from within (Gilroy, 1992: 53). The new right in Britain and in France also give expression to these fears using metaphors of emasculation, or by identifying their enemies as forms of microbes disturbingly located inside as well as outside the national 'body politic'. For members of the French *Front National*, as Eleanore Kofman puts it: "[i]mmigrant men undermine the virility and primary protective functions of French men and threaten French women". This sense of vulnerability is heightened by "speaking of the nation as a female person to be defended by men against an aggressor" (Kofman, 1993: 9).

During the colonial period, the European colonisers projected an idealised image of the home country in the colonies. These images were to have a long-lasting impact on the European-educated minority. Idealised images of democracy in the metropolis have sometimes also played a subversive part in inspiring democratic anti-colonial movements, and in protests against the worst injustices of forced labour and authoritarian rule in the colonies. However, the shattering of such illusions usually took place on arrival in the colonial metropolis.

In this context, simply demanding equal rights to citizens of the metropolis can be seen as a form of anti-colonial liberatory practice. As Robin Cohen observes in the post-independence context of immigration into France, "for migrants to demand full parity and equality with French workers was not a reformist but a revolutionary demand" (Cohen, 1987: 138-9). This in itself could explain why so many obstacles have been placed in the path of full legal and political assimilation of formerly colonised immigrant communities.

In both Britain and France, a post-colonial sense of confusion exists. It is aggravated by the heavy burden of post-imperial guilt, combined with resentment at what is perceived as rejection and ingratitude from the people of the former colonies. Both the guilt and the sense of impotence and frustration are largely unacknowledged in the public domain, but both are exploited by the Right, which seeks to legitimise the anger, and delegitimise the sense of collective guilt. A common thread in the discourse of the Right is the denial of any historical responsibility for the present poverty and wretchedness of the former colonies. Anger at the 'invasion' of the mother country by people who only recently demanded independence is turned into an anti-immigrant lobby, influencing professional attitudes and even setting the tone of legislation.

Increasing colour prejudice and xenophobia are signs of the "painful transition this country [i.e. Britain], and the overdeveloped world as a whole, is undergoing" (Gilroy, 1992: 51). The pain of loss and the fear of national decline is a commonly expressed feeling among voters for the far Right (for example, Powell, 1968). It is derived from the loss of international stature, and the weakening of national identity domestically in the absence of the common enemies of the past. These included the 'savage hordes' of the colonial imagination. Illusions of cultural superiority and the sense of invulnerability to the opinions of others cannot be sustained after the end of Empire and the appearance, not coincidentally, of mass immigration from the former colonies into the metropolitan heartland.

## Individual Solutions: Immigration and Citizenship

It may be that "...a collective drama will never be settled through individual solutions" (Memmi, 1990: 192). Even so, the struggle for full citizenship rights (both formal and real) within a single state can be seen as a form of individual and even collective self-determination. It can also be seen as a way of subverting, though not ending, the former colonial relationship by overcoming legal and political inequality. Legal and political integration facilitates (even if it does not ensure) the transcendence of the clearly distinct categories of insiders and outsiders, the colonisers and the colonised. This can be contrasted with the strictly limited outcome of conventional decolonisation:

> Decolonisation resulted from a major political change inside the colonial powers and, by creating the Third World, changed the political structure of the world. Nonetheless, decolonisation has not produced true liberation. (Buenor Hadjor, 1992: 95)

Thornton, agreeing with this, argues that decolonisation was a reaction to events that the imperial powers could no longer bring under their control (Thornton, 1978: 280). In the process of hastily granting independence, usually without the complication of referendums or public participation, collective national rights were clearly given precedence over the securing of individuals' economic, social and civil-political rights. There was in the Charter of the UN, according to Kenneth Robinson,

> ...a marked unwillingness to agree that people may cease to be non-self-governing not only as a result of securing international recognition as constituting an independent state, but also as a result of incorporation in a larger unit, more especially...if that larger unit was a colonial power. (Robinson, 1954: 186)

This was sanctioned by the 1960 Declaration on the Granting of Independence to Colonial Countries and People.[3]

In Algeria, France was unable to resolve the colonial conflict and had to pull out. It was observed at the time that, "In order not to be like Guinea, she [i.e. Algeria] would have to be like Brittany" (Aron, 1960: 133). In other words, by 1960 only by granting full legal, political and social equality to all the Algerian population could the French state conceivably have persuaded them to remain within the French Republic. The cost of this was simply too high, and Algeria's national sovereignty took precedence over individual emancipation and individual economic, political and social rights.

The nationality status and citizenship rights of the three million or more Algerians who settled in France after 1962 is now one of the most controversial issues on the national political agenda. It is no coincidence that the nationality code became a burning issue in 1989, the year of the bicentenary of the French Revolution. Any state's definition of nationality underpins that state's claim to popular legitimacy. In May 1993, the newly elected right-wing government placed reform of the country's nationality laws at the top of its political agenda. Before the election of Jacques Chirac as president in 1995, changes made had already undermined the principle that anyone born in France is entitled to become a French national at age eighteen (*Guardian*, 17.8.1993). Those born in France of foreign parents are no longer be able to obtain French nationality automatically. As a result, the principle of *jus solis*, which has existed since 1789, has been violated. According to the International Federation of Human Rights Leagues, the new nationality laws "attack territorial rights in a way that only the Vichy government had previously dared to do" (*FIDH Newsletter*, 1993: 1).

It could be argued that this narrow concern with legal citizenship affects only legal rights, not social conditions or equal opportunities in the real world. But as Stuart Hall reminds us,

> It is true that social identity cannot be reduced to formal legal definitions...but if you are a black woman trying to secure rights of citizenship from the local [social security] office, or an Asian family running the gauntlet of the immigration services...'formal legal definitions' matter profoundly. (Hall, 1992: 7)

The importance of securing fundamental legal rights should be more openly acknowledged now that these very rights (e.g. to freedom of movement, to nationality in the country of residence, to welfare, health and education) are increasingly coming under threat in Western Europe. In this context it starts to become apparent that basic legal rights are a vital terrain of conflict, not only for non-nationals or the children of immigrants, but for the citizens or native population as well.

## Self-determination and the Integration Option

In the case of the former *vieilles colonies* of France (Martinique, Guadeloupe and French Guyane in the Caribbean, and Reunion in the Indian Ocean) full integration and French citizenship were demanded by the Communist Party at the end of the Second World War. These objectives have been retained up to the present time, and there is no serious challenge to the status quo. The status of the DOM (*départements d'outre-mer*) is analogous to that of Hawaii within the United States. All can be regarded as examples of decolonisation through integration. Under international law, this form of decolonisation is regarded as quite acceptable, provided that it is the outcome of a genuinely democratic consultation process, through a referendum for example (Thürer, 1987). According to international law,

> [t]he right of self-determination is the right of a people living in a territory to determine the political and legal status of that territory; for example, by setting up a state of their own or by choosing to become part of another state. (Akehurst, 1984: 248)

The right to choose integration as the outcome of self-determination is formally acknowledged by United Nations Resolution 1541 (1960). From the 1960s until the 1980s, European sovereignty over geographically non-European territories was nonetheless generally regarded as anachronistic and undesirable (Rapaport, 1971: 20-1; Thürer, 1987). This picture may be changing in the 1990s, as the world becomes an increasingly restrictive place, and infringements of asylum rights and freedom of movement make the high cost of formal 'independence' for the former colonies much more apparent than before. Pressures to emigrate have been exacerbated by the impact of economic recession at the global level.

Increasingly, inhabitants of fully integrated territories with rights to freedom of movement within one of the OECD blocs (EC, US) can be regarded as the fortunate few. People from the DOM are among the very few former colonised people who have not been excluded from the division of the wealth of empire, which Ian MacDonald's quotation describes at the start of this chapter. Inhabitants of the DOM have freedom of movement, residence and employment within France and the European Community as a whole. They are also entitled to virtually the same social and welfare provisions as other French citizens. A similar interpretation of recent developments has been made in the case of Puerto Rico (Rivera-Ramos, 1991).

The notion of fixed, phenotypically determined cultural traits was not fashionable in France after the Second World War. The discredited Vichy regime had associated itself with Nazi theories of the hierarchy of races. In this context, the demand for integration by the Communist deputies was intended to transform social relations; as specifically class-based, this demand could be contrasted with the white planters' desire for continued autonomy from the mainland. As one of the overseas deputies said at the time of the debate on the law of departmentalisation: "After fraternity and liberty, we have come to ask you for equality before the law, for equal rights" (*JORFAN*, 14.3.1946: 754). The historical background to this included the reality of forced deculturation through slavery and labour within the plantation system. The formal emancipation of slaves first took place in 1790, ensuring a certain allegiance to the Republic among the non-white population of the French *anciennes colonies*. The law was also self-consciously anti-colonial and anti-racialist, as Aimé Césaire explained in 1946:

...the assimilation of these colonies to the metropolis will be the best possible reply of France to the theoreticians of racism, as well as providing protection against foreign ambitions. (Cited in Nicolas, 1973: 52)

It is significant, however, in explaining some of the problems of legitimacy later encountered by the French state in the Caribbean and Indian Ocean DOM, that 'departmentalisation' and equal citizenship have delivered "advantages for those individuals who happen to be born in the peripheral communities, rather than for those peripheral communities themselves" (Faber, 1984: 19). The implication of this is a process of economic and social integration, in the course of which there emerges a paradox: the more prosperous the individual inhabitants become, the less self-sufficient is the territory in each DOM (Constant, 1992). Collective economic development seems to be sacrificed for the sake of the economic and social advancement of individuals. The perception of the French overseas departments as relatively disadvantaged regions or communities may explain why forms of peripheral nationalist politics have emerged there in the past three decades. This is discussed further in Chapters 2, 3 and 4.

## Resistance to Equality

The British Empire has been dissolved via a prolonged and continuous process of separation, or what one could term segregation. Independence has been the fixed policy of Britain in even the tiniest territories. A logical extension of this has been the internal transformations of British nationality and immigration law. As a result of such changes, most so-called 'New' Commonwealth people without recent ancestral links in Britain have lost access to full citizenship and immigration rights within the old metropolis. As a consequence of this juxta-position of 'New' Commonwealth status and immigration controls, "A person from Grenada or St Lucia may have been a patrial one day, and ceased to be so the next following independence" (MacDonald, 1983: 51). As such, he or she would have lost any rights to enter the 'mother country'.

Ideally, as has been pointed out already, post-colonial relations would take place on the basis of formal equality and respect for cultural difference. If this is to come about, it is necessary to see the former metropolis as itself in need of decolonisation. Transforming a relation of domination and subordination into a more equal one requires changes and adjustments on both sides, and this often seems to be forgotten. The oppressors, in this case the former colonial powers, may also be in need of some kind of liberation: a decolonisation of the mind of the coloniser as well as the colonised (Ngugi, 1986).

The malaise of British and French society since independence of the colonies is apparent in the rise of far right parties, including the *Front National* in France and the National Front and British National Party. As has been mentioned, such revanchist nationalists claim that the end of colonialism leaves the former colonial power vulnerable to a 'reverse colonisation'. In this way, the far right intuitively denies the possibility of more equal post-colonial relations, suggesting instead that one form of hierarchy will be followed by its reversal, and the resulting subjugation of the former oppressors.

By 'flooding in' in excessive numbers, former colonial subjects are seen to be wreaking their revenge on the dominant society. In an incoherent way, the far right may be expressing the collective fear that the former colonised will become fully equal to the former colonisers, thus disproving all the assumptions of superiority on which imperial history, and Britain's or France's sense of greatness, were built. Enoch Powell's words seem to express graphically a subconscious fear that the former slaves' descendants will take revenge for the sins committed against their forebears: "the black man will hold the whip hand over the white man" (cited in Gilroy, 1988: 84). Greater equality is unthinkable to the xenophobic right; it would result in take-over and white men's emasculation.

The sheer destructive power attributed to what are, after all, proportionally relatively small numbers of former colonial people resident in the metropolis is quite remarkable; the whole language of the new fascists is a sort of perverse, undesired and backhanded compliment. The spectre of "white female vulner-ability" also haunts this exclusionary political universe (Kofman, 1993). The military, sexual, botanical, zoological and medical metaphors used increase the emotional impact on potential voters (ibid.; Siedel, 1986).

In the light of such panic, it is difficult to disagree with Ernest Gellner when he says that: "One can hardly feel very confident that Europeans-in-Europe...would behave in a way markedly better than did or do the *colons*" (Gellner, 1964: 178). The West Europeans are currently faced with demands for equal rights within their own state boundaries, from immigrants and their children. The response of the far right is to try to exclude, and eventually to expel, as many as possible of those who, in Ian MacDonald's words, "stake their claims".

## The Single EC Frontier: a New Iron Curtain?

Replying to questions from the *Guardian* newspaper in July 1992, Kenneth Clark, then British Home Secretary, claimed to be startled to hear that the draft

European frontiers proposals, drawn together by the Trevi group of ministers, were a secret document, not open to the press or any other public scrutiny (*Guardian*, 2.7.1992). A press officer from the Home Office commented: "The external frontiers convention...is a secret document because it's not regarded as a completed document and we need the agreement of the other 11 in order to publish it, apparently." The difficulty, according to John Carvel, Home Affairs editor of the *Guardian*, was that "Once the document was completed, it would be unalterable", having been agreed (ibid.).

The serious problem of public access to such negotiations is complicated by the association of the Trevi group with issues of security and counter-terrorism. Why immigration and asylum issues should have been included in these discussions at all is difficult to understand. Even well informed organis-ations and legal groups were not invited to give their advice or opinions on the likely consequences of the proposals, let alone migrants' organisations (*Plein Droit*, 1993; JCWI, 1993a).

The contrasting modes of post-colonial relations among member states of the European Community can be illustrated in the comparison between the British and French non-sovereign territories in the Caribbean (see Chapter 2). Another example is the contrast between Hong Kong and Macao. Whereas the population of Hong Kong have been effectively deprived of British citizen-ship, Macao residents have retained full freedom of movement within the European Community up to 1997 and their incorporation into the People's Republic of China (BBC Radio 4, House of Commons Debate, 19.4.1990). In effect, therefore, the external frontier of the European Community extends to Macao in the same way that it includes the French Overseas Departments.

The contrast between the apparently responsible attitude of Portugal's government in the case of Macao and that of Britain in Hong Kong was pointed out by the MP Bernie Grant, in a Commons debate on the 'points system' for extending full British citizenship to a limited number of Hong Kong residents (ibid.). Similar paradoxes have emerged in the case of Gibraltar, whose inhabitants were almost excluded from full British nationality in 1981, even though they were within the EC boundary from the Spanish point of view (Dummett & Nicol, 1990: 250–51).

Within the single external frontier, freedom of movement is limited to full citizens of EC member states.

People who are not EC citizens will not benefit in any way from the reduction of internal barriers. If they are resident in one EC country, they will have no right to move to another but will still be subject to the immigration laws of the country they wish to move into. (JCWI, 1992: 84)

How are these border controls to be effected? With the Schengen accords of 1992, which abolished internal passport controls between the Benelux and France, there is a danger that colour and appearance may become determinants of whether or not passport control is carried out (House of Lords, 1992: 22). As Gellner noted several decades ago, pigmentation is one visible and ineradicable sign of difference in an anonymous society. It can become a "means of exclusion for the benefit of the privileged" (Gellner, 1964: 168). This will be discussed in more detail in Chapter 6.

At the same time, there is increasing co-ordination between migrant groups within the member states of the EC. An Immigrants' Charter in Europe was drawn up by SOS Racisme in France in 1988. In 1990 a European Migrants Forum was launched in Brussels (JCWI, 1994). Citizenship rights based on residence and birth, and free movement within the EC are among the main demands (*Le Monde*, 20.12.1988; Szondi, 1991: 189). The European Migrants Forum has called for a boycott of passport controls by all foreign residents of the EC.[4] The demand for equal rights is indeed a radical demand and much feared as such. In almost every way, the position of those who might be termed 'immigrant citizens' in Western Europe and the position of the inhabitants of the French overseas departments are exceptional. Their status is exceptional in that they have apparently achieved a more or less equal share in the wealth of Western Europe: wealth to which the imperial possessions made a significant contribution.


## Conclusion

As we have argued, the extension of citizenship that Ian MacDonald mentions is rare. Yet cases where the underprivileged have indeed "conceptualised their discontent in terms of...a struggle for full citizenship within the existing imperial units" are not so rare. Not only is this the case in South Africa for the black majority, but it was equally the case in parts of the Caribbean during the colonial period, and among some of the African population of West Africa. In apartheid South Africa, the theory of separate development effectively meant that all black Africans who lived in designated white areas were allocated to so-called native homelands. One ILO Report describes their situation thus: "often having only the remotest connection with their areas of ethnic origin, in addition to being deprived of the most basic rights, they are increasingly reduced to the status of aliens in their own country by the loss of citizenship" (ILO, 1964: 10). The ANC has conceived the black South African population's liberation in terms of integration within a single polity, with the extension of full citizenship and equal rights to all. The same exclusionary principles that they opposed have, however, been used to structure UK immigration and nationality law, most recently in both the 1981 Nationality Act and the 1988 Immigration Act. Both laws instituted unequal citizenship rights between categories of people solely on the basis of their ancestral kith and kin links with Britain.

Almost nowhere has decolonisation in the West European empires resulted in assimilation and integration on an equal basis. The possible exceptions to this are mainly in the Caribbean, where the Dutch, French and American islands are closely tied to their respective 'mother countries', and the people have varying levels of citizenship rights. In the following chapter, we confine ourselves to comparing the French territories of the Caribbean with some remaining British colonies in the region. The legal and material position of the inhabitants of these territories will illustrate the differences in national policies of the metropolitan states, as well as differences in local political responses at the community and individual levels.

## Notes

1. This chapter is based on a paper first given at the ECPR Workshops in Paris in April 1989, and draws on an article by the author published in *Politics*, 10(2), 1990: 15-19 "Assimilation, Integration, Citizenship and Decolonisation".

2. For an attempt to describe comprehensively the variety of these relations of colonial domination in the context of European colonialism, see Mason (1970), chapter 6, "The European Expansion".

3. Rupert Emerson, for example, considers the referenda of 1958 in the French colonies to be the only examples of "the preordained acceptance of self-determination in the entire decolonisation process" (Emerson, 1960: 300). In fact the DOM are another example, and Puerto Rico another. The most recent cases of collective self-determination through democratic means are the South African bantustans, whose populations voted overwhelmingly for parties that support their reintegration into the Republic of South Africa.

4. *Towards Free Movement? Immigration policy in the European Union after the Maastricht Treaty*, Day Conference organised by JCWI, 26 May 1994, London.

# 2 Post-Colonial Conundrums: Caribbean Examples

*Everything is mobilised so that the colonised cannot cross the doorstep, so that he [sic] understands and admits that this path is dead and assimilation impossible. This makes the regrets of humanists in the mother country sound very hollow.*
Memmi, 1990: 191

*Since the concept of political autochtony assumes a distinction which does not exist in the plantation polities - that between the native institutions and the foreign import - either it cannot be applied, or if it is, it is indistinguishable from its political opposite - political assimilation.*
Munroe, 1972: 178.

## Introduction

1990 was declared the start of the Decade of the Eradication of Colonialism by the United Nations. To mark the thirtieth anniversary of the Declaration on the Granting of Independence to Colonial Counties and Peoples, two regional seminars were held: one in the Caribbean and one in the Pacific. Island developing countries generally were to be regarded as a new category of territories meriting special attention from the international community. There was nothing new about the UN's commitment to ending colonialism. What was perhaps more surprising was the willingness to consider alternatives to outright independence in the case of the smaller, remaining dependencies (Jordan, September 1989).

This chapter will focus on the integration of the former French colonies of Martinique and Guadeloupe into the French Republic since 1946. This will be presented as a possible alternative to independence and sovereignty. The decolonisation experience of the French Caribbean regions will be broadly contrasted with that of former British Caribbean colonies. In particular, attention is paid to another special case, that of Anguilla, a formerly independent island reincorporated into Britain's Empire following the so-called Revolution in 1967-9 against St Kitts and Nevis, with whom the six thousand or so islanders had been incorporated at independence.

This reincorporation has not resulted in integration, however, and so far in the British context demands for full integration have been consistently rejected. Instead, the Anguillans, like the Montserratians, St Helenians and other colonial 'Brits', inhabit constitutional and political oddities known as British Dependent Territories. These are neither colonies in the usual sense (Britain no longer reports to the UN Committee on Decolonisation concerning these territories), nor are they states under international law. They are hybrids; the nationality status of their inhabitants is neither British nor foreign, and is in some ways parallel to that of what were once the 'citizens' of South Africa's former bantustans.

Little places, whether in the Caribbean, the South Atlantic or the Pacific, can and do throw up big principles, especially where the evolution of post-colonial relations are concerned (*Hansard*, 26.10.1983: 308; Thorndike, 1989; Winchester, 1985: 304). In the words of Ted Rowlands, former Minister for the Overseas Countries and Territories at the Foreign and Commonwealth Office (1975-9):

> ...these specks on the horizon, apparently on the surface minor issues, had a propensity to suddenly loom and smack the government straight in the face when it least expected it. The whole history of the dependent territories...has proved that point absolutely. (Quoted in Drower, 1992: 82)

This was certainly the case with Anguilla.

Another feature of the small Caribbean islands is the intensive comings and goings through emigration and return. This high degree of mobility belies the idea of sleepy backwaters, cut off from the outside world. The societies themselves arose out of a forcible admixture of people of European, African and Indian origin, creating societies with a high degree of class and colour stratification, and with strong links with the metropolitan society and culture.

Even in the smallest, most isolated islands, where the geographical boundary seems so 'naturally' to delineate the social and political community, this is not the case.

> Status obsesses many West Indians but colour groupings are blurred and fragmented rather than dichotomized, and the attrition of the white and light elite forces black mobility. The numerical weakness of the elite forces cognizance of pressures from below, and the entire class hierarchy is knit together by intermixing, acculturation and assimilation. (Lowenthal, 1972: 139)

There is a need to avoid neat separations, made for the sake of convenience to the social scientist.[1] Social boundaries of community do not coincide with the borders of the islands. As studies of migratory processes in the Caribbean have so clearly shown, the fluidity of social boundaries is reinforced by the high rates of movement in and out of the islands (Philpott, 1973; Richardson, 1983).

In his study of Jamaican independence, Trevor Munroe discusses the connection between the notion of autochtony, or indigenous identity, and the pro-independence politics of the post-war period. He suggests that the very idea of inside/outside is problematic in its application in the context of plantation societies (Munroe, 1972: 178). The same point has been made by Jean Houbert in the case of the plantation societies of the islands of the South-West Indian Ocean (Mauritius, Seychelles and Reunion), where "the European dimension was not superimposed on indigenous societies from outside, but was an intrinsic part of their whole genesis" (Houbert, 1986: 146). Even the culture and language of the islands can be described as a melting pot of African, European and Asian elements. In the Guyanas, Amerindian elements are added to this stew. The result is a unique synthesis in each territory, and even in different regions within one territory.

The complexity of identity in this context is expressed in the use of the term 'creole', which is used in many different ways: in some places it refers to Caribbean-born whites, sometimes to non-whites, and sometimes only to mixed populations. Overall, the term denotes the product of a process of transplantation and cultural fusion (albeit a highly stratified fusion) which can be found throughout the region in different forms (Lowenthal, 1972: 32-3). Creole-type societies emerge wherever colonial plantation society forced diverse people together, with no hinterland to which they could escape. These people created a common language for communication (Creole) and some shared belief systems. Creole societies are not unique to the Caribbean, but also exist in the Indian Ocean and in some parts of former French West Africa.

Forced assimilation of slaves and indentured labourers took place throughout the Caribbean. After the mid-1800s emancipation was followed by vehement denials from the local planter class that they had any common ground, politically, culturally or socially, with the former slaves and indentured workers, and with the mulatto middle class, where it existed.

## Decolonisation and Independence

Usually, decolonisation is taken to mean the process by which former colonies, or non-self-governing territories, become self-governing states. Using this definition, we could include the independence of the United States and Haiti two centuries ago, alongside the independence of St Lucia or the Seychelles in the past two decades. This very broad definition cannot help us much in exploring post-colonial relations; it describes the form but neither the causes nor the content of the changes that have been said to constitute 'decolonisation'. This term has also been used to refer to national liberation; the aim is to free the colonies from the economic, psychological and political control of the former colonial power (Gardinier, 1982: 515-16). False decolonisation, then, as described by Frantz Fanon, for example, is independence without an accompanying process of democratisation and national liberation. The idea of false decolonisation has been used in the case of Jamaica, for example (Munroe, 1972: 178-81).

In content, decolonisation must be about undoing the colonial relationship. This operates at several levels: at the inter-state level of politics and economics, at the inter-personal level in terms of perceptions and relationships; and at intermediate levels which mediate groups' relationship with the state. Immigration and nationality law, for example, can be seen as intermediate institutions. Another is the process of incorporating culturally distinct groups into the education system.

If decolonisation is to be equated with post-colonial liberation, it cannot be confined to national liberation; it should result in previously excluded and segregated people securing access to improved levels of economic, social and political rights. "The larger family created by colonialism need not necessarily split apart at the time of national liberation. Its members can create new relationships" (Moutoussamy, 1988: 141).

This may be possible in a context of separate sovereignty, or it may be more likely through integration or some form of association. Since 1960, and until fairly recently, the United Nations has simply equated collective self-determination with independence, and independence with decolonisation

(Akehurst, 1984: 252). Even so, it was also acknowledged by UN resolution 1541 (XV) that self-determination might logically result either in one of three possible outcomes: free association, integration with an independent state, or independence and separate statehood. Some rare examples of post-colonial integration exist today, including the French DOM, but also Alaska and Hawaii, which are both recognised as integral parts of the United States. But such is the bias for independence that, as one commentator wryly commented of the French overseas departments,

> the tragedy of the situation is this...that even if, in the total absence of fraud, eighty per cent of the [electorate] declared themselves in favour of remaining French, almost no-one would believe them. (Defos du Rau, 1968: 77)

Not surprisingly, this situation causes some insecurity among the electorate and among the political elite, highly assimilated to French national norms in living standards and lifestyles. On the other hand, their very degree of assimilation leads to a paradoxical tendency for local politicians in the French Caribbean to emphasise local distinctiveness and separate identity in their relations and negotiations with central government in Paris.

## Colonialism and the Demand for Equality

It is common to draw a distinction between British and French political cultures and public administration systems. Being insular in outlook, the British tendency is said to be to separate and to devise special administrative arrangements for geographically distinct areas, however well integrated they may be in cultural and economic terms. In England, special status has long been reserved for such tiny island territories as the Isle of Man and the Channel Islands (McCartney, 1984: 41-71).

France, on the other hand, has long been viewed as a comparatively a-territorial state. That is not to say that French policy makers have not been concerned with the extension of the national territory; undoubtedly they have. But the highly reified and abstracted nature of the Republican system, its encoding in clear written form, and the universalism of the Jacobin values that underlie it ensured greater uniformity in administration in the metropolis and overseas in the colonies. This made it possible to argue that the overseas departments were among the longest-lived members of the French 'family' (Hintjens, 1992a: 64-75; Burton, 1993). Undoubtedly, the family was paternalist and unequal, but it nonetheless appeared to function as a coherent whole.

What is remarkable during colonial rule is the extent to which the plantation coloured and free blacks in both the British and French Caribbean colonies claimed the culture of the mother country as their own (Comitas & Lowenthal, 1973; Munroe, 1972: 148, Constant, 1988: 30-48). When compared with the local planter elite, central government in London appeared to be the champion of liberalism and racial equality, as Richard Hart notes of Jamaica. The local planter aristocracy firmly resisted any central government encroachment on what they saw as the internal, local affairs of the colony. This was particularly true of abolition of the slave trade and of slavery itself, both of which were violently opposed by the plantocracy throughout the Caribbean.

> In these circumstances, and with these experiences, it is not surprising that free persons of African descent became more and more loyal to Britain, more and more partial to the concept of British rule. (Hart, 1972: 277)

Independence in the nineteenth century would have produced a sort of UDI of the white planter class, and the unmediated domination of this class would almost certainly have been accompanied by a further deterioration in living conditions for the poorest, and an intensification of exploitative labour practices in order to reduce costs. In the former Caribbean colonies of both Britain and France, it was the local planter class that was the most ardent advocate of local autonomy, particularly when faced with liberal reforms. It was not just the mulatto elite, but also the ex-slaves and indentured workers, who demanded intervention by, and protection from, the central state. Haiti's example, while containing huge potential for subversion in the remaining slave plantation colonies, did very little to enhance the attractions of political independence.

From at least 1960 onwards, the equation between political independence and national liberation was more or less taken for granted. In the present system, the break–up of a number of multi-ethnic states (e.g. Ethiopia and Yugoslavia) seems to confirm this idea. This was not the case in earlier decades; even Marcus Garvey, the champion of a return to Africa for all peoples of African descent, at one time found himself torn between demanding "representation in the Imperial Parliament, or a larger modicum of self-government for Jamaica" (Hart, 1972: 273). Among the mulatto middle class, the striving for greater inter–personal equality often implied a rejection of all that was associated with Africa and their African ancestry. Cultural assimilation was only earned at the cost of losing any claim to historical distinctiveness; yet the mulattos were excluded by the white elite and reminded of their slave roots at every opportunity. During the colonial period, the difficulty was that,

> The advantages of being white were so obvious that race prejudice against the Negroes permeated the minds of the Mulattos who so bitterly resented the same thing from the whites. (James, 1973: 101)

In this context of alienation, demands for equal rights could still be seen as anti-colonial since they sought to erode existing class and colour stratifications, and eventually to dismantle them altogether. The aim was to arrive at a social structure both more just and more equitable. Political rights for the as yet unenfranchised former slaves were also demanded. As C.L.R. James notes, "Within a West Indian island the old colonial system and democracy are incompatible. One has to go" (James, 1963: 406). Taking this as a point of departure, it may be possible to gauge the extent of decolonisation in the Caribbean by the extent to which there has been a real 'democratisation' of political and social structures since the end of formal colonial rule.

This choice between democratic reforms and a continuation of the existing colonial system was quite starkly perceived by Aimé Césaire and other advocates of the French Caribbean colonies' integration into France in 1946. The proposal to transform the four *vieilles colonies* (Martinique, Guadeloupe, Guyane and Reunion in the Indian Ocean) into French departments arose out of a long tradition of legal and political assimilation, which can be traced back to the French Revolution, and the abolition of slavery in 1790 (see Document 1). The right to vote was initially extended to the adult male population of the *vieilles colonies* under the Second Republic in 1848, and was definitively restored in 1870. Women obtained the vote in 1946, at the same time as in metropolitan France. Aimé Césaire described the new law as "the end point of a historical process and the outcome of a doctrine" (*JORFAN*, 5.3.1946: 659); this was the doctrine of Jacobin assimilation.

Fully incorporated into the French colonial system, each of the *vieilles colonies* already had a marked individuality at the time of the Revolution, in terms of social structures and local politics. The First Republic's abolition of slavery was firmly resisted by planters in Martinique, whose interests influenced Napoleon's decision to restore slavery in 1804. By contrast in Guadeloupe abolition could not be resisted, and open slave revolts in 1802 forced the planter class to leave the island altogether (Jolivet, 1987; Burton, 1993: 75). Meanwhile in French Guyane the problem of escapee slaves had never been resolved due to the nature of the territory and the vast and densely forested interior (Jolivet, 1990). The forced deculturation of the population of these islands (and to a lesser extent of Guyane, given its densely forested interior) deprived the people of any 'authentic' pre-colonial culture to which they could have 'returned' after independence.

Throughout the Caribbean, colour segregation was sharpened after the abolition of slavery, and was used as a weapon to exclude blacks and mulattos from political and economic power (Lowenthal, 1972: 70-3). Emancipated mulattos and blacks obviously wanted an improvement in their daily living conditions. But the local planter elite firmly asserted that, "[e]mulation by non-whites...ought to stop short of such goals as social equality and high status" (Lowenthal, 1972: 74). Or indeed the right the vote.

In the French colonial context, national legislation was not imposed uniformly or consistently. The position of freed black slaves in the new Republic did not accord with official policy. In Haiti's case, for example, one researcher has suggested that indigenous mulatto nationalism was inspired by the racial prejudice encountered not only in the colony but also in mainland France (La Guerre, 1986: 205). Personal contact of the colonised people with the metropolitan society may well reduce the feeling of attachment to the mother country (Hart, 1972: 150, 181).

In one respect, at least, the difference between Britain and France during the colonial period was striking. As Harold Mitchell notes, "[u]nlike Great Britain, France offered equality of citizenship with direct representation" in French political institutions from 1870 onwards (Mitchell, 1963: 24). In the British Caribbean, the adult male franchise was only extended in 1944, and then only for a fairly weak local council. Britain also failed to distinguish its old Caribbean colonies from the more recently acquired sub-Saharan African colonies. By including all Afro-Asian and Caribbean colonies within the so-called New Commonwealth, Britain divided the Commonwealth along colour lines. The myth was thus created that the Caribbean colonies, like sub-Saharan Africa or India, could somehow revert to self-government. This decolonisation option was then imposed on islands like Jamaica, where there was a sizeable body of opinion against independence, led by Bustamante's Workers Party (Munroe, 1972). Where there was support for independence, this was often based on promises that levels of social provision, wages and economic development would come to resemble those in Britain (Figueroa, 1990). In order to become independent, the former British colonies were to adopt replicas of British political institutions, to prevent a return to pre-colonial barbarism (Davidson, 1992: 73-5). As has already been suggested in this chapter, this idea was doubly absurd; in the context of the Caribbean colonialism had been so all-encompassing that it left no "cultural hinterland of identifiable political structures" which might operate as an alternative to the colonial administration (Munroe, 1972: 176).

It was not just the question of economic 'viability' that made the remaining small island colonies of the Caribbean reluctant to accept independence after the Second World War. It was also the fact of their close ties with Britain, their assimilation into the national popular culture, and their hopes for equal treatment and improved working and living conditions. Mike Faber suggests that, if Britain had offered the inhabitants of the smaller former colonial territories a referendum in which they were asked whether they wanted to opt for full UK citizenship and integration into the United Kingdom, "there is every chance they would have voted overwhelmingly to do so" (Faber, 1984: 19).

## Integration: the Path Less Travelled By

In the French Caribbean colonies in 1946 it would equally have been impossible to mobilise the entire population politically behind a demand for separate sovereignty and political independence. Aimé Césaire, and other leaders of the Left, did however rally the majority of the electorate behind the demand for equal citizenship rights and full departmental status (*Documentation Française*, 1948: 17; Sablé, 1955). The aim was to obtain an immediate improvement in social conditions through attaining legal equality within the French state (Moutoussamy, 1988: 20-22; *JORFAN*, 14.3.1946: 757). The French Republic appeared to offer the best chances of improving material conditions for the poor in the *vieilles colonies*. It was therefore to France that Césaire, an ardent advocate of *négritude*, but also a Communist, turned for support for this liberatory project. In the 1920s and earlier, demands for integration had repeatedly failed (Lemery, 1925). As we saw, prior to 1946, such proposals were generally regarded as highly subversive.

After the war the planter class in the French Caribbean colonies, who had been Vichy collaborators, were completely discredited politically, and the *vieilles colonies* elected Communist and Socialist deputies to the National Assembly. They were unanimous in their support for the proposal to transform the former colonies into fully-fledged French *départements* (Hintjens, 1994). Integration had wide appeal among the electorate in Martinique, Guadeloupe and in French Guyane. It was hoped that under departmental status there would be funds available and rights guaranteed, which together would ensure better living and working conditions for the vast majority of the population.

Indeed, this expectation has been the cornerstone of local politics and the whole integration project in the French Caribbean ever since. It is noticeable that, even in the 1990s, new policies extended to Guyane and the French Antilles are judged by local politicians and by the electorate in terms of their equivalent in metropolitan France. The impact on state expenditure in the DOM, and on economic, social and other rights of individuals in these regions will be crucial to the degree of support; this tends to be true across party lines, making for some unusual alliances between the Left and the Right in the overseas departments (Hintjens, 1991a).

That the demand for departmental status and legal assimilation was so readily agreed to by the National Assembly in Paris was undoubtedly exceptional. This reflected the unusually generous mood after the Liberation towards the colonies, which had played their part in preserving France's honour by providing troops for the French forces and rallying to de Gaulle. It also reflected the strong position of both the Communist Party and the Gaullists in the National Assembly at that time (Sablé, 1955; Jacquemart, 1983: 19-26).[2]

If the law had been proposed only two years later, once the Communist Party had left government, it would almost certainly have been rejected outright. In 1946, however, it was seen as the French government's duty to provide decent living conditions for the poor of these former colonies. During the war, the French Antilles had been cut off from the French mainland for several years, and their dependent colonial economies had withered, resulting in near-starvation conditions. In addition, in order to persuade the National Assembly to vote in favour of the new law, a certain amount of flattery was used. Aimé Césaire stressed the sentimental ties between France and its Caribbean islands, and spoke eloquently of the 'genius' of France (*JORFAN*, 12.3.1946: 659). The Republic was the crow that dropped the proverbial cheese; Césaire the flattering fox who picked it up, and distributed it.[3]

At a time of patriotic fervour the Gaullists were especially keen to extend departmental status to the former *vieilles colonies* in order to prevent the United States from acquiring them (*JORFAN*, 14.3.1946: 754-5). The Communists believed it was time to show solidarity with their overseas brothers and sisters, the latter having been newly enfranchised (Sablé, 1955: 143,172; Girardet, 1972: 275). The idea in 1946 was to remove disparities in working conditions and welfare provisions between metropolitan and overseas workers, through the application of a common legislation (Betts, 1961: 8). This included the retrospective introduction of the full range of existing labour protection laws, which was one of the main demands of Aimé Césaire and other proponents of the law (*JORFAN*, 14.3.1946: 757).

Having opted for integration immediately after the end of the war, the French Overseas Departments are now in an almost unique position in the Caribbean, as peripheral but integral parts of a former colonial power. The scale of the material transformation of the colonial economies and societies is almost unparalleled elsewhere in the Caribbean (with the possible exceptions of Puerto Rico and the Netherlands Antilles). There are also continuities with the colonial period. The white *béké* minority in Martinique remain economically powerful and racially exclusivist (Kovats-Beaudoux, 1973: 243-8; Allen, 1979). Such continuities are outweighed by a fundamental shift in the basis of the entire economic, social and political life of the population (Miras, 1987: 87; Hintjens, 1991a: 46-51; Mathieu, 1988: 52-9). In the course of fifty years, the plantation economy has all but disappeared, and has been replaced by an economy based on the expansion of the public sector, state expenditure, and related services. Incomes, employment, education, and social and political relations are mediated by a massive net transfer of resources through the institutions of the French state (Guillebaud, 1976; Constant, 1988; Reno, 1994).

This transfer of resources is not aid or assistance; it is part of the normal transfer of resources within the French public sector. As one scholar of public administration has pointed out, in a modern system of public accounting, under uniform provisions:

...a poor area relative to the rest of the country will pay less than average in taxes and receive more than average in expenditure, unless the system is deliberately manipulated against it. (Stanyer, n.d.)

Transfer payments from the metropolis support two-thirds of so-called 'GNP' in Martinique and Guadeloupe, and more than three-quarters in Guyane (Dupont, 1988: 24-25; Aldrich & Connell, 1992: 143-5). Agriculture accounts for only one-tenth of total employment and even less in terms of overall production. This compares with 37 per cent of employment in 1967 and 50 per cent in 1954 (INSEE, 1991: 39). It can be argued that the DOM are no longer separate economies; they act as relays for the circulation of French and EC capital in the Caribbean. A similar model of Puerto Rico's economy as a relay for US capital has been elaborated by Dietz (Dietz, 1983: 268).

The French state has effected a substantial redirection of incomes towards consumers in the DOM. This public expenditure has been transformed into demand for goods and services, most of which are produced in mainland France. The enormous 'trade deficit' between each of the DOM and the rest of France is visible only because a system of separate regional accounts exists for each territory. Less than a quarter of all 'imports' are directly covered by income from 'exports' from the Antilles, and less than one-tenth from Guyane. In 1991, for example, the proportion was 13 per cent in Guadeloupe and 16 per cent in Martinique (INSEE, 1991: 19). This apparent trade imbalance does not have to be made good by the local authorities in the DOM, however, since it is automatically covered by the national accounting system of the French economy as a whole. It is therefore not in fact a trade deficit at all, but the result of a net transfer of resources from the French state to the DOM through the national accounting system.

During the colonial period, the mulatto middle class in the French Caribbean colonies put its faith in equality within a republican, Jacobin France. At the same time, it was fighting against that 'other France' that was represented by the local planter class, both colonial and reactionary in their outlook (Constant, 1988: 30-48).

Since 1946, as contact has intensified between Martinicans and Guadeloupeans and their supposed motherland, the former enchantment with the greatness and generosity of France has worn somewhat thin. It has not disappeared, but has given way to a sense of creole, island nationalism, born out of disillusion. By the early 1960s, C.L.R. James observed that the mass of the population in the French Caribbean was already disappointed by the record of the French central government. Yet this dissatisfaction arose out of high expectations, and these remain. This may explain why anti-French feeling has not readily been translated into support for independence parties, as James assumed it would (James, 1963: 408). There were protests, numerous strikes and demands for changes in policy, but until the early 1980s, the independence movement was hardly visible. Instead, the Left mobilised opposition to existing policies around a demand for *autonomie démocratique et populaire*. In 1958 the referendum on de Gaulle's presidency showed that his support in the overseas departments was even higher than in the metropolis; 81 per cent voted 'Yes' in the Antilles, and 94 per cent in Reunion, compared with a national average of 77 per cent (*Année Politique*, 1958: 157; Jacquemart, 1983: 115-7).

In fact, disillusion set in soon after integration, since the reforms demanded were not implemented with the expected speed; but only after long delays. Rule by decree, much hated during the colonial period, was continued by default after 1946. There were delays in the extension of basic administrative services into the new departments (Sablé, 1955: 172; Turpin, 1979: 49-51).

The source of the disappointment, then, was not so much integrationist or assimilationist policies; rather it was the failure to implement them fully and the difficulty of translating identical legislation into substantial equality between overseas and metropolitan French citizens. Already in 1946, some deputies had foreseen that the integration process would create impatience, by raising expectations to an unrealistic level. Paul Valentino, at the time a Socialist deputy for Guadeloupe, expressed his feelings on the matter in the following terms:

> I have the inner conviction that a form of assimilation which hands over responsibility for deciding the fate of these colonial peoples to central Government will end up destroying the ties of affection which attach them to the metropolis. (*JORFAN*, 14.3.1946: 760)

Serious difficulties arise out of the distinction between real and legal equality. The inhabitants of Martinique, Guadeloupe and Guyane are full French citizens, but this has not brought them material conditions which match those in metropolitan France. Economic conditions in the DOM do not match even those in the poorest regions of metropolitan France. Unemployment has reached levels of over 30 per cent, records for the European Community regions (INSEE, 1991: 19; Aldrich & Connell, 1992: 129-64). Yet these high unemployment levels can be seen as a sign of the raised expectations of the population. Indeed, there has been such a shortage of agricultural workers in the French Antilles that St Lucians and Dominicans have been allowed in to do this work (*Politis*, 28.3.1990). The legal and illegal movement of other Caribbean people into the Caribbean island DOM has resulted in a complex pecking order, in which the Antilleans inhabit a middle position in the overall scheme of things:

> The black West Indian sees the Frenchman as an exploiter, only marginally better than the *béké*; at the same time he is angry about the presence of Dominican and Haitian immigrants for whom he reserves an intolerance similar to the intolerance the French West Indians meet in the dormitory suburbs of Paris. (Williams, 1984: 7)

The whole departmentalisation process has had deceptive and ambiguous results. On the one hand, appearances suggest that the French Antilles are the most prosperous and 'developed' areas of the Caribbean, with much conspicuous consumption, and impressive standards of public infrastructure, with roads, schools and hospitals second to none in the region (Williams, 1984: 6; Constant, 1988: 68-85; De Lépine, 1990).

On the other hand, there are striking inequalities, and efforts to encourage industrial production, or indeed any production, have largely failed. The productive economy is moribund, and does not respond to economic initiatives from the French government. Only service activities such as construction, trading and finance, and the public sector, appear able to thrive and the DOM have become overwhelmingly service-oriented economies. The most lucrative jobs are in the public sector or in the supply of the public sector. Indeed, the very economic and political changes in the French overseas departments that brought higher wages, and social welfare benefits akin to those in the rest of France, all but ruled out rapid industrial growth based on a cheap and 'flexible' labour force, as seen in Puerto Rico during the 1950s and 1960s, for example. Furthermore, so long as the French state continues to provide the means to reach material plenty for a significant part of the population, there will be no mass support for independence (Burton, 1982; Hintjens, 1991a: 65). The idea of outright independence is anathema to many Antilleans (Burton, 1993: 87).

The 1990s have witnessed some new developments in electoral politics in the two islands. Whereas in Guadeloupe the nationalist UPLG (*Union pour la Libération de la Guadeloupe*) abandoned its pro-independence stance in 1989, after the devastation of the island by hurricane Hugo, in Martinique the destruction caused by another hurricane twelve months later was shortly followed by a record vote for two pro-independence parties, the Ecologists and the MIM (*Mouvement pour l'Indépendence de la Martinique*). These two obtained 9 of the 41 seats in the Regional Assembly in elections of October 1990 (*Le Monde*, 16.10.1990) and the main party of the island, the PPM (*Parti Populaire Martiniquais*), lost its majority for the first time since 1982, when the first regional elections were held.

The Left's traditional dominance in the French Antilles was weakened in the 1993 legislative elections, however, with Lucette Michaux-Chévry, an RPR candidate and former government Minister, being elected as one of Guadeloupe's three deputies (*Caribbean Insight*, March 1993). In Martinique, the MIM refused to support the PPM candidates against the Right, resulting in the defeat of the party of Aimé Césaire in two out of three seats in the island. Abstention rates reached unprecedented levels in the first round of the legislative elections: 56 per cent in Guadeloupe, and 57 per cent in Martinique, compared with 42 per cent in both islands in the legislatives of 1992 (*Le Monde*, 30.3.1993). The pro-independence vote was minimal, pointing to the tactical, and fickle, electoral alignments in the French Antilles.

There are strategic and economic as well as sentimental and political reasons why France wishes to retain a national presence in the Caribbean. The DOM act for France as "bases for displaying and selling its products to their neighbours in the Caribbean and Indian Ocean" (Aldrich & Connell, 1992: 278). As a result of its continuing presence in the Caribbean, the Indian Ocean, the North Atlantic and the Pacific, France can claim with some degree of credibility to be more than just a West European state; it can claim world power status (ibid.: 279).

## Anguilla: the Exception that Proved Unruly

Perhaps it was because the colonial responsibilities of Britain were far heavier than those of France that it became imperative in the 1960s and 1970s for Britain to grant independence to the remaining colonies as quickly as possible. By the 1950s, like the old lady who lived in a shoe, the British government simply did not know what to do with all her proverbial 'children' (interview R. Webster, 31.3.1990).

When Anguillans rebelled against incorporation into the independent state of St Kitts-Nevis-Anguilla, one of the many interesting expressions that were used to appeal to the British government for understanding of their cause was "Seeking the choice of mother's care" (Westlake, 1972: 40). Most Anguillans' preferred option after two years of separation from St Kitts-Nevis was to return to colonial status under Britain's wing (Webster, 1987: 88; Petty & Hodge, 1987: 57-8).

Exercising 'Anguillan self-determination' did not prove to be a simple matter and resulted in a great deal of misunderstanding between an unwilling colonial 'mother country' and six thousand assertive islanders. Their choice, starkly expressed by the leader at the time, Ronald Webster, was between the colonial dominance of St Kitts and Nevis, under the autocratic Robert Bradshaw, or the domination of the United States (Petty & Hodge, 1987: 63-73). Literally hundreds of articles appeared on the Anguilla affair - the Anguilla 'Revolution' as the Anguillans still call it - between 1967 and the early 1970s (see Webster, 1987).

A very small island with a population of only six thousand people had seriously embarrassed the British Government and damaged the careers of some senior politicians. Anguillans simply demanded that their right to self-determination be respected. Furthermore, they had made very effective use of the international media, and had made their voices heard in the United Nations. They refused to form a part of the new island state of St Kitts-Nevis-Anguilla under Bradshaw because of his unwillingness to allow elections to be held, the introduction of flogging, summary expulsions of foreigners and bans on the free assembly of persons (Webster, 1987: 71). Prepared shortly after secession from St Kitts-Nevis, the first paragraph of the Constitution of Anguilla read as follows:

> The people of Anguilla establish this Constitution to govern the Territory of Anguilla...The ultimate political power shall remain with the people of Anguilla. No constitutional arrangement connecting Anguilla with other islands or countries shall be effective unless it shall have been submitted to a referendum and approved by a majority of those voting. (Webster, 1987: 32)

The leaders of the 'Revolution' insisted that they were simply defending the human rights of Anguillans, and their collective right to national self-determination. As was repeatedly emphasised in their demands for a hearing with the UK government, 98 per cent of the Anguillan population had voted in favour of secession, uncomfortably close to unanimity. This gave the leaders considerable confidence in their claims to represent all Anguillans. Interviewed after a meeting with Lord Caradon on the future of the island, in March 1969, Ronald Webster, at that time leader of the Anguillan government, concluded confidently, and without irony, of the six thousand islanders,

> ...we will insist that the British troops be pulled out of Anguilla before direct negotiations are conducted. I think the British are beginning to recognise the will of the people which is the one that should determine the future of Anguilla. (*San Juan Star*, 27.3.1969)

The policy over the years 1967-9 was to hold out against any compromise involving return to St Kitts-Nevis, using bluster to claim to be "well armed against any invasion", and attempting to embarrass the British Government to the negotiating table. "Even if there is no overseas aid to help Anguilla," said Peter Adams, the first Prime Minister, "we shall hold out indefinitely. We are against slavery" (Webster, 1987: 35). Various offers, including one from France to incorporate the island of Anguilla within the department of Guadeloupe, were reportedly rejected (*San Juan Star*, 20.2.1969).

British troops were shortly sent in, ostensibly to prevent a supposed Mafia-style take-over of the island. They met Union-Jack-wagging islanders and no resistance whatsoever. The British troops were popular, but the local Commissioner Tony Lee, who had recommended bringing the troops in, was not, as he had totally failed to understand what the islanders wanted.

The Anguillans soon took their case to the Committee of 24 in the United Nations, who asked Britain, via Lord Caradon, to assist in finding a peaceful resolution to the conflict (Webster, 1987: 122). Anguilla was the subject of jokes, by Art Buchwald, for example, who satirised the invasion, asking how the "lightly armed British paratroopers and marines managed to break through the heavy Anguillan defences which consisted of one Napoleonic cannon, 12 shotguns, three Ford trucks and 2,000 sheep" (*Daily News*, 28.3.1969). Undoubtedly, Britain had egg on its face.

The Labour Party's policy in the remaining colonies, like that of the Conservatives before them, was to grant independence wherever possible (Faber, 1984). With so many demands to listen to special cases, it was easier to ignore them all, and to declare Britain's unilateral withdrawal from Empire rather than negotiating the details. To continue with the metaphor of family life, it seemed at the time that "Britain [was] saying in effect, that it [was] no longer in the orphanage business" (Lowenthal & Clark, 1980: 302). Britain was also responding to pressure from the United Nations, and the strong consensus after the momentous constitutional hand-overs of the early 1960s in sub-Saharan Africa, in favour of equating self-determination with independence. Only in 1980 did Britain finally accept the demand for the reintegration of Anguilla as a British dependent territory (colony). This was finally agreed by the Anguillan islanders to be the best possible option (Drower, 1992: 167).

In the 1990s, there is a widely shared perception that British policy in Anguilla is 'aggressively non-interventionist', leading to widespread corruption in political life (interview, F. Hughes, 29.3.1990). Those in power deny that the island is being pushed towards independence. For all sorts of reasons, however, the present Anguilla government is asking Britain, in the shape of the local Governor, to intervene more actively in local affairs. In particular, they are keen to see a more interventionist approach being adopted in the regulation of offshore banking activities in order to prevent and prosecute cases of fraud and money laundering (interview, E. Gumbs, 30.2.1990). One explanation for Britain's behaviour towards Anguilla is that 'she' has so many colonial 'children' that she is obliged to foster them out. In this rather sentimental account, Britain loves all her (colonial) children, but can no longer afford to look after all of them (interview with R. Webster, 30.3.1990). Such homely images of family are used very frequently in describing relations between Anguilla and the colonial power. The same images also recur persistently in French Caribbean discourse on politics.

By the 1990s, local opinion in Anguilla concerning the events of the 'Revolution' of 1967-9 has become divided. Some feel that the significance of this period is not much diminished, and that it is faintly ridiculous to talk now of an Anguillan Revolution. However, the self-proclaimed leader of those events, Ronald Webster, claims that the Revolution will not be over until each Anguillan is his (*sic*) own boss (interview, R. Webster, 30.3.1990). In the island, generally, it seems that independence at the personal level is fiercely asserted, whilst political independence is utterly rejected. By general consent, any politician who campaigned for independence in Anguilla would not be elected. In spite of this continued attachment to its status as a British dependency, what is most notable about Anguilla in the 1990s is the rapid pace of Americanisation, of the population, of the culture and of consumption patterns (interview, C. Harrigan 30.3.1990). For those in power, this is the only way forward: the island must expand its tourist activities in order to prosper and survive.

### The Case of Montserrat: Being Forced to be Free?

In Montserrat it also seems that very few people are asking for independence. One of its most ardent advocates, the former Prime Minister, John Osborne, was found guilty of corrupt dealings in offshore banking (Winchester, 1985: 232-41). Montserratians generally, especially with the passage of Hurricane Hugo in 1989, are aware of their need for continued and substantial financial support from Britain. Howard Fergus, a local historian and sometime Acting Governor, has written a calypso-style poem against independence. It is certainly unusual music to our ears, but expresses feelings commonly heard in the remaining British dependencies of the Caribbean:

> Recently there have been talk of independence.
> But to the majority this is utter nonsense
> Be careful on whom you place your dependence
> For God's sake, banish the thought of independence. (Cited in Thorndike, 1989: 117)

Interviews carried out in the island in 1990 also confirmed that most people regarded the prospect of independence with some suspicion (H. Bramble, 21.3.1990, field notes 19-26.3.1990). There is a rich understanding locally of the techniques used by the colonial power to foist independence on unwilling populations: one such technique is to associate a particularly popular politician with a pro-independence position (field notes, 22.3.1990).

The islanders are also acutely aware that most of the fully-integrated islands in the Caribbean, like the French DOM and the Dutch Antilles, have considerably higher per capita aid and income levels than dependencies like Montserrat. As David Marlow has pointed out, the comparison with independent states is not attractive, since "very few former British colonies in the West Indies have, after political independence, achieved even Montserrat's level of per capita income" (Marlow, 1992: 47). There exists a strong feeling in the remaining territories that they do not want to be pushed into independence. Yet integration on an equal basis, or intermediate options such as autonomy have generally been regarded by the Foreign and Commonwealth Office as 'inappropriate' and 'politically unattractive' (Thorndike, 1987: 14).

Independence has not yet been imposed on Britain's Caribbean colonies, but the people who live and were born there have been excluded in other ways from the benefits generally associated with full citizenship of a larger state. In particular, they have been granted neither freedom of movement within the UK and colonies, nor access to national welfare benefits (Robinson, 1984). As early as 1962, the Montserrat Constitution established by the West Indies Act ensured freedom of movement and prohibited discrimination only within the geographical confines of the island of Montserrat itself. Indeed by the 1990s, Montserratians sometimes feel it necessary to obtain a visa simply in order to visit the UK, even if they are going on holiday to see friends or relatives who are resident there. Since 1981, Anguillans and Montserratians, like all other colonial subjects (with the exception of the Falklanders and Gibraltarians) have been classified as British Dependent Territory Citizens (BDTC) under the terms of the Nationality Act. As one immigration and nationality lawyer described it, the new law effectively deprived Anguillans and Montserratians of any rights of abode or residence, employment or welfare cover in the UK.

> Acquisition of this citizenship [i.e. BDTC] does not denote any connection with a particular territory, and consequently, no right of abode under the immigration law of any particular territory...[it] is intended to die out with the generation at present living. (MacDonald, 1983: 3)

## Nationality Law and Decolonisation

The British Nationality Act of 1981 also violated the principle of *jus solis*, according to which place of birth determines nationality and thereby confers citizenship. In all the remaining British colonies, there is great unhappiness and resentment at this situation. Ten years ago, journalist Simon Winchester noted with dismay that the proposals faced hardly any political opposition within Britain itself (Winchester, 1985: 87). After all the efforts of the Anguillans to make their position understood, this piece of legislation sweeps away their basic right to freedom of movement within the 'national' territory, and deprives them of all the rights that this freedom opens up. The Caribbean islanders feel all the more offended since the Falklanders have been granted full citizenship since 1982 (interview, F.Hughes, 29.3.1990). Similarly in St Helena, a population very loyal to Britain has expressed its utter dismay at the imposition of what amounts to an informal apartheid policy. "Why does Britain not take them in?" asks Simon Winchester. "[Why] exclude them from the privileges of Britishness and yet rule over them?" (Winchester, 1985: 134-49).

There were those in the 1980s who hoped that London would relent in its 'aggressively non-interventionist' policies towards the remaining colonial territories (ibid.: 204). This seemed unlikely:

> Innovation in constitutional measures is off the agenda in London, except for the offer of independence. This approach seems inadequate in terms both of the genuine needs of small island citizens in the 1990s, and also, perhaps more poignantly, in terms of the interests of Britain in administering its residual responsibilities. (Marlow, 1992: 49)

Belatedly there may in the 1990s be a realisation that the effects of this policy have been unnecessarily harsh on the smaller remaining dependencies and colonies; attitudes at the Foreign and Commonwealth Office may be softening. In a recent report to the United Nations Special Committee on Decolonisation on the colony of St Helena, the British Representative announced that,

> his country's aim was to ensure that the people [of St Helena] decided for themselves what kind of political future they wanted, whether it be independence or some other status. (St Helena, 1989a)

Shortly afterwards, Britain's representative addressing the Committee declared the government's decision to withdraw from its proceedings (St Helena, 1989b). In the same vein, it was suggested by a British official, interviewed in Anguilla, that once the Hong Kong issue was resolved in 1997, the people of Britain's remaining colonies might be treated more kindly; certainly, no change in nationality law is likely until after 1997 (field notes, 6.4.1990).

Until recently, therefore, the prospects for the remaining British colonies in the Caribbean appeared to be independence or nothing, whether the islanders themselves agreed to this or not. The much-trumpeted respect for self-determination in the Falkland Islands is clearly not seen as 'appropriate' for islanders under British rule in the Caribbean. Belatedly, both the government and some academic commentators are beginning to recognise that independence is unlikely to prove a realistic option for the remaining UK and US dependencies (Drower, 1992: 233; Sutton & Payne, 1993: 1). This was explicitly acknowledged by the then Foreign Secretary, Douglas Hurd, when he met representatives of the fifteen remaining British colonies in London in November 1993. His reasoning was that even the United Nations Decolonisation Committee, the so-called Committee of 24, was no longer pressing for British withdrawal (*Times*, 27.11.1993). Alternative forms of constitutional status for very small remaining British dependencies are now being seriously explored for the first time, both in London and in the United Nations.

Another reason for the discernible shift away from a policy of independence at any cost may be the United States' increasing concern to control illegal drug movements and money-laundering activities in the Caribbean. These have been connected with the very rapid growth in offshore banking, especially in the Turks and Caicos, the British Virgin Islands and Montserrat. The need for policing the waters of the islands has led to a strengthening of the defence role of the Governor of each of the British colonies. Since 1991 the number of officials responsible for British Dependent Territories, located in the territories and in the Foreign and Commonwealth Office in London, has been doubled (Sutton & Payne, 1993: 6).

Meanwhile, France seems keen to reinsert its island territories and Guyane within their regional environments (Burac, 1994; *Times*, 27.11.1993). One of the features of the regional reforms of the 1980s was an attempt to link the DOM to their neighbours in terms of French and EC investment and trade. Ideally the DOM would serve as links in a chain of investment in cheaper production in neighbouring countries, linked to France not only through the Lomé Convention of the EC, but also through special regional co-operation associations in the Caribbean, the Pacific and the Indian Ocean (Aldrich & Connell, 1992: ch. 9). As we have seen, part of the challenge to the present departmental status of the Caribbean DOM comes from internal pro-independence forces, with the recent swing in the regional elections for the MIM in Martinique causing some alarm about the future of the island (*Le Monde*, 16.10.1990). Yet the picture in this respect is not clear, since the vote has fluctuated since the early 1990s. In Guadeloupe the UPLG (*Union pour la Libération de la Guadeloupe*), recognising that equal rights were an absolute priority in the liberatory struggle, abandoned the demand for immediate independence in the early 1990s (*Le Monde*, 28.3.1990).

A much more likely cause of any future rupture in relations between the metropolis and the Caribbean DOM is the perception that the retention of these territories is not only anachronistic, but also very expensive. Polls carried out in the late 1980s in metropolitan France indicated that two-thirds of the population would not be opposed to the idea of granting independence to the remaining DOM-TOM. The main reason given by those who were questioned was that the DOM had the right to separate self-determination (*Le Point*, 31.10.1988). It can be argued that, whether under the French Constitution, or in international law, this right does not formally exist (Maestre, 1976; Thürer, 1987). With the onset of long-term economic recession, it seems that French public opinion may be moving away from the Gaullist vision of a greater, global national identity, towards a more insular, continental version.

## Responsibility and Post-colonial Relations

Crudely speaking, one could argue that independence in the former British colonies in the Caribbean produced a 'shell' but no 'yoke' and that integration into France of the former French colonies produced more ' yoke' but no 'shell'. If bread-and-butter issues were central in the French Caribbean's decolonisation process, they were generally sidelined or underplayed in the Anglophone Caribbean's move towards independence.

Although expressed incoherently, bread-and-butter issues (or what is sometimes called stomach politics) lay behind the popularity of Bustamante's trade union in Jamaica after 1945. In the struggle between a politics of content versus a politics of form, form was given priority by the colonial power and the British colonies rapidly moved towards independence. Only in those territories which today remain associated with the United States, the Netherlands and France can individuals' socio-economic and political rights be said to have been given priority in the decolonisation process. Writing of the US Virgin Islands, Gordon Lewis notes that during the 1960s there was "not so much a struggle against American rule as such, but rather an effort to gain for the Virgin Islanders, as many of the rights and privileges that pertained to that rule as possible" (Lewis, 1972: 21). A similar situation existed in Puerto Rico (Lewis, 1963; Martinez, 1977). Lewis uses an analogy with slavery, arguing that, on balance, the Virgin Islanders, like the Puerto Ricans, preferred even second-class American citizenship to "a position of equality within the Antillean slave barracks" (Lewis, 1972: 22). The same could be said of the French Antillean islanders, the Anguillans and Montserratians.

In this context, it does appear (rather as in South Africa) that the neat and tidy separatist nationalism of the independentists fitted in well with the designs of the colonisers, who denied any responsibility for the daily living conditions of the colonised people, in this case the people of the Caribbean. The challenge of integrating white, black, East Indians and others living in the Caribbean was totally neglected (Mitchell, 1963: 73, 95). Furthermore, in the name of the principle of national self-determination of 'peoples', the Caribbean was pushed willy-nilly into sovereign statehood without proper financial settlements after independence.

Implicit expectations and explicit demands for the free movement of persons were disappointed straightaway by the 1962 Immigration Act. For the smaller islands in particular, it is difficult to exaggerate the importance of ensured international freedom of movement to their economic sustainability (Philpott, 1973: 34-5). The final nail in the coffin of free movement for Commonwealth people came in 1981, when UK nationality law was changed, with the effect that inhabitants of most of the British colonies were deprived immediately, and even retrospectively, of any rights to full British citizenship (MacDonald, 1983; Dummett & Nicol, 1990: ch. 13).

The non-existence in the Caribbean of an autochtonous political tradition can be seen as a key constraint on any 'genuine' form of decolonisation through independence. This was the point made by Munroe in the quotation used at the start of this chapter. Along with "[n]atural disasters, internal dissensions and vulnerability to naval attacks", cited by Lowenthal, this may also explain why, up to the early 1960s, even the "most ardent advocates of freedom [had] hesitated to press for final severance from Great Britain" (Lowenthal, 1962: 39). Lowenthal also draws a parallel with the situation in South Africa, noting that, during the nineteenth century, "[f]or the British enclaves in South Africa, the imperial tie [was] a buttress against apartheid" (ibid.: 39-40).

In certain situations, then, external colonial rule may appear as the lesser of two evils. If there is no other choice than that between internal settler rule and administrative control by distant but perhaps apparently 'neutral' colonial power, the latter may be preferred as the less directly oppressive option. In other cases, the relationship of colonised and coloniser can even be transformed through a process of incorporation. The main obstacle to this solution is that it requires the transformation of the coloniser. This is never an easy task, since

> To say that the coloniser could or should accept assimilation, and hence the colonised's emancipation, means to topple the colonial relationship...In other words the end of the colony as a colony, and the end of the mother country as a mother country. To put it bluntly, the coloniser would be asked to put an end to himself. (Memmi, 1990: 193)

Among the means that can be used to transform the relationship, Memmi includes: paying the colonised labour force the same wages as the home labour force; promoting the colonised through legal and administrative means; and economically developing and industrialising the colony. It is interesting that these are the measures demanded in the French overseas departments by the architects of the law of integration of 1946. They have become the basis for the legitimacy of the French presence in these territories ever since.

## Conclusion

In conclusion, it seems that relations between France and her former colonies in the Caribbean region have moved towards relatively more equal status for all French citizens, whether of the mainland or overseas French territories. In the case of Britain's relationship with its Caribbean possessions, the relationship is now arguably more colonial and less equal than at any time since the end of slavery. Britain uses immigration legislation to keep inhabitants of the former Caribbean British colonies at arm's length across the Atlantic, and neglects these new states, as well as the remaining colonial dependencies, with impunity. Through summary arrest, internment without trial, deportation, police brutality, policing of welfare entitlements, and removals of rights to appeal against immigration decisions, the rights of Caribbean people living in the United Kingdom are routinely 'legally' violated.

In the case of the French Caribbean, relations between the Antilleans and the metropolitan French are far from smooth or trouble-free. There is discrimination in the metropolis towards Antilleans who live and work there, in spite of their high degree of cultural assimilation. This in turn hardens attitudes towards metropolitan French and other white Europeans in the Antilles, feeding into nationalist sentiment which is based at least in part on resentment at the dominance of the metropolitans and *békés* at the top levels of business and in the public sector. In terms of civil and political rights, and economic and social rights such as minimum incomes, social protection and other substantial freedoms, however, the French Antilleans, like their Dutch Antillean counterparts, have almost identical rights to those of the metropolitan-born French population.

## Notes

1. As Eric Wolf suggests, "...social and cultural facts do not present themselves in units in which social space and geographical space coincide...On the contrary, we see various activities cross-cutting one another in manifold intersects, yielding pluralistic patchworks, rather than a bounded homogeneity of social warp and woof" (Wolf, 1988: 757).

2. The National (Constituent) Assembly elected in October 1945 was made up as follows: French Communist Party - 161; French Section of the Socialist International (Socialist Party) - 150; Gaullists (MRP) - 150; Moderates - 64; Radicals - 28; others - 33. There *Année Politique 1944-45*, 1946: 512-18; *Année Politique 1946*, 1947: 580.

3. An example of one author who takes a similar view to this is Frédéric Constant. His study, *La Retraite aux Flambeaux: Société et Politique en Martinique*, is one of the most original and thoughtful books to have appeared on local politics in the French Caribbean. He sees local politicians as the brokers or 'gatekeepers' between the state and the local electorate.

# 3  Reunion Island: Being there and Being French

Reunion prospers in the same way as Martinique and Guadeloupe, accepting jobs, roads, hospitals and subsidised camembert in exchange for just being there and being French.
Neil MacLean, *Sunday Times*, 1.10.1989.

**Open Your Eyes, Close Your Eyes**
*Imagine a Reunionnese person showing a foreign visitor*
*Round our native land*
*Asking him to open his eyes*
*And look at the beauty of our island*
*And close his eyes*
*To all the misery and poverty.*
*"There is the airport, with the runway just redone.*
*Boeing 747s land there.*
*Open your eyes.*
*Over there is a village full of poor people*
*Who work in the factory nearby*
*In endless fear that it will close down*
*In the next two or three years.*
*Close your eyes."*

*"We're going to take the four-lane*
*National Express highway to the capital.*
*Open your eyes.*

*There are still slums near*
*Those tall buildings in town.*
*The people who live there have no curry to go*
*With their rice.*
*Close your eyes."*

*"All those field stretching from the mountain*
*To the sea*
*Planted with cane and fresh green trees*
*Belong to just one owner.*
*Open your eyes.*
*And creole workers live in those*
*Tiny shacks with tin roofs.*
*Close your eyes."*

*"There are the white sandy beaches*
*Lined with pretty villas and beautiful houses*
*Where a few 'nice white people'*
*Come all year round to tan themselves.*
*Open your eyes.*
*In this fishing village nearby*
*They have lived in misery for a long time.*
*Close your eyes."*

*"We are now going through the property of the Monsignor,*
*With its sprinkled gardens and laden fruit trees.*
*Open your eyes.*
*Those badly dressed children are walking*
*On the hot tarmac road in bare feet,*
*Going to fetch water, carrying their little buckets.*
*Close your eyes."*

*"You see my friend*
*That my island is lovely*
*And everything is fine.*
*But only when you...*
*Open your eyes."*
Zemia Yves, *Combat Réunionnais,* Journal of *Union Générale des Travailleurs Réunionnais en France,* 1989.

## Introduction: the Indian Ocean Context

The French influence in the islands of the South-West Indian Ocean is considerable, and is rooted in historical and linguistic ties. In the Seychelles and Mauritius and Reunion, variants of francophone creole are spoken. Rodrigues, a dependency of Mauritius, has an entirely creole-speaking population, mostly of African origin and seeing themselves as distinctive from mainland Mauritians. In the Comoros, too, France has left its mark. In 1974 a referendum resulted in the detachment of the island of Mayotte from the rest of the archipelago, when a majority of the Mahorais voted against independence. The territory of the Comoros was then dismembered in contravention of the principle of territorial integrity enshrined in the UN Charter. Mayotte is now a *collectivité territoriale*, an administrative category for an overseas possession that falls somewhere between a fully-fledged overseas department and an overseas territory (Aldrich & Connell, 1992: 88).

In the Post-War years, the South-West Indian Ocean became an area of marked strategic significance. During the Cold War, a sizeable United States 'facility' was established in the island group of the Chagos, centring on the island of Diego Garcia, where by the late 1980s an estimated one thousand US troops and technical personnel were stationed both on- and off-shore. This 'facility' (in reality a base) is capable of servicing Polaris submarines, has acted as a relay for US military operations in the Gulf, and has a sophisticated missile and satellite tracking station. It is serviced by almost two thousand civilian Filipinos and Mauritians, as well as forty British administrators (interview, S.Turner, 20.1.1989). To create this military installation required the involuntary removal of almost two thousand inhabitants, many of whom had lived in the islands for more than a hundred years (Madeley, 1982; Winchester, 1985: ch. 2). As Jean Houbert notes:

> What was novel about the excision of the Chagos was not that it was carried out in defiance of the United Nations Resolution 1514 condemning the dismemberment of colonies, but that it was carried out with the collaboration of the government of Mauritius. (Houbert, 1992: 97)

To avoid embarrassment to both the UK and Mauritian governments, a myth was created that the islands had not been permanently settled (Drower, 1992: 65). The fact that the *zilois* (the creole name given to the islanders from Diego Garcia) continue to demand, and to receive, compensation from the British government more than twenty years later suggests otherwise. In most cases the islanders were offered 'shopping trips' to Mauritius and then unceremoniously dumped on the quayside in Port Louis, the capital (Madeley, 1982: 4). Only the left-wing parties (mainly what was MMM - *Mouvement Militant Mauricien*) have been prepared to raise the issue of compensation for the islanders as a bargaining stake with Britain. The MMM was in power for a short time in the early 1990s, and managed to revive the whole question of compensation. A £1.25 million settlement in 1979, seen as final, was followed by a payment of £4 million in 1982. Further demands for compensation have been made since (Walker, 1986: 3).

Broadly speaking, French policy in the Indian Ocean has relied on the courting of friendly states such as Mauritius and the Seychelles, and normal relations with other regional powers. Both the main regional powers, South Africa and India, officially recognise the legitimacy of the French presence in the Indian Ocean (field notes, 22.11.1988; 1.12.1988). France maintains particularly close relationships with the creole island governments, providing them with special cultural and economic co-operation arrangements (Houbert, 1992). More generally, in the 1970s and 1980s, France attempted to maintain a military presence in the region that would make it relatively 'independent' of the two super-power blocs. To the extent that Cold War bipolar rivalry permitted France to make the most of this 'independence', the end of the Cold War has created a crisis in the role which France might be seen to be playing in the Indian Ocean. Prior to the second Gulf War in 1991, it could be argued that France kept somewhat aloof from super-power conflicts. Thereafter, France appeared more unambiguously aligned with the United States.

In Franco-British relations in the Indian Ocean there appears to be a tacit agreement not to 'rock the boat'. Thus, according to one Foreign and Commonwealth Office official interviewed in 1989, there had long been an understanding between the two governments, to the effect that, if France did not raise the issue of Diego Garcia in the United Nations, then Britain would remain silent on the splitting of Mayotte from the Comoros. Britain has also adopted a neutral position in the Franco-Mauritian and Franco-Malagasy disputes concerning French occupation of Tromelin island and the *îles éparses* around Madagascar and in the Mozambique Channel (interview, S. Turner, 20.1.1989; Oraison & Miclo, 1978; Aldrich & Connell, 1993: 265).

As the Gaullist picture of France would have it, during the period up to the early 1990s, the United States and the Soviet Union were concerned with strategic interests in the Indian Ocean, and Germany and Britain with economic profit. France's concern on the other hand has been with what is termed *rayonnement*, a cultural flowering and influence that is more than purely political, and has to do with prestige and being loved (interview, A. Legros, 5.12.1988; Klen, 1992). Reunion's place within the Indian Ocean, then, is supposed to be as an example of the historical grandeur of France and the extension of its influence throughout the world. Certainly, without the DOM-TOM, France could not claim world power status as a major nuclear, spatial and maritime power. In the Indian Ocean alone, there are 7000 French troops and around half as many sailors (Aldrich & Connell, 1992: 153-4, 267).

Although the reason that Reunion originally became a French department in 1946 had relatively little to do with French machiavellian designs in the Indian Ocean, strategic considerations may at least in part explain why the island is likely to continue to remain a part of France in future. One long-term observer of local political life in Reunion comments, more prosaically, that *départementalisation* policies are rather like a train that is set on a track: there is little room for manoeuvre in any direction and a momentum develops which makes it difficult to reverse (interview, A. Oraison 28.11.1988).[1]

## Approaching Reunion Island

The island people of Reunion, now numbering over half a million, do not fit well into any predefined category such as 'plural society', 'multicultural', African or Asian. As a creole island, Reunion's population is characterised by a remarkable hybridity. In this chapter we will be considering some of the particular cleavages of class, gender and ethnicity which are themselves expressive of the complex island identity, as both part of France, and part of the Indian Ocean islands sometimes called 'Franconesia' (Houbert, 1992; Gerbeau, 1992).

My own connection with Reunion island goes back to the early 1980s, and the start of a doctoral thesis on the process of economic, social and political integration into France and the European Community from 1945 to 1981. When I had reviewed the material available in mainland France on the island's history, social structure, population, economy and political life, the opportunity arose to visit the island itself, thanks to a grant from the Nuffield Foundation. The sheer richness of the research experience means that field notes have been relied on particularly heavily in this chapter.[2]

Over the past fifty years, the plantation economy based on sugar has undergone a complete transformation, somewhat akin to that described already in the French Antilles. The remarkable expansion of the public sector has allowed some individuals to escape pre-existing social cleavages, giving them greater autonomy from creole social structures. This has been particularly true of women, who have been affected in interesting and unexpected ways by the changes that have taken place since 1946. Their key position in Reunion's society is remarkable, even when compared with that of Antillean women.

For some groups, and particularly for poor creole men, working in agri-culture or plantation work, the changes in the economic base have pushed them into a marginal class position. In fewer than fifty years, the whole foundation of employment and of the economic, social and political life of the

Reunionnese has shifted from small-scale agriculture and plantation production to employment (and unemployment) structures mainly oriented around services and the public sector. The effects of this have been a mixed blessing. As suggested in Chapter 1, collective benefits of 'self-reliance' have been sacrificed in the pursuit of maximum benefits for individuals. As in the Antilles, *départementalisation* in Reunion has resulted in large-scale migration to metropolitan France, where almost a quarter of a million Reunionnese and their children are now more or less permanently settled.[3]

On the whole, Reunion has had a reputation as a place where there is not much to report; a "patois of peace in a patchwork culture" in the words of one travel article (*Sunday Times*, 1.10.1989). The Reunionnese are conventionally regarded as *gentils*, sweet-natured, trusting and hospitable. Left-leaning metropolitan French people are prone to complain that the Reunionnese are less 'conscious' than the Martinicans or Guadeloupeans, whose relations with the metropolitan French tend to be more overtly conflictual and competitive (field notes, 2.12.1988).

The lack of much explicitly expressed hostility between the island's so-called 'ethnic communities', and the high degree of inter-marriage and inter-mixing generally, have led some commentators to consider Reunion an almost unique haven of peaceful multi-ethnic relations. It is seen by some as living proof that harmony between the 'races' is possible, and as an answer to theorists of apartheid (Lochon, 1992). The rate of inter-mixture has been high in the past, with the result that more than half the population can only be described as creole. Despite this, local group names are mostly colonially derived. The terms which persist for purposes of identification and self-identification, such as: *cafres, malbars, zindous, zarabes, tiblancs* and *zoreils*, have not changed at all since departmentalisation in 1946 (Klen, 1992: 151-2).[4]

The reality behind the appearance is more problematic and complex than could be guessed from the gushing of tourist writers that this is "a tiny Eden" (*Sunday Times*, 1.10.1989). As the poem puts it, Reunion is indeed a lovely place if one chooses to be blind to the marked relative deprivation of part of the creole (i.e. island-born) population. Sharp distinctions continue to be made between people, particularly for women, on the basis of their features, African features generally being regarded as less desirable than Asian, which are in turn regarded as less desirable than European features. Persistent and sometimes harsh discrimination continues to take place in the social and work setting on these bases.[5]

Light skin colour still denotes success and wealth. Strangely this association persists in spite of the abundant evidence that being white does not equate with prosperity, as evidenced in the miserable poverty of most *petits blancs* (poor whites) who still compose around a third of Reunion's population. Advertisements in the 'lonely hearts' columns of the local newspapers stress light skin colour as a desirable attribute. We return to such advertisements when we consider the politics of gender and colour in a later section of this chapter.

## Inequality, Unemployment and Citizenship

According to Gilbert Annette, a former mayor of St Denis, the capital city of the island, "Reunionnese people produce like Tanzanians but want a Parisian lifestyle" (*Libération*, 9.4.1991). The experience of the last fifty years in Reunion is certainly an interesting one for development economists. It would, for example, be difficult to find an example anywhere in the world where redistribution has been given the same priority over economic growth objectives (Rivera-Ramos, 1991). One outcome of the economic and administrative incorporation of a poor plantation economy into an industrialised state with a strong welfare orientation has been the almost complete disconnection of the social welfare of the Reunionnese from productive activities within the island.

Like the Antilles, Reunion officially has a negative net trading balance with the rest of France. The island economy exports only "a little sugar, a few spiny lobsters and some perfume oil" (*Economist*, 23.3.1991). Almost everything that is consumed has to be imported, even refined sugar. In the early 1990s the value of what the island's population imported was almost ten times the value of what was exported to the mainland (INSEE, 1991: 36). Public-sector employment and service employment continue to grow each year in relation to the total, and at the same time conventionally productive employment in agriculture and industry has declined steadily since the early 1960s. In 1990, employment in agriculture, industry and services represented 14, 15 and 71 per cent of the total, respectively (INSEE, 1991: 15). This represents a complete reversal of the situation up to the start of the 1960s, when over half the active population was employed in agriculture.

Such statistics cause dismay to local economic nationalists, a group which includes part of the business class. They also vex the Planning Commission of France (CGP - *Commissariat Général du Plan*) which insists on treating each overseas department as a distinct mini-economy. However, as is the case for the French Caribbean territories, there is no need for Reunion, as an entity, to make good the deficits in official accounts, since its import and export accounts are internal to the French economy. Any international deficits are subsumed within the national trading balance of the French economy.

As in the French Antilles, almost any proposal designed to bring about economic growth in Reunion involves recommendations for more rather than less state intervention. These might take the form of subsidies, training or special tax concessions, for example. Yet any further increases in public expenditure, efforts at job creation through incentives to private business, in subsidies or in training, will only tend to reinforce the existing structural dependence of all incomes and forms of employment on the expenditure and welfare policies of the French state. In spite of this the idea that each DOM needs to develop more economic 'self-sufficiency' is apparently appealing, and lies at the heart of local and regional development (Miras, 1987). According to one local businessman, the 'dependency' of Reunion on the metropolis is not due to the island's remoteness, since:

> Reunion's economy is very similar to that of regions like Brittany or Lozère, but because it is an island, one measures the figures, and then repeats them frequently. (Interview, J.Payet, 30.11.1988)

Comparisons with the economic and fiscal position of some of the poorer departments of metropolitan France would be enlightening in this respect. Unfortunately, accounts for inflows and outflows of goods, grants, incomes and other resources are not available for metropolitan departments or regions, and statements such as this one can therefore be neither confirmed nor refuted. In the case of the DOM, data collection is facilitated simply by virtue of their physical separation from the mainland. This makes it easy to record the movement of goods, people and capital across their geographical borders (Miras, 1987: 23; Hintjens, 1988). In terms of standard national accounting, therefore, there is no difference between the overseas and metropolitan regions; in both cases, inter-regional deficits in finance and trade are simply absorbed by public transfer payments.[6]

With the vast state expenditure on housing, roads, school construction, small enterprise development, health services, job creation and social benefits, it is hard for the Reunionnese to accept that the French state can do nothing to alleviate unemployment. In 1990 the official unemployment level was 36.9 per cent, the highest in any of the French overseas departments (INSEE, 1991: 19). For under-25-year-olds, the rate is closer to 60 per cent, making unemployment the major economic and social problem in the island (*Le Monde*, 31.10.1991). By 1993, the overall level had increased to 39.6 per cent (*Indian Ocean Newsletter*, 25.9.1993). This has serious consequences at the micro, household level, as we will see. It also undermines state legitimacy, whilst simultaneously increasing the population's dependence on employment, social security benefits and incomes transferred through the state.

As we noted in Chapter 2, high unemployment may be taken as an indicator of some kind of economic development and social and political transformation. After all, with-out unemployment benefit and social security provisions, formal unemployment could not reach such high levels. Thus it is no contradiction to note that, alongside very high unemployment, there is also a serious labour shortage in the construction industry, and, on a seasonal basis, in cane cutting and refining. This requires the periodic importation of labourers from the Comoros and Mayotte, for example. As a recent study concluded, in none of the overseas departments of France "do local residents, whatever their origin or skin colour, willingly cut cane or perform menial jobs" (Aldrich & Connell, 1992: 157). Periodic labour shortages also emerge in Reunion's construction industry, largely because of low wage levels.

Class conflict, like gender relations, are expressed through competition and collaboration oriented around access to public-sector employment, welfare benefits and other forms of petty or informal employment. Mayors' officers are the main employers in the island, as in the Antilles, and play an important economic and social role as well as acting as brokers for political support and patronage. The form of politics that characterises this society is centrally concerned with the redistribution of the 'goodies' arising out of the transfer payments and public expenditure of the French state. The Reunionnese version of what has been called 'stomach politics' is described later in this chapter.

By being part of France, all the overseas departments have been largely insulated from the price shocks that have affected the independent Caribbean economies. Even the comparative prosperity of other Indian Ocean islands, notably Mauritius and the Seychelles, is highly dependent on their ability to attract both tourists and highly mobile international capital. The basis of Reunion's economic prosperity, on the other hand, lies in the French state and national economy, in the economy of the European Community and in the redistributive policies of both. As Dudley Seers has commented, "peripherality within a large country allows for fiscal transfers from the rich to the poor" (Seers, 1980: 11). The same can be said of regional, social and agricultural policies at EC level.

In Reunion, in times of national prosperity, this redistributive bias has had the effect of reducing economic competition and mitigating the social and political conflict which can arise out of the whole *départementalisation* project. In times of recession, however, when the welfare state becomes more difficult to sustain and public expenditure is cut, competition for increasingly scarce resources and employment is likely to lead to greater social and political conflict. Welfare provisions may be threatened. This could undermine the legitimacy of the whole integration process and of the departmental and regional institutions. In 1993, for example, the Regional Assembly budget for Reunion was cut by one-eighth compared with the previous year, with a higher cut in investment expenditure as compared with current spending (*Indian Ocean Newsletter*, 16.1.1993). It was the second year of cuts in absolute terms, representing a reversal of the usual trend for the overseas departments within the French budget.

There are some signs of a crisis of state legitimacy emerging in Reunion, and being expressed in disillusion with both local and national government, as well as a desire for protection from the implications of the widening and deepening of the Common Market. There is a reassertion of a distinctively creole identity, and a growing debate about the educational and political implications of ignoring creole as the first language of the majority of islanders in favour of French. Creole identity has been articulated with a form of revanchist nationalism, which appears to be aimed mainly at the marginalised creole men among the local electorate (Hintjens, 1992b).

In the past, the gross economic inequalities between classes and 'ethnic groups' in Reunion's society have been softened by welfare payments to the poorest. Basic minimum income guarantees provided by the French state have been particularly important to a large number of families, as well as child benefits, free medical care, pensions and disability allowances. Since the start of *départementalisation*, it has been in Paris, and not in neighbouring states such as Mauritius or Madagascar, that the norm by which the Reunionnese measure their own standards of living has been set. *Départementalisation* itself has created a sort of institutionalised dissatisfaction with its own record among the electorate of the French overseas departments.

In Reunion there is certainly a sense of disillusion with the record of central government policies. Yet no clear alternative to existing policies is being proposed by either Left or Right. It may be the intensified level of contact with metropolitan French people, rather than direct control under central government, that has brought new tensions into the local political debate and in relations with the French mainland. Local politicians deplore the fact that metropolitan people occupy most of the top administrative and business positions in the island, even fifty years after the original law of integration (*Le Monde*, 28.2.1991).

Meanwhile, Reunionnese people continue to seek work in poorly paid jobs in mainland France. The rate of unemployment among the islanders living there increased from 2 to 3 per cent in the 1970s to 10 to 15 per cent by the late 1980s. This compares with a national average for France in 1989 of 6 per cent (INSEE, 1991: 24). Many of those who find themselves in the mainland without work return to Reunion, often adding to unemployment levels there. There is some anger, particularly among young educated creole men, at the number of metropolitans living in Reunion and able to find work, while creoles remain unemployed (*Le Monde*, 28.2.1991).

It is in their position as French, and yet distinctive, that the Reunionnese come face to face with the complexity of their citizenship status and its limitations. There is much ignorance concerning the overseas departments, and Reunion in particular, which is often located in the Pacific or the Caribbean by metropolitan French people. On the part of the Reunionnese themselves, a feeling of being second-class French citizens co-exists with a deep desire to continue being included within the Republic, and to retain the benefits conferred by membership of that political community. Moreover, by virtue of history and political identity, the Reunionnese feel entitled to such benefits. The shock of recognising their own distinctiveness as French citizens has been particularly traumatic for the Reunionnese living in mainland France, insofar as they will previously have "considered themselves to be fully French" (Tal, 1976: 80; also see Jardel, 1984: 225; Meyer, 1987: 893).

Conflicting loyalties and identities are not purely metaphorical or cultural. Most families are divided by work and marriage relations between Reunion and the mainland, and the airport at Gillot operates more like a bus station in a provincial town than an international airport. This complexity is seen as confusing by Paul Vergès, leader of the PCR (the Reunionnese Communist Party - *Le Parti Communiste Réunionnais*). Speaking of the creole people, he comments:

> Every Reunionnese person is like a walking civil war. In other words, the individual has been influenced by French culture, has a way of thinking that might be described as French, but still feels [s]he belongs to the island. (TRF, *Le Miroir Colonial*, 30.11.1988)

His observation is interesting. It suggests that creole and French identities are mutually exclusive and discrete. It could be argued that, on the contrary, most Reunionnese people "move easily between the metropolitan and Creole worlds" (Aldrich & Connell, 1992: 177). In addition, to equate French with metropolitan French culture is to exclude the DOM from France, symbolically and perhaps in the future also in fact. A survey of interviews carried out by the local press in 1988 suggested that people's main concerns were to do with improving living standards rather than with abstract questions of identity that preoccupy politicians. Most young people expressed concern at unemployment; those out of work wanted to find a job, and those in work wanted better pay and security; young people also wanted more leisure activities; older people wanted to improve their homes; others asked for better roads, improved sanitation in rural areas, and better child care provision (*Quotidien de la Réunion*, 22 & 29.12.1988).

Violence in Reunion is usually expressed in non-political ways: in a very high level of suicide, and exceptionally high rates of domestic violence and homicide within families compared with metropolitan France (*Le Monde*, 6.3.1991).[7] Their position of utter dependence on a state that seems increasingly inward looking and almost indifferent to the fate of the overseas departments and territories cannot but leave the Reunionnese feeling isolated and frustrated (see Cartoon 1). Some local politicians will admit that there is a widespread fear that, at some future time, the French central government could impose independence, or grant it after holding a national referendum, whatever the opinions of the Reunionnese, and in the name of the 'national self-determination' of the DOM-TOM (J.Pinna, questionnaire, July 1990).

## Caught Between Two Worlds

The fact that the Reunionnese are full French citizens has made all the difference to their material levels of income, health and life expectancy. Among the inhabitants of the Indian Ocean islands, they are the best off on all these counts. In comparison with metropolitan French citizens, however, the Reunionnese are very poor, and income is very unevenly distributed within the island.

This was shown starkly by the introduction of the RMI (*Revenu Minimum d'Insertion*) in 1989. A year after its initial extension to Reunion, over 50 000 individuals had obtained some form of public financial support under this system. They were supporting an estimated 140 000 people, more than a quarter of the total population (Catteau, 1992: 52). According to INSEE estimates, this accounted for 10 per cent of the total RMI allocation for the whole of France, when in population terms Reunion accounted for only 1 per cent of the French total (*Economie et Statistiques*, 1992: 51). At the same time, the region of Reunion has the highest proportion of individual taxpayers subject to the *impôt des fortunes* (a tax on significant assets) of any French region.

This alarming social inequity has prompted proposals by the government for reform of the salary scale for local civil servants. Public sector salaries in Reunion are almost one and a half times those in the French mainland. The proposals of the *Rapport Ripert* were intended to impose cuts of 50 to 70 per cent, but this idea was shelved after strikes paralysed the administration in the early 1990s (*Le Monde*, 15-16.9.1991). The proposals have never been implemented. Business interests in the island have been strongly supportive of the civil servants, arguing that a cut in public sector salaries would affect all sectors of the island's economy by causing a contraction of the local market (Chane Tune, 1991: 94). This argument has proved persuasive.

So long as there are such marked inequalities in income, there will be room for social unrest and discontent with the outcomes of official policies. This happened in 1990 and again in 1991 and 1992, with the first serious public riots witnessed in the island since the Second World War. A sense of relative deprivation of a section of the population, and of social injustice, as well as absolute poverty, can explain a major public riots which took place in February 1991 in parts of the capital city, St Denis. The unrest began and ended in a housing estate known as Le Chaudron, an area of high unemployment. Le Chaudron estate was once hailed as a great achievement in slum improvement. Built in the 1960s, it soon became home to the poorest Reunionnese creoles, including many unemployed people and many single-parent families (Wolff, 1991). The people who lived there were mostly disregarded by the authorities until the riots took place (*Le Monde*, 2.3.1991). It was a part of Reunion where visitors were asked to 'close their eyes' as they drove through (field notes, 3.12.1988). Next to Le Chaudron are the University of Reunion and commercial developments, where French department stores and supermarkets were constructed in the 1980s. The contradiction between the affluence of these shops and the inability of those who live close by to buy most of the consumer goods displayed, was pointed out by the rioters themselves in 1991 (*Le Monde*, 6.3.1991).

The targets of the rioters were primarily the official television and radio stations. The protest started over the decision of the French Audio-visual Commission to close down the unlicensed cable TV station *Télé Free-DOM*, which provided non-stop American movies, sports and pornography, but also local news and discussion programmes in creole rather than French. Creole is not allowed on RFO, the official channel, and the name *Télé Free-DOM* had became highly symbolic of access by previously excluded people to the media. This may explain why the decision to close the station down provoked such an immediate and violent response (*Le Monde*, 25.5.1991; *La Croix*, 19.6.1992). The rioters' targets were not confined to the administration, however. They also looted supermarkets and large chain stores, particularly those selling cars and household equipment. It was in a burning warehouse that seven people died on the first day of the unrest. A few months after the riots, two bombs exploded, destroying an electrical goods shop and a garage (*Le Monde*, 11.6.1991). It is to these shops that many *RMIstes* (those receiving RMI) are indebted (Gerbeau, 1992). Almost exactly one year later, new protests took place. On this occasion no-one died, and protesters, most of whom were long-term unemployed young men, took over a local mayor's office and staged a sit-in demanding work (*Le Monde*, 12.3.1992).

Reunion's remoteness means that problems are not always taken very seriously in Paris, or dealt with promptly. Cases of corruption rarely come to trial, are referred for judgement to the national courts, and never heard of again. "We are so far away, on our little confetti, and we feel completely abandoned" complained one local magistrate (*Le Figaro*, 11.6.1992). In this context, it is not surprising that local politics has become more and more concerned with protecting the interests of the island vis-à-vis the metropolis and the European Community. The Community, and the metropolitan French, after all, are themselves increasingly preoccupied with internal affairs. Xenophobia and racism are on the increase throughout Europe. French governments appear to have become more forgetful of the DOM, except where they are of strategic usefulness or commercially convenient as overseas 'relay points' in relations with neighbouring countries.

The fear of being abandoned is a powerful mobilising force, and is used in Reunion by both the Left and the Right. The Left implicitly acknowledges the assimilationist basis of departmental policy in making social and legal equality the central plank of its political demands (Hintjens, 1991a: 52). On the walls in Reunion, it is common to see the slogan in creole *Egalite Comme de Moun de Frans* (equality like the people of France) (field notes, 27.11.1988). The riots were not the result of ethnic tensions, nor a surface indicator of a deeper desire for independence, but a demand for more equal treatment. So far, independence has been unpopular with the Reunionnese electorate (Aldrich & Connell, 1992: 217).

Demands for recognition of the right to equal treatment were recently expressed by Camille Sudre, metropolitan founder of the pirate radio and television 'Free-DOM' stations. Among the immediate demands put to the government in 1991 after the riots, was the reopening of the *Télé Free-DOM* station, which was agreed to in May 1992. Other demands included identical levels of minimum wages, family allowances and unemployment benefits to those in metropolitan France, as well as more job training and subsidised air travel to the mainland (*Indian Ocean Newsletter*, 28.3.1992). These priorities originated with a list of fifty proposals presented to the Minister of the DOM-TOM, Louis le Pensec, during a visit to Reunion shortly after the riots. Issues of employment and social rights were prominent among the rioters' concerns (*Libération*, 25.3.1991, 24.11.1991). There was a strong sense of *déjà vu* about the proposal to encourage migration to the mainland; free air travel and training for migrants to work in the mainland was first introduced by Michel Debré during the early 1960s. The agency he established to carry this out (BUMIDOM - *Bureau pour le développement des Migrations des Départements d'Outre-Mer*) was so severely criticised as neo-colonial by the Left in the DOM that it was disbanded in 1982 when the Socialist government came to power (Debré, 1974: 40-8; Anselin, 1994: 213-7).

When the measures promoting migration to the mainland were first introduced in the early 1960s, one of the French government's main concerns had been population growth, as well as the assumed consequence in the form of high unemployment of young people. As a result of a recent demographic upturn, politicians from all sides of the political spectrum once again express concern at keeping the birth rate down (*Le Figaro*, 8.3.1991; *Politis*, 14.5.1992). In the 1990s, the problem of unemployment has replaced population in the minds of those recommending a revival of state-assisted migration programmes.

In April 1991, a new development plan for Reunion was agreed through a *pacte de solidarité* signed with the regional authorities. This introduced a series of sixteen measures, including a youth training scheme fund, sports facilities, community participation funds, housing improvements and the recruitment of more creole teachers to replace metropolitans (*Année Politique*, 1992: 400). The following year, the EC committed itself to a massive programme of financial and technical support for small and medium businesses in Reunion, involving telecommunications upgrading and a job creation element (*Indian Ocean Newsletter*, 6.6.1992). In addition, the EC allowed the extension of the local import tax, known as the *octroi de mer*, until 2003. This was a special exemption from the normal terms of the common external tariff (*Indian Ocean Newsletter*, 25.7.1992). Clearly, Reunion is not being completely forgotten in Paris or in Brussels.

Invited to visit the Elysee palace with Paul Vergès, leader of the Reunionnese Communist Party (PCR) in June 1992, Camille Sudre asked for equality for the Reunionnese in social benefits and minimum wages (*Le Monde*, 23.6.1992). Mitterrand agreed that the process of equalisation in wage rates and social benefits would be speeded up (*Indian Ocean Newsletter*, 20.6.1992). In the elections of June 1992, Sudre's Free-DOM electoral list obtained almost one-third of the vote, making it the largest single party in the Regional Council (*Le Quotidien de Paris*, 8.6.1992). This was strengthened by an electoral alliance with the PCR, which until quite recently managed to retain its popularity among the working-class electorate. Local

Socialists were accused of neglecting the problems of the long-term unemployed, and were among the targets of the rioters (*Indian Ocean Newsletter*, 2.3.1991). It will emerge in discussing more recent elections, however, that, rather like the pro-independence vote of 1990 in Martinique, this vote for the Free-DOM-PCR list represented a protest vote rather than a permanent switch in the Reunionnese electorate's alignments.

It is interesting to note that the UDF and the RPR, both parties of the Right, which were once defenders of total legal and cultural assimilation of the DOM to the rest of France, are today those who are keenest to emphasise the need for 'specificity' in policies for the DOM. As Claude Miras observed, social equalisation was mostly achieved under the Right in the 1960s and 1970s, whereas cultural specificity and regional politics have become the order of the day in France since the Left came to power in the early 1980s. Locally, the Reunionnese Left is generally opposed to any measures which are based on seeing the DOM as 'special cases' unless such measures discriminate in favour of the inhabitants of these departments (Miras, 1987). This difference between the Left in mainland France and in Reunion has happened at a time when local business interests, and right-wing politicians, have started for the first time to look to the economic success of the neighbouring island of Mauritius and wonder whether this could somehow be replicated in Reunion.

Advocates of a more 'capitalist' path for Reunion point to the high levels of wages and social provisions in the overseas departments, as parts of France, when compared with real productivity. They argue for the need to balance economic growth with social equality. Yet they also need to recognise, and are forced to accept, that any reduction in the wage rate in Reunion would be politically most unpopular. Locally, only representatives of the Chamber of Commerce and local businessmen (who do not owe their positions to elections by the public) will admit openly that it may be necessary to bring wages down in line with productivity if further private capital investment is to be attracted into the island in future (field notes, 6.12.1988). To openly proclaim such a policy remains taboo, since it would be electorally disastrous for any politician in an island where the 'politics of the belly' is likely to continue to reign supreme.

## Gender Cleavages and Uneven Integration

The most striking lesson which arose out of being in Reunion rather than reading and talking about it was the importance of sexual politics in its widest sense. The relations between women and men, and their respective roles, provide a microcosm of Reunion's relations with metropolitan France and the French state more generally. The nature of these relations is crudely expressed in the lonely hearts columns of the local paper, which are avidly read and widely commented on. Usually, metropolitan (often military) men seek creole mistresses. Creole women, on the other hand, tend to be looking for husbands, and often for metropolitan men as partners. Being passed over in this way causes anger among creole men, who see these women as alienated and mentally colonised, and metropolitan men as sexually aggressive and colonising.

Speaking more generally, these small ads are expressed within a context of rapid changes in local gender relations between men and women. There has been a dramatic shift in employment from mainly manual and agricultural work, performed largely by creole men, to clerical and service employment, where creole women almost equal men. Statistics on employment, education, income and status by sex have now been painstakingly collected by the local INSEE office in each of the DOM, including Reunion (INSEE, 1988a; Pasquet & Squarzoni, 1988). They indicate that the relative position of the two sexes has altered as dramatically as employment patterns.[8]

This apparent gender bias in women's favour is the almost accidental result of structural changes rather than of any conscious favouring of women over men. The effect, overall, has been to marginalise poor creole men from economic life. Women in Reunion have a life expectancy on average ten years longer than men. This can be compared with a difference of eight years in metropolitan France, where average life expectancy is in any case somewhat higher than in Reunion (77 compared with 74) (INSEE, 1991: 43). Creole men have high mortality levels generally, and this is particularly true of younger men: as INSEE estimates, between the ages of 20 and 30, men are three times more likely to die than women. This gap between male and female mortality levels has grown more than proportionally since 1946 (*L'Economie de la Réunion*, 1989: 3-5). To explain this marked difference between male and female mortality patterns, it is worth examining the politics of gender relations more closely. This is rarely done in studies of the DOM, and it is hoped this may shed some light on wider economic, social and political structures in the island, and relations with the rest of France and the EC, as well as being of interest in itself (Gautier, 1994).

Reunionnese women's health has also improved dramatically. This has accompanied an unusually rapid drop in the birth rate, possibly the most rapid ever documented anywhere in the world (Hamon, 1979; Le Cointre, 1982; Festy & Hamon, 1983). The average number of children per woman was 2.8 in 1986, compared with 4.6 in 1970 and 7 in 1952 (Pasquet & Squarzoni,

1988: 17). This decline in fertility has been affected by migration, improvements in health and education and an exceptionally high level of female participation in the expanded public sector and other tertiary employment. By 1990, infant mortality levels in Reunion were 8 per thousand, compared with 7.5 per thousand for the rest of France (INSEE, 1991: 19, 21). This contrasts markedly with the situation in the island before 1946, when infant mortality levels were among the highest recorded in the world, at 165 per thousand. Until the early to mid-1950s, deaths in Reunion exceeded births (Demographic Yearbook UN, 1963: 522-5; Pasquet & Squarzoni, 1988: 17). It is fair to speak of a demographic revolution in Reunion, one which has had especially positive implications for women's health.

The change from a primary, commodity-based economy to a tertiary, service-oriented economy has resulted in a greater proportion of jobs being made available for women. In 1982, it was estimated that 38 800 women were employed in the tertiary sector, compared with 42 800 men (INSEE, 1988a: 36). Since 94 per cent of women's employment is in the tertiary sector, compared with around 55 per cent of men's employment, the expansion of services and government employment has tended to benefit the sexes unevenly in terms of new job opportunities (Pasquet & Squarzoni, 1988: 35). It is apparent to any visitor that working-class creole men, formerly employed in cane planting and cutting, in fishing, in sugar mills and distilleries, have lost much of their economic role and financial independence. In common parlance, the working woman has become a desirable asset - a *pied à riz* - providing for her children and for her male partner, if he is unemployed.

At the same time, social problems have increased, partly as a result of male unemployment, and partly because of rising disposable incomes. Alcoholism and domestic violence reach chronic levels in the island. Murder levels are seven to eight times the French average, belying the image of happy creoles (*Le Monde*, 6.3.1991; *Témoignages*, 6.12.1988). Reunionnese men have a very high rate of fatalities from drink-related violence, road accidents and diseases (*L'Economie de la Réunion*, 1989: 9-11). In the first ten months of 1988, for example, sixty people were killed on Reunion's roads, and most of these were young men (field notes, 25.11.1988). These are among the reasons why substantially more young men between the ages of 20 and 30 die than women in the same age group.

Men remain predominant in the labour force of the non-state and non-service sectors of the economy, where wages are generally low and the need is largely for unskilled labour. In addition, women do better than men in higher education: 62 per cent of university students, and 72 per cent of para-medical and public health trainees (but only 30 per cent of agricultural students) are female (INSEE, 1988a: 33-4). The uneven distribution of employment for women and men between the public and private, primary, secondary and tertiary sectors of the economy may also explain why, in the late 1980s, Reunionnese women's incomes were estimated to be only 9 per cent below those of women in mainland France, compared with a difference of 62 per cent on average for creole men compared with the average for men in the metropolis (*L'Economie de la Réunion*, 1988: 4). Similar discrepancies in the degree of relative inequality can be observed in Martinique and Guadeloupe (INSEE, 1988b; 1988c). In the particular case of Reunion, some studies suggest that women's greater financial independence from men has enhanced their autonomy and confidence (Pasquet & Squarzoni, 1988: 33, Wolff, 1991: 91-107). There is certainly a paradox, in that,

> Generally speaking, whereas in the hexagon [mainland France] women have jobs which are generally less well paid than men, the opposite is true in Reunion: the average income of women is higher than that of men. (*L'Economie de la Réunion*, 1990: 4)

The myth of the woman as a *pied à riz* ignores the fact that many more women are unemployed or impoverished than men (Gautier, 1994: 159). The number of single-parent women-headed households has increased very sharply, and these households generally have much lower income levels than households where there is a working man. Attempted suicides are also high among young women as well as young men, particularly those women living in more remote rural areas who may feel excluded from the benefits of the 'modern life' (*Témoignages*, 1.12.1988).

In poorer urban communities such as Le Chaudron, nuclear families are very much the exception since men are rarely in a position to 'provide'. Serial fatherhood is common, and the French state benefit system provides for single parents, which can place a premium for a creole woman on being sole tenant of her living space rather than sharing it with a male partner on whom she would be assumed to be 'dependent'. There is also considerable 'extension' of the family structure, expressed in the strong material solidarity between women-headed households, involving mothers and daughters, friends and neighbours. This mutual assistance extends to child care and sharing of food (Wolff, 1991). Such households can hardly be described as matriarchal, since the solidarity between women represents a coping mechanism to deal with their poverty and exclusion, rather than any intentional subordination or exclusion of men.

In recent years, women-headed households in poorer urban areas of Reunion have become the objects of anthropological study. They are seen to display many of the features of poor inner-city households in metropolitan

France (Wolff, 1991). Yet their problems are peculiarly Reunionnese to the extent that relations between the sexes have been totally transformed by the economic and social impact of the integration process as it has affected this plantation island since 1946.

Returning to the lonely hearts columns, it was sometimes remarked that Reunionnese women, in looking for metropolitan male partners, were expressing their disgust with some of the more destructive forms of male behaviour prevalent in Reunion: drunkenness, violence, sexual infidelity and an inability or unwillingness to provide financially. There is a tension produced by the apparent mismatch between traditional 'family values', which remain strong, and the dramatically altered possibilities of finding employment for unskilled men in particular. The metropolitan man may also become drunk, violent and unfaithful, but on the whole he has the distinct attraction of being more able (even if not necessarily more willing) to provide the financial security needed, for example to bring up children (field notes, Pasquet & Squarzoni, 1988: 27). Only very rarely is it possible for creole women to take advantage of this, since metropolitan men tend to regard creole women as mistresses rather than as potential marriage partners.

It is quite ironic that most wealthier creole men, and many prominent creole politicians, prefer to marry metropolitan French women rather than creole women from Reunion. This includes some of those who are the most adamantly *créoliste* politically, claiming to defend the *petit créole* man and woman against the imperialistic designs of metropolitans (field notes, 21.11. 1988; 3.12.1988).

In many ways the cleavages between men and women have been aggravated by forces over which they have little or no control. It is not until this aspect of unevenness in departmental policy is appreciated that one can make much sense of the political tensions that have emerged in recent years over the use of creole in the media. There is much resentment among creole men, among the young unemployed, but also among students, that metropolitan men are more attractive to creole women and 'take our women away'. The resentment can be exploited politically: it is an undercurrent to which allusion is made. The slogan *Réunion aux Réunionnais* appears to have more resonance among young men than among young women, reflecting the formers' feelings of hurt pride and economic and social marginality.

Marriage relations between the average creole man and a metropolitan woman would be even more unlikely than between a metropolitan man and a creole woman. Most metropolitan women in Reunion come as wives of officials and businessmen or for a holiday. There is also a continued colonial mentality of 'untouchability' in relation to white women. There are few creole men who would be able to fill the role of provider for a metropolitan woman. Indeed, young Reunionnese men may have more chance of intimacy with a metropolitan person through homosexual relations. On the whole, metropolitan French people living in or visiting Reunion stick to Paris-style cafes, eat patisserie and visit the theatre, where it is still possible to see white people portray Africans as savages (field notes, 21.11.1988). One cannot help feeling that, although Reunion may indeed be France, the metropolitan French who live there have a lifestyle that is distinctly colonial in feel. They do not frequent the poorer urban areas, do not buy food from Chinese corner shops or go to creole cafes and rum bars. They remain on the boulevards, sipping coffee and eating croissant for breakfast, away from the side-streets where they might glimpse squalor or poverty; they have creole maids to care for the children, and generally regard the locals as good or naughty children, depending on their outlook.

Everyone you meet in Reunion has family in metropolitan France and elsewhere in the world. Until the 1980s, many younger people emigrated to the mainland, and today almost 150 000 people, one-fifth of the population, live in mainland France (INSEE, 1991: 45). Social contact between poorer creoles and metropolitans, both in the island and in the metropolis, is still marked by stark inequality and some abuse of power. Creole women are vulnerable to mistreatment and harassment in their work as maids, nannies, shop assistants and secretaries. Young creole men in towns work mostly in low paid jobs as bus drivers, guards, clerks or administrators in the public sector. They may do odd jobs, and sometimes double as jovial, but always subservient, drinking and sporting partners of metropolitan men.

In Reunion, the poor white men tend to be the most isolated of all, being little involved in the urban centres where creoles and metropolitans mix socially. Poorer blacks in the main towns have come to depend almost exclusively on benefits and occasional manual labouring jobs in construction and road-building. This kind of temporary employment is often provided by local municipalities, sometimes in exchange for political 'favours'. Such favours may include acting as informal security guard during election periods, or simply voting for the nominated candidate.

Much of the nationalist and official 'planning' literature on the DOM regrets the present marginality of the productive economy. There is a widely-held view that the service and public sectors are 'parasitic' and embody 'artificial' forms of economic activity, compared with real production in the agricultural and industrial sectors. Yet it is worth remembering that the productive economic base in Reunion was the plantation, which formed the social, economic and political unit of the colonial society. Departmental policies have aimed to transform social structures associated with the past. As such, it is hardly surprising that the plantation, which was the main economic, social and political institution of French colonialism in Reunion, has gone into sharp decline. By the same token, however, departmental policy has ruled out the possibility of an industrialisation strategy based on comparative advantage by introducing levels of pay based on national norms in France as a whole, which are out of all proportion to labour productivity levels in Reunion itself.

If economic option are expressed solely in terms of a choice between honest toil on the land or in the factory, or idle dallying in service employment and financial dependence on 'Papa welfare state', this has some serious implic-ations for the politics of gender roles. The nationalist formulation expresses a bias not only against types of employment generally carried out by women, but also against the principle of equal access to welfare provisions for inhabitants of the DOM. The argument is that familiarity with the welfare state has created a 'hand-out mentality' among recipients.

Most women in Reunion carry a double burden of work at low pay and unpaid housework. Their access to benefits is not automatic, but depends on having access to regular, officially declared and insured forms of employment. Single mothers who live on state benefits are also subject to policing of their sexual relations. The same can be said of women in other regions of welfare states where there is high unemployment and many women-headed households. Controversies about welfare dependency and single mothers in the US and more recently in Britain have expressed the same concern with moral laxity and the so-called dependency culture (Baca Zinn, 1989). The idea that welfare dependence causes the break-up of families and marginalises the male provider has been described as "...the generative example of blaming the victim" (Baca Zinn, 1989: 858).

At a metaphorical level, such images of the ideal economy express a fear of collective 'emasculation'; the fear that Reunion and the other DOM-TOM have become mere decorations for France; the 'dancing girls', 'pretty girls in rags' or 'artificial creations' of French policy (de Baleine, 1981; Guillebaud, 1976). The implication seems to be that 'the people' should be earning their living by the sweat of their brow rather than in an office, and that men rather than women should be the main breadwinner. In the context of Reunion, the inadvertent result is to glamorise colonial plantation labour, hardly an attract-ive option for most Reunionnese today.

What is really at stake in Reunion is whether women and men living in the island should have equal rights with the population of the rest of France.. Almost all Reunionnese now depend for the largest share of their income on continued expansion of the public and services sector. The rhetoric of economic nationalism therefore appears to be used for symbolic rather than practical reasons.

## Stomach Politics and Regional Reforms

The dominant mode of politics in Reunion appears to be what Jean-François Bayart has called the 'politics of the belly'. One of the distinctive features of this form of politics is the fusion of the private and public spheres, and of economic and political power structures (Bayart, 1993: 96-8). Unlike the case of the Antilles, where the characteristics and causes of this clientilistic form of politics has been well documented and researched (Constant, 1988: Daniel, n.d.; Moutoussamy, 1988), there have been few serious studies of local politics in Reunion. Various forms of political patronage have become institutionalised and routinised in the operation of municipal, departmental and regional government. As in the Antilles, the local state in Reunion "rather than being a representative of the people, is a surrogate father - a fixer and an employer" (Nabajoth, 1985:145). This takes place within a context of reliance of the population on the state for a large part of its income. Clientilism therefore has as its foundation the legal entitlement of the Reunionnese to social benefits and wage levels close to the national level. The former Minister for the DOM-TOM, Louis Le Pensec, stated the public view of all local politicians when he claimed that, although

> the economic development of these areas [i.e. the DOM-TOM] is to the detriment of social development...it would be a terrible error of judgement to start levelling wages and work conditions of Reunion with those of neighbouring states in the Indian Ocean to ensure competitive standards. (*Indian Ocean Newsletter*, 16.11.1991)

This statement came in response to proposals in the French National Assembly to create a deregulated, low-wage economic 'free zone' in Reunion. As always, the main aim of such a scheme was to try and resolve the chronic problem of unemployment. Not only do wages remain high, in addition the riots of 1991 may have adversely affected prospects of attracting private investment. It thus appears that for the foreseeable future the French state and the EC will need to continue subsidising capital investment in the DOM if any more jobs are to be created (*Indian Ocean Newsletter*, 29.8.1992).

During the 1960s and 1970s, the Gaullist politician Michel Debré explicitly advocated increased expenditure on social and physical infrastructure as the best means of retaining the hearts and minds of the Reunionnese (Debré, 1976). In addition public employment has been provided through massive investment in infrastructure, social services, education and health. As has been mentioned, this has led many commentators to conclude that Reunion's economic and social structures are 'artificial' because they are so highly dependent on French state intervention (Albertini, 1965; Benoist, 1974; Mathieu, 1988).

Yet it needs to be emphasised that this 'artificial' structure supports and maintains the incomes and consumption levels, education and health of real human beings who might otherwise find themselves considerably impoverished by comparison. State expenditure in the DOM is not charity or aid: most of it comes automatically as the counterpart of the French citizenship of the islanders. Indeed, as noted in the case of the French Antilles in the last chapter, Reunion's population, being on average poorer than the population of metropolitan France, is subsidised indirectly through the French state's unitary system of public accounting.

Regional reforms introduced in the early 1980s were intended to transform the formal institutional relationship between local politicians and the central organs of the state from one of subordination to one of more equal partnership (*Le Monde Dossiers et Documents*, 1992: 1). They were also supposed to make such relations more transparent, and more democratic (Mény, 1985). The overseas regions now enter into 'contract plans' with the central organs of the state, and these plans are supposed to be publicly debated and freely negotiated between the region and the state. An integrated regional development plan for the DOM, known as POSEIDOM, has also been discussed between the European Community, the French government and the regional authorities of the four overseas departments (Reno, 1993; Jos, 1994: 256-8). This kind of 'equalisation' of relations between the central organs of the state and the regional authorities may have reduced centrifugal political forces in the DOM, but has not allayed fears of abandon.

Regionalisation was the Socialist Party's response to territorially based demands for autonomy and independence from left-wing parties in the DOM. The immediate result was a general moratorium on the status and autonomy issue, declared by the Communist Parties and the PPM (*Le Naïf*, 10.5.1981; Constant, 1988; Hintjens, 1991b). By satisfying local demands for greater local involvement the reforms led to a renewal of political life. There was a move beyond the stalemate of the 1960s and 1970s, when the local political debate in Reunion, as in the French Antilles, appeared stuck between the grooves: Left - autonomist or separatist and anti-French; Right - departmentalist and pro-French. When the Left was re-elected to power after more than twenty years of Gaullist monopoly, this equation dissolved. This was once again that 'other' France, a radical, anti-colonial and egalitarian France. Only this time, the state appeared in a decentralising mood, more concerned to recognise regional specificities, and markedly less Jacobin than before (Kesselman, 1985).

The Reunionnese Communist Party, the PCR, has remained one of the largest in the world in terms of its proportional electoral support, and one reason for this is undoubtedly its continued insistence on equal rights as the central plank of all other policy demands and programmes. Historically assimilatory, the Left in the overseas departments of France retains this basic materialism. This can be contrasted with the sometimes 'folksy' approach of the Right, which tends to romanticise the creole identity, characterising the islanders as sweet, tropical children with quaint ways, not quite mature enough to be given the heavy responsibilities of full French citizenship.

In the late 1980s and 1990s, a series of corruption scandals have emerged in Reunion, in connection with the tax incentive scheme known as *défiscalisation*. There are frequent complaints of corruption by local politic-ians of all parties, which have in recent years been taken more seriously by the central authorities in Paris and their local legal representatives, including the Prefect (*Le Figaro*, 11.6.1992). In 1993 two politicians of the Left, accused of fraud, were 'on the run' in the island to escape arrest (*Indian Ocean Newsletter*, 17.7.1993). The imprisonment of one of these, Eric Boyer, a former Senator and Socialist President of the Regional Council, and of another Socialist, Gilbert Annette, former mayor of St Denis, has added to popular perceptions that the local political scene needs to be 'cleaned up' (*Guardian*, 26.3.1994). The son of the leader of the PCR, Pierre Verges, who was also wanted for financial malpractice, was in hiding for over a year. In spite of this, the Left remains popular with the electorate in Reunion. In the Presidentials of 1995, Jospin received 56 percent of the vote (*Le Monde Hebdomadaire*, 10.5.1995).

Low overall participation rates among Reunion's electorate may reflect disillusion with all politicians, creole or otherwise. National politics appear to be of more interest than regional or even departmental politics. Participation rates in European elections are lowest of all, with 23 per cent taking part in 1989 and 26 per cent in 1992 (*Le Monde*, 20.6.1989; Jos, 1994: 257). This compares with abstention rates of 30 to 40 per cent in most legislative elections, 20 to 25 per cent in presidentials and over 40 per cent in regional elections (*Le Monde*, 10.5.1988; 13.3.1993; 21 & 23.3.1993). The abstention rate in the second round of the Presidentials of 1995 was 25 per cent (*Le Monde Hebdomadaire*, 7.5.1995).

Clientilism is not an anomaly, or something which only operates at election time. It is the major mode of legitimation for the entire integration project, involving local politicians acting as brokers between the French state and local electorate (Constant, 1988). Violence is also used, and it is common at election times for politicians to hire paid *nervis*, or thugs, who intimidate and threaten voters and political opponents. The popularity of the PCR until very recently was due to its ability to create a local version of 'municipal socialism'. This involved a sophisticated and technocratic form of inter-municipal patronage, creating jobs for party members and supporters, and instituting public works schemes involving close and considerable co-operation between the various municipalities under PCR control. In the last legislative elections in 1993 the PCR-Free-DOM alliance was defeated in four out of five constituencies. Only Paul Vergès, PCR General Secretary since the late 1950s, was re-elected (*Le Monde*, 23.3.1993). Unusually, these elections were a victory for independent, right-wing dissident and Socialist candidates.

Low overall participation rates among Reunion's electorate may reflect disillusion with all politicians, creole or otherwise. National politics appear to be of more interest than regional or even departmental politics. Participation rates in European elections are lowest of all, with 23 per cent taking part in 1989 and 26 per cent in 1992 (*Le Monde*, 20.6.1989; Jos, 1994: 257). This compares with abstention rates of 30 to 40 per cent in most legislative elections, 20 to 25 per cent in presidentials and over 40 per cent in regional elections (*Le Monde*, 10.5.1988; 13.3.1993; 21 & 23.3.1993). The abstention rate in the second round of the Presidentials of 1995 was 25 per cent (*Le Monde Hebdomadaire*, 7.5.1995).

The 1990s have been marked by a more inward-focused political debate in Reunion, and this is broadly true of each of the other overseas departments as well. Whereas in the 1960s and 1970s, there were many parallels in the terms of political debate in each of the DOM, increasingly there has been a fragmentation in the internal political debates and logic of elections in Reunion, Martinique, Guadeloupe and Guyane. It may well be that the regional reforms have contributed to this process; perhaps

> the adoption of some form of regional planning by a government can have the unintentional effect of mobilising political groups which demand more resources and rights for 'their' region. (Gore, 1984: 262)

A new form of creolist nationalist politics emerged in the 1980s. The argument of the PCR from the late 1950s to the early 1980s was that Reunion needed a completely new political status, called *autonomie démocratique et populaire*. Once regional reforms opened up the political space for local alliances between Left and Right, a broad consensus emerged on the need to give priority to island interests. Creole politicians of all political stripes declared their willingness to work together for this purpose. To be able to speak creole, once reminiscent of slavery and manual labour, has become an asset for any politician who wishes to be taken seriously. It has become clear also that the old creole elite, still partly based in the sugar industry, agrees on certain important points with the Communist Party: the Reunionnese must be given priority in jobs, and the island must be enabled to develop in a more self-reliant way economically. As one creole man said when interviewed by a local paper, "*Bande zoreil y occupe trop de postes importantes. Apres na pie la place pou nous*" ("The metropolitan French take all the best jobs, and then there is no more room for us": i.e. us creoles) (*Quotidien de la Réunion*, 10.12.1988). Stated this simply, a creolist policy has wide appeal among the unemployed (Lacoste, 1991: 12,14).

As was suggested earlier, the recent work of Jean-François Bayart on the 'politics of the belly' may be useful in interpreting local politics in Reunion. Although the setting of his work is the post-independence state in francophone black Africa, the following observation may shed some light on the combination in Reunion's case of a continued dependence on the French state with the undoubted and considerable achievements that have resulted from pursuing an integrationist policy since 1946.

> The daily process of creolisation, far from reflecting an inherent cultural alienation to the supposed extraneity of the State, suggests instead a real ideological interiority which is capable of inspiring institutional or administrative innovations in the pure constitutional and bureaucratic register of power. (Bayart, 1993: 244)

In language, too, new phrases and categories of identification have emerged which express the fusion and complex articulations characteristic of the politics of clientilism. One example is the word *zoréoles*, coined to describe those metropolitans who have lived so long in Reunion and identified so closely with the creoles that they are no longer entirely outsiders. This fusion of the words *créole* and *zoreil* is a typically humorous creole device.

Local politicians have considerable scope to adapt national political institutions and procedures to the local context. There is a complex process of cultivating an ever-greater financial dependence on the central institutions of the French state, and yet asserting the right of control over the use of those resources and their distribution at local level. The agenda of local politicians is to enhance their redistributive powers and leverage over the electorate and to increase their executive and fiscal autonomy from administrators and politicians in central government. This bargaining and renegotiation of boundaries found a kind of resolution in the context of the regional reforms. By creating an additional level of administration and political representation in the DOM, these reforms led to an increase in the overall budget. Politicians' main concern remains first and foremost to secure continued public funding at the highest possible levels. In 1991-2 the budget for the DOM was cut by 10 per cent, which seriously undermined future prospects for economic growth in the four regions (*Le Monde*, 4.8.1992). Increasingly, in this context of recession, public policy and local and regional politics have become concerned with the distribution of a shrinking pie.

## The End of a Model of Integration?

The whole Post-War history of Reunion might be regarded as an unusual and interesting colonial social and welfare experiment, were it not for the fact that the integration option was initiated by the Reunionnese themselves. Popular sentiment was fully behind the proposal for departmental status in 1946 (Sablé, 1955; Mémorial de la Réunion, 1968).

With regionalisation in the 1980s, a paradox has emerged. As the regions have acquired greater control over resources and public expenditure, recession has deepened. In practice, the recent history of regionalisation in France has been about the administration of declining budgets and unpopular liberalisation measures. There is now greater control over resources at the regional level, but the context is of industrial restructuring away from France and other former industrial heartlands and towards the newly industrialising countries, including Mauritius in the Indian Ocean. It is clear that the overseas departments have not been "exempt from the budgetary squeeze that is hitting public expenditure in France" (*Financial Times*, 18.12.1985).

Recent demands for a second department in Reunion, to be located in the south of the island, may reflect an attempt to consolidate public expenditure at existing levels by creating a new tier of administration in the island. The overseas departments are already the only French regions to be composed of a single department each, so that regional and departmental authorities have identical constituencies. With a second department in the South, the Communist Party of Reunion (PCR) would have a stronger position in the island (*Démocratie Moderne*, 7.3.1991).

Liberalisation in the DOM took a particular form, with five years of tax relief on investment, starting in 1985 (known as *défiscalisation*). This encouraged a temporary boom in construction in the private sector, but it produced no sustained growth in production or employment. Competing for investment funds in this way heightened the sense of insecurity in Reunion about the commitment of the French state to maintain its present level of public spending. It has been predictably very difficult to attract much private capital to invest in the island, given the very high wage levels relative to labour productivity (interview, J. Payet, 30.11.1988).

With declining government revenues and stringent fiscal policies, the parental generosity of the French state appears less reliable. It may be that, as a Planning Commission report put it, "there is no longer any point waiting for Godot" (*"plus rien ne sert d'attendre Godot"*) (CGP, 1983: 11). The same sense of hopelessness was expressed by Michel Rocard when he visited Reunion shortly after the riots. "I am not related to Father Christmas" he complained, when faced with the high level of expectations from representatives of the Reunionnese population (*Le Monde*, 19.3.1991). He reminded those he addressed in Chaudron that things were not all that rosy in mainland France either, especially for inhabitants of the poorer suburbs of big cities. The crowd responded by resuming riots that night, burning cars and shops (*Libération*, 18.3.1991).

According to Michel Debré, interviewed shortly before Michel Rocard's visit, the greatest threat to Reunion's status as a French overseas department was the continuing neglect of the Socialist government (*Le Figaro*, 8.3.1991). On the whole, the Reunionnese are against any prospect of independence. There is a danger, however, that social and political unrest will be confused with separatist agitation by relatively uninformed observers in the French mainland (Gerbeau, 1992). Public opinion in France is shifting concerning the best future option for the remaining overseas possessions, the DOM-TOM. Any debate on their future takes place in the light of the creation of the construction of the European Union and the ongoing conflicts in New Caledonia. It seems likely, in this wider context, that independence might one day seem a desirable and realistic political option. However, France's quite major strategic interests in the Indian Ocean mean that, of the four overseas departments, Reunion is perhaps the least likely to be 'abandoned'.

## Notes

1. When I mentioned this idea later to some students, they replied, yes indeed, and the train is full of people who are having a party, happily unaware that the bridge ahead has collapsed, and making so much noise they cannot hear the nationalists warning them to apply the brakes before it is too late (field notes, 30.11.1988)! Such is the wealth of different interpretations that can be made using a single metaphor.

2. The experience could be likened to time travel, since, like a mediaevalist, I had not expected to visit the society I was studying. There was considerable interest in why a Scottish-Belgian woman should be interested in Reunion. How had I come to know

the names of the plants, of towns, details of historical events, important families, and even one or two recipes for creole dishes without ever having set foot in Reunion? There were surprising discoveries, including the importance of sexual politics, which has been included as a section in this chapter.

3.  The major study on the Reunionnese in mainland France, which is now very dated: Tal, 1976. Another important source of information is Albert Techer's study (1983).

4.  *Cafres*: population of African and Malagasy origin, imported as slaves from the seventeenth to nineteenth centuries; *malbars*: population of South Indian origin, probably from Tamil Nadu and Karnataka, imported as indentured labour in the nineteenth century; *zindous* (*les hindous*): overlap with *malbars* and *tamouls* non-muslim people of Indian origin and still practising some hindu rituals, not necessarily exclusively; *zarabes*: muslim Indians, mostly from Gujerat, mainly came as traders in the late nineteenth and early twentieth centuries; *tiblancs* (*petits blancs*): poor whites, some of them descendants of first settlers. They are quite mixed with Malagasy and European elements; mostly live in the interior, known as Les Hauts; many emigrated to French mainland in the 1960s. Other groups are the *chinois*, most of whom run small shops selling almost everything at a price, and the *Grands Blancs*, descendants of the white settlers who did not lose their land after the abolition of slavery, as the *tiblancs* did; still dominate commerce and the sugar industry. *Zoreil*, also used in the Antilles, refers to the metropolitan French. The expression can be roughly translated as 'ears'.

5.  In many families of *petits blancs* any physical manifestation of negro features is treated as a form of disability, and children in such families who have negro hair, African facial features or any other signs of 'not being Caucasian' may even be kept hidden, socially ostracised, and not regarded as members of the family. An example of a student with this experience was given by an interviewee (Jacques Tual, 28.11.1988, field notes).

6.  Legal minimum wage levels in Reunion are slightly below the national minimum wage. The difference is less than 5 per cent, however, and cannot be compared with the difference between wages in Reunion and in Mayotte, for example, where the inhabitants do not have full French citizenship. In 1988 a teacher with the same qualifications would earn 2500 French francs per month in the Comoros, compared with 20 000 French francs in Reunion (Marcel Philippe in TRF's programme, *Le Miroir Colonial*, transmitted November 1988).

7.  There is a certain level of everyday violence associated with economic interests. One old *tamoul* woman, from whom I bought the poor person's supper of stew in a piece of French bread, showed me her broken fingers. She had twice been attacked by hired thugs, who had broken three of her fingers, in an attempt to move her out of the tin shack which she occupied in one of the main streets of the capital, St Denis. She said the police were sympathetic but that the businessman who wanted the land lied in court, and was not prosecuted owing to lack of evidence (field notes, 29.11.1988).

8.  For a comparison with women's economic and social position in the Antilles, see INSEE, 1988b,c and also Gautier, 1994.

# 4 An Unsettled Colonial Question: French Guyane

*If the Japanese had DOM-TOM of their own, they would transform them into economic showcases. Let's make the most of overseas France!*
G. Grignon (deputy St Pierre & Miquelon), *Le Monde*, 17.4.1987.

*Is not the fact that we provide French Guyana with the means to protect itself against violence and destruction from outside justification enough for the French presence in this far-away land?*
*Le Monde*, 12.5.1987.

## Introduction

There is some contradiction in these two statements of desired policy. In the context of French Guyane,[1] protection and security of the existing social and natural resources are hard to reconcile with the further exploitation, settlement and economic development of the territory. The society and politics of French Guyane are beset by tensions between the drive for a *mise en valeur* of the Guyanese interior, on the one hand, and the protective centralism of the French state, on the other.

The colonial question in French Guyane is unsettled in two senses. In the first place the internal settlement of the territory is far from complete. In addition the form that self-determination in the territory would take, and whether it would result in independence, are questions that are yet to be resolved. These two incomplete forms of colonialism tend to reinforce each other. So long as the French state retains its control over French Guyane, the creoles will look to the state for assistance with their development plans. So long as the local creole settlers are unable to extract significant resources from the territory, they will continue to depend on the expenditure of the French state for their basic livelihoods. Independence is unlikely to become a popular option under these circumstances.

The three Guyanas differ remarkably in several respects, and these differences may largely be traced to differences in the nature and degree of colonisation itself (Scherm, 1987). We are using the term here in its original sense, to denote the settlement of non-indigenous peoples in 'foreign' lands, and the exploitation of the resources of those lands. To this day, settlement patterns in the three Guyanas exhibit the differing colonial practice of Great Britain, the Netherlands and France. The population density of Guyane is around 1 person per square kilometre ($km^2$), with a total population of around 100 000 for an area of 90 000 $km^2$. This compares with an average of 2.4 people per $km^2$ in Surinam and 3.7 people on average per $km^2$ in Guyana. Given the very similar ecological, climatic and geographical features of Guyana, Surinam and the French territory, Guyane emerges as by far the least 'colonised' or economically developed of the three Guyanas. In spite of this, per capita incomes in the 1990s compare favourably with those in the other two Guyanas.

Integration into France has resulted in a drastic loss of economic autonomy; again in 1985, Guyane's total exports and imports amounted to $32.9 and $239 millions, respectively, compared with $214 and $209 million for Guyana and $314 and $266 million for Surinam (Dupont, 1988: 58-9). However, this deterioration in the 'trade balance' has little meaning as Guyane has no need to balance its budget with the rest of France. As in the Antilles and in Reunion, the increase in imports and fall in exports have been the direct result of a rapid improvement in per capita incomes. In Guyane the trade gap is particularly spectacular, being between 10:1 and 20:1 (i.e. exports cover only between 5 and 10 per cent of imports into Guyane).

The apparently vast potential in natural resources: in timber, in gold and other minerals and forest products makes Guyane potentially the wealthiest of the overseas departments. Yet there have been great difficulties in realising this potential. One plan after another has failed to produce results. The main export, shrimps, is not produced in the territory of Guyane at all, but offshore. There has been a steady decline even in timber exports (Brasset, 1987: 3-5).

As Bridget Jones and Elie Stephenson recently remarked, the territory of Guyane is "torn between its marked economic dependence and the challenge of taking up its destiny" (Jones & Stephenson, 1994: 101). The challenge may be an illusion, particularly under French colonialism. French colonisers, deseredly or not, have on the whole gained a reputation as less destructive of indienous Amerindian society than their Dutch, Spanish or British counterparts (Berkhofer, 1978: 115).

This chapter explores the historical origins of the 'colonial' problem in French Guyane, and the specificity of French development policy in the territory. In particular, it examines the developmental ambitions of the main creole political party of the post-war period, the PSG (*Le Parti Socialiste Guyanais*). Are their proposals for 'internal colonisation' realisable with state assistance? The history of previous attempts to exploit Guyane's natural resources suggests that such proposals are doomed to failure. What alternative forms of development could exist for Guyane? France's main satellite-launching base is located in Kourou, which until the 1970s was a sleepy fishing village on the coast. Given the difficulties of expanding the use of natural resources in the territory itself, can Guyane perhaps base its future economic development on the exploitation of outer space?

## Has French Guyane a History?

This surprising question is asked by the French Guyanese historian Elie Stephenson. He posits a connection between the lack of internal settlement, the underexploitation of resources and the difficult task of establishing a French Guyanese identity and discovering the real history of the population (Stephenson, 1978). It could almost be said that the history of French Guyane is the history of what failed to take place in successive periods. In particular, it is the history of failed settlement efforts organised by the French state. This history really starts in 1763, with the so-called disaster of Kourou, when two-thirds of 10 000 French settlers transported to Guyane died within a few years of their arrival (Schwarzbeck, 1986: 174). Coming shortly after the cession of Canada, the Kourou experiment was followed by a similarly fated settlement project in 1820. These failures, combined with the fear of depopulation within France itself, discouraged any further efforts at large-scale European settlement of Guyane.

The importance of the Kourou experience in French colonial history can be gauged from the fact that more French settlers were sent to Guyane in 1763 than had been selected for emigration to Canada during the entire colonial period there. The project 'came to ground' in the mangrove swamps, and the idea of large-scale European overseas settlement was abandoned. To this day, partly as a result of this, "French America [is] essentially an insular America" (Morisset, 1986: 262) both geographically and in terms of mentality. It is confined to the narrow coastal belt of Guyane, and includes the islands of Martinique, Guadeloupe, St Pierre et Miquelon and the social and cultural island of Quebec.

In its potential (and in its likely future were it to become independent), French Guyane is more Brazilian than Caribbean. Anthony Payne agrees that for the Guyanas, the Brazilian connection may "represent a greater opportunity for political and economic development than active participation within the Caribbean region" (Payne, 1984: 135). As a rather unproductive plantation enclave, Guyane has been Caribbean by default, as it were, by failing to expand internally the frontier of the colonial society. Seen from the settlers' point of view, the jungle of French Guyane often appears as a wilderness, or a desert, with Cayenne an outpost of civilisation, an oasis lost in its midst (Lémery, 1925:15, Audige, 1985: 64).

Since 1946, the French state has ostensibly been decolonising its relations with Guyane's inhabitants, creole and Indian, through the introduction of the legal, political and social rights of French citizenship to the population. But in another sense, whatever the formal legal status of the population, it is clear from the priorities of the creole population (the population of outside origin, born locally, but excluding the Amerindian and Bush Negro populations) that the much hoped-for colonisation of Guyane is still expected to take place in the future.

Stephenson furthermore sees French Guyane as a 'pseudo-society', with a constant process of cultural fragmentation taking place. Researchers have stressed the pronounced individualism of the Creoles (Jolivet, 1990: 22; Jones & Stephenson, 1994). The natural environment of the rainforest is a part of this, since it acted as a sieve through which slaves, indentured labourers and other immigrants seeking freedom and fortunes could escape the control of the French colonial authorities (Girondin, 1986: 5). This was not possible in the much smaller island colonies of Martinique and Guadeloupe.

The same centrifugal process has been identified in French Canada, where extreme political centralisation undermined the economic autonomy of the settler society. In both French Guyane and in French Canada, the colonial society was 'headless' in the sense that the economic elite was unable to develop its own separate economic interest and nationalism. Most profitable economic activity was the work of isolated settlers, rarely supported by the French state. In Guyane the gold rush of the late nineteenth century was an example of this. As we shall see, the creole population continues to look to the French state for support even when proposing the exploitation and settlement of the Guyane interior. This is paradoxical because, unless it obtains its own state, the settler society of Guyane is unlikely to be able fully and 'freely' to exploit the interior (McRae, 1964: 225-70).

In its early stages, the fragmentation of French Guyanese society took the form of a refuge into the jungle and the creation of so-called Bush Negro or maroon societies, based on the partial reconstruction of West African modes of living. The plantation system did not fully recover from the first abolition of slavery in 1794, when most slaves abandoned the plantations for good. After 1848, when slavery was again abolished, efforts were made to recruit contract workers from Madeira, West Africa, India and China (Girondin, 1986). Mortality levels were extremely high, and of those who survived many did not stay in French Guyane. For example, by 1885, of 8472 Indians recruited between 1860 and 1877, 4621 (or 55 per cent) had died, 1184 had returned to India, 184 had left for Guadeloupe and 2483 remained in Guyane (Girondin, 1986: 28). The constant departure of labour from the plantations could not be prevented by the introduction of strict controls. In the late nineteenth century agriculture was almost entirely abandoned as creoles moved into the interior in large numbers to prospect for gold.

French Guyane was a penal colony. Efforts to encourage free French citizens to settle permanently in this tropical wilderness having failed, the policy from 1851 onwards was simply to send French prisoners, and Guyane was mainly known as a penal colony until the early twentieth century. This was never a serious project of settlement, and not surprisingly it did not create an independent local pioneer class who might have been capable of exploiting the region's resources. At no time after the early nineteenth century was the colony of Guyane of any special economic interest to France. As Frank Schwarzbeck sees it: "During the first Empire, it was part of the larger possessions which were of little economic importance." At this time, the Caribbean islands were by far the most profitable colonies. By the nineteenth century, however, during the second empire, Guyane became "one of the smaller possessions which were of little economic importance" (Schwarzbeck, 1986: 176).

As has already been suggested, relative neglect was combined with a high degree of centralised state control. Guyane's colonisation and settlement were constantly hampered by the tight control of the ministries in Paris over all economic and legal affairs in the colony. Under the *pacte coloniale*, the state had a monopoly on land, and stringent regulations governed the recruitment and treatment of labour, which served to limit internal economic activity, and placed a brake on colonisation. French colonial rule generally was much more about exercising political control than about maximising economic returns from the colonies. The Empire was retained first and foremost for reasons of national prestige.

There is a more general point to be made here relating to the nature of French colonial rule. In British colonial policy, mechanisms of indirect rule often facilitated liberalisation and commercialisation of the colonial economy. By contrast, the centralised, direct control of the French state (in both its Republican and monarchical form) inhibited local moves towards greater economic autonomy.

Unlike indirect rule in the British manner, where the preservation of custom was left to 'traditional' authorities, in the French colonies it was generally the central state legislation which tried to preserve pre-existing economic autonomies and to prevent their erosion through commerce. In French Guyane, the preservation of the indigenous Amerindian people has resulted in part from the failure of all large-scale settlement efforts throughout Guyane's colonial history.

The insularity of creole society and of the 'modern' enclave introduced since 1946 may be related to its external orientation. By the same token, the absence of an inwardly-directed project of colonisation and 'development' may account for the continuing fragmentation of the society into a number of discrete and relatively autonomous economic, social and cultural entities. To reiterate the argument so far: it appears that in the peculiar nature of French state, and in the French capital's lack of industrial and commercial dynamism, we may find an explanation for the frequently observed insularity and frag-mentation of contemporary French Guyanese society.

We can of course look for alternative explanations. But if we do accept that: "nothing fundamentally distinguishes the British, Dutch and French possessions [in Guyana] from each other, either in climate, in the natural environment or in the wealth of resources" (Girondin, 1986: 37), then it is the political history of French Guyane that distinguishes it from the other two Guyanas. On the other hand it is largely territorial differences that distinguish Guyane so markedly from the French Antillean islands, Martinique and Guadeloupe.


## Preservation or Development: Amerindians and Creoles

French Guyane, like its neighbours, is an area where nature is in control almost everywhere. The rainforest environment is 'voluptuous', filled with "rampant reproduction and frenzied fructification" (*Guardian*, 28.11.1988). The delicate eco-system of the rainforest is also highly vulnerable to more intensive human intervention. The *Guardian* report cited above concludes that the interior of French Guyane "is no place for humans". For the 5000 or so Amerindians, and the 7000 'Bush Negroes' the tropical rainforest environment provides part of the means for their day-to-day existence. It is not the sole basis of their economies, since what is obtained from the natural environment has long been supplemented by commercial river transport among the Galibi Indians and the Boni maroons. More recently, access to welfare payments and temporary jobs provided by the municipalities have become the norm for many of the more 'integrated' coastal Indians and maroons.

As in Venezuela and north-western Brazil, the tropical rainforests are considered by creoles and European settlers and immigrants as a sort of treasure chest to be raided. There is a booming illegal trade in protected species of animals, which for some years was co-ordinated through French Guyane (*Libération*, 14.7.1987). This commercialised hunting and gathering for export is highly profitable. One French reporter described how eggs of a preserved species of giant turtle were watched around the clock to deter thieves. Local police were helped in this task by German environmentalists (*Le Monde*, 21.4.1987)! From the earliest days of European settlement to the present, proposals to exploit the resources of French Guyane commercially have always included proposals to increase the felling of trees, increase the acreage of cleared agricultural land, and to undertake more intensive fishing of the rivers and sea, as well as mining of bauxite and panning for gold. Recent experiments have involved more elaborate programmes of tree clearance, cattle ranching (as in Brazilian Amazonia), and in some areas fruit and vegetable crops and rice planting, the latter involving immigration of Hmong tribes people from Indochina. The fairly dismal record of these plans is now universally acknowledged.

During the period of colonial history in French Guyane, official policy tended to protect the Amerindian population (Berkhofer, 1978: 115). It continues to do so by controlling the right of people to move into, visit and settle in the interior of Guyane, which is known as Inini. This land is owned by the state, although leases of ninety-nine years are granted to the Amerindian populations, subject to the land being used. Within the province of Inini, any land leased to Amerindian communities, which is deemed not to be used for traditional activities, reverts to the state (Castor & Othily, 1984: 107). Even if this protective policy smacks of paternalism, it is noteworthy that the Amerindian population does look to the French state to protect them against the encroachment of creoles, of tourists and of prospectors and profiteers of all kinds.

Citizenship was first extended to the Amerindian population in 1969, under a reform which officially placed the interior territory of Inini on the same footing as the rest of French Guyane. The first group of Amerindians to organise themselves were the Galibis, coastal dwellers who had more contact with creoles than with other Amerindian groups living in the interior. In December 1984, for the first time, local politicians and administrators met representatives of the six Indian Communities, grouped together in EPWWAG (the Emerillion, Palicour, Wayana, Wayampi, Arawak and Galibi Indians). EPWWAG demanded that the state should respect the Indian communities' "land rights as the original occupants" (*Le Monde*, 8.4.1985). The same demand had been made less publicly in 1983 by the *Groupement des Amérindiens de Guyane Française* (*Le Monde*, 8.6.1983).

The echo from New Caledonia was unmistakable, and very discomforting for the PSG (*Parti Socialiste Guyanais*), which, as the main creole nationalist party, prides itself on representing the whole body of *le peuple guyanais*. It was galling for the PSG to find the locally-born creole population excluded from the category of 'authentic' Guyanese in the discussion of who was to be regarded as truly indigenous.

Once again, as in Iberian America during the colonial period, the creoles find themselves torn between a growing resentment of the control of the metropolitan power, and a strong sense of their own superiority vis-à-vis the Amerindians and the 'Bush Negroes' (Morse, 1964: 136-8, Stephenson, 1978: 36). In French Guyane, as elsewhere in the Americas, "American Indians are outside the Creole structure, but generally regarded as below it" (Mason, 1972: 295). Yet this may be changing, as one study on schoolchildren's attitudes suggests. A good number of the children were aware that the Amerindians were the first inhabitants of what is now Guyane, and there were few who associated them with negative images of 'savages' or 'primitives' (Chalifoux, 1990: 33-40).

Local responses to the Indians' demands are of considerable interest because of what they tell us of the complex structure of French Guyane's society. The Left in Guyane is even more integrationist than the Right as far as both Amerindians and Bush Negroes are concerned. It is noteworthy that the PSG refused to co-operate with a committee set up to examine how to satisfy the EPWWAG demands for secure communal lands. The French Prefect, Claude Silberzahn, suggested to local politicians that they take an "intelligent, French view" (*sic*) of the Amerindian minority problem, revealing the French government's conciliatory approach to demands by indigenous groups in the overseas departments and territories (*Le Monde*, 8.4.1985).

Among the Amerindians, there are wide disparities in the degree of contact with creole and French society. The Galibi, who live in the coastal region, are the most integrated economically, and depend largely on fishing and river trade for subsistence and money income. The militancy of this group has increased in recent years, in part due to developments in neighbouring Surinam, where the Galibi have been persecuted (*Libération*, 30.8.1985). In 1986, of 8800 refugees who had fled into French Guyane from neighbouring Surinam, 5000 were Galibi Indians whose lands had been seized (*Le Point*, 29.12.1986). The almost frenzied concern of the PSG leaders to have the refugees repatriated quickly needs to be viewed in the light of the shifting structure of community politics in French Guyane. In particular, with a large minority of immigrants and refugees from Brazil, Belize, Surinam, Haiti, Martinique and Guadeloupe, the Guyanese creoles feel they will be 'swamped'. Deprived of an absolute electoral majority, Guyanese creoles fear they will lose control over the local political agenda. There is also concern that the whole issue of the Amerindians' land rights could become more politicised in future.

Since the start of the Fifth Republic, successive French governments have favoured the protection of the Indians from violence and destruction from outside, and above all from disease. "Here in the heart of the jungle, three days' canoe ride from the coast, colonialist France is walking on eggshells, and she knows it" (*Le Monde*, 11.9.1984). Media attention has helped in bringing about greater awareness of the susceptibility of the Amerindians, through disease and threats to their environment, to cultural collapse and extermination. In 1987, after protests from Survival International, a proposal by the Thierry Sabine Organisation to race motor boats up the Oyapock and Maroni rivers was turned down. Jacques Chirac expressed his 'hostility' to the idea, as did the then Prefect, Dewâtre. However, local politicians were disappointed by the decision (*Le Monde*, 12.5.1987). Visits into territory set aside for the Wayana are very strictly controlled. Since 1962 they have been subject to prefectoral authorisation. For this more isolated community in particular, the French state, the 'First World', is attempting to protect the tribal 'Fourth World' within its national borders, not just from external aggression, but from the creoles, full French citizens themselves

There is little understanding among the orthodox French Left of the demands of the Amerindians. Thus *Lutte Ouvrière* complains that the French state allows the Amerindians in Guyane to vote, but does not provide them with the material means of escaping from their condition of economic underdevelopment (*Lutte Ouvrière*, 21.9.1985). It has been reiterated by representatives of the Amerindian communities in recent years that they do not want to be assimilated into creole society, since this would inevitably mean the disappearance of their culture altogether. On the other hand, their citizenship does open up the possibility of obtaining material benefits (such as family allowances) which may make life more comfortable for them. Locally the PSG is perceived as a party of creoles with ambitions to settle the interior. This may explain why the Amerindian communities of French Guyane have voted overwhelmingly for the republican and right-wing parties since the start of the Fifth Republic (*Le Monde*, 4.2.1983).

The protection of the Boni maroons has been much less consistent. In part this is because they are less vulnerable to disease than the more isolated Amerindians. Survival International has nonetheless condemned the forced assimilation of the Boni, who, it claims, are rapidly abandoning their traditional ways of life to settle in the slums of St Laurent du Maroni at the mouth of the river dividing Guyane and Surinam, with a resulting deterioration in their health and the disappearance of their cultural traditions (*Le Monde*, 4.10.1984). The French state's decision in the early 1980s to police the river frontier was due to territorial disagreements with Surinam, the perceived radicalism of Bouterse's regime, and the increase in illegal immigration from Haiti via Surinam. It is this change in policy, above all, which explains the demise in prosperity among the Boni, since they previously moved freely between the two countries, and enjoyed a virtual monopoly of river transport by canoe.

It is certainly difficult for the French state in Guyane to find a balance between its commitment to protection of the tribal people's autonomy, demands to tighten control of the territory's borders, and the principle of uniform French citizenship for all inhabitants of French Guyane. The threat of disease is often even greater than the oft-cited danger of cultural alienation for Amerindians. Many Indians are gradually becoming part of creole society and taking on a multiple French/Guyanese/Amerindian identity. One of the leading spokespeople of the Wayana, Antécume, worked for many years in a foundry in Lyons, and was known to his fellow workers as André. His case is just one example of the complex adaptation of Amerindian society to the nation state within the contemporary Guyanas. So long as it remains possible for the Amerindian communities in Guyane to retain their traditional means of living, electronic watches, Jacques Brel songs and reggae music are welcomed, and are seen to represent the positive rather than the negative effects of the coming of Westerners (*Libération*, 30.8.1985).

However, not everyone is satisfied that the French state protects the African maroons and Amerindians of Guyane. Survival International has, for example, declared that "the actions of the French administration...have led to exactly the same situation as in the most retrograde countries of South America, that is to say it has led to *clochardisation*; the only difference is that the same result is obtained by spending a lot of money" (*Le Monde*, 4.10.1984). The organisation asks for more autonomy to be granted to these groups. French anthropologists, such as Jean Hurault, have also seen difficulties with imposing French citizenship on the tribal peoples, arguing that it is unfair to unilaterally declare tribal peoples French citizens without their participation. Uncomfortably, but for different reasons, the same objection is made by the far right *Front National* in France to the automatic acquisition of citizenship by the children of foreigners born in France. This is discussed in further in Chapters 5 and 6. The same message may have a different meaning in Guyane, but the removal of French citizenship would surely leave the Amerindian population even more vulnerable than before, faced with the designs of explorers of different stripes.

## The PSG: Dreaming of Subsidised Conquest

The French state seems as unable to organise the economic exploitation of the territory of Guyane in the post-war years as it was during the colonial era. It is telling that, since Guyane became an overseas department of France in 1946, the only major developments projects have been concerned with outer space and with the sea. By 1990, 30 Ariane rockets had been launched from the space centre at Kourou (BBC News, 1.4.1989). The fishing fleet which trawls the Atlantic waters for shellfish has been majority French-owned only since the late 1980s (*La Croix*, 31.12.1986). Even the little tourist activity in Guyane has been largely on a number of tiny offshore islands, the Iles de Salut. In spite of numerous plans, the Guyanese interior remains as sparsely populated, and its resources virtually as untapped, as they were one hundred years ago.

In the deep interior of French Guyane is the 'frontier' hamlet of Saul. According to official statistics, its population fell from 119 in 1974, to 67 in 1982. It is here, in the geographical centre of the territory, that the PSG proposes the construction of a new capital for French Guyane. The siting of the new capital in the geographical centre of post-colonial states may be proposed because it is seen as a factor of unity and a symbolic departure from a coastal-oriented colonial past. In French Guyane, the project also expresses the objective of intensifying the exploitation of the land and other resources of Inini, the interior, in order to achieve a greater degree of self-reliance.

A book written several years ago by two PSG deputies, Elie Castor and George Othily, and remarkable for its precise detail and the exhaustive technicality of its proposals, was ambitiously entitled *La Guyane Les Grands Problèmes, les Solutions Possibles*. The book was written as a virtual blueprint for Guyane's economic development. It advocated more intensive exploitation of the territory's mineral resources (mainly bauxite and gold) in the national interest, as well as a rapid expansion in agricultural production, in lumber and fisheries activities. Most of these proposals pre-date *départe-mentalisation* in 1946. As in much of Latin America, colonial questions have not been settled in Guyane; they cannot be "placed behind us. They are still alive in our own century" (Morse, 1964: 168). The tendency for all development proposals to resemble each other is expressed in the title of a newspaper article *L'Aventure toujours recommencée*; the constantly renewed adventure (*Le Monde*, 14.9.1984). The adventure of Guyane's economic development, often begun, is never completed.

At the start of their book, Castor and Othily lay down the foundations of a regional development plan, under the title 'the conquest of the South'. "For several decades the conquest of the South has been a major preoccupation for the Guyanese!", they say, implicitly excluding the Amerindians from their definition of Guyanese (Castor & Othily, 1984: 22). They state that this will only be possible through the settlement and economic development of Saul. Elsewhere, the authors describe Guyane as "Brazil in microcosm" (ibid.: 21-3). For each detailed proposal of the PSG, there is a demand for corresponding additional technical and financial support from the French state. The national interest of France is invoked in defence of the national interest of French Guyane. Concern is expressed, for instance, that key economic sectors, such as bauxite and fisheries, are for a large part in American hands.

Put very simply, the PSG represents the dream of the creoles of Guyane, including the wealthy and the poor, to conquer the Guyanese interior. The party sees this as the basis for greater economic autonomy, and for Guyanese independence in the longer term. However the creole elite, who might fulfil the role of pioneers, are too small in number and too dependent on France to break out of the urban society (Jones & Stephenson, 1994: 120). The most impoverished creoles, who might be motivated to clear land and farm, are sufficiently cushioned by welfare payments to find settlement in the forest an unattractive option. Few will ever go to Saul.

In effect, the PSG seemed to be asking the French state to act as a surrogate coloniser, by subsidising the cost of exploring the development potential of the interior of Guyane. The French state is asked to instil a spirit of enterprise and initiative in young Guyanese through appropriate training; at the same time, the French state is criticised for not providing the Guyanese with a standard of living, wages and health treatment identical to those in metropolitan French departments. The PSG claims to represent all the people of Guyane, and asks that development should benefit them first of all. However, the party rejects the independence option and instead campaigns for a special autonomous status for Guyane within the French Republic. In recent years, the PSG has been split by personality conflicts between its two main figures, none other than Elie Castor and George Othily. As a result, the party has lost the pre-eminent position it once held in local political life.

## Xenophobia and Human Rights Abuse in Guyane

Integration into France has transformed Guyane from an extremely poor part of the Latin American sub-continent into one of the wealthiest and fastest growing economies in the region. This prosperity, which is not dependent on the resources of Guyane itself, attracts immigrants from poorer and neighbouring Caribbean islands, and to a lesser extent from Brazil, Surinam and Guyane (Gorgeon, 1985: 68). Temporary immigration has been required to provide labour for construction and infrastructure work at the Kourou space centre.

Porous borders have made it difficult to prevent immigration and the illegal movement of people across the border from Surinam. Of the three Caribbean regions of France, Guyane is experiencing the greatest social and political unrest in the 1990s. The treatment of Haitian and Surinamese refugees has become particularly ruthless, with summary deportations becoming routine since the late 1980s. The right of appeal of applicants for asylum has also been denied.

Permanent immigration from Haiti has become more important since the mid-1970s, and there are now roughly 25 000 Haitians in Guyane. Many enter illegally, but because they are francophone, in the past, many have obtained French citizenship on favourable terms (Cherubini, 1985: 97). Meanwhile, unemployment among Guyanese has increased. The real figure of 1990 was probably several percentage points above the official level of 24 per cent (INSEE, 1991: 19). When the creole politicians contrast their own position with that of the Haitians and other immigrants, however, they feel in a very superior position.

As their numbers have increased, Guyanese creoles have started to identify Haitians as different from themselves, even though they share a French-based creole. Haitian immigrants are blamed for the increase in crime, for AIDS, for witchcraft and for drug trafficking (Jolivet, 1990: 14, 21). The cultural closeness of the Haitians may mean they appear more of a threat to the Guyanese creoles, since they are rapidly able to assimilate (Jones, 1989).

In 1988 a conflict in Surinam sent both Galibi Indians and maroon Africans into French Guyane seeking asylum. Haitians have also sought asylum after being turned away by the United States and other neighbouring states. Brazilian military forces are suspected of organised incursions into Guyanese territory in the South. The local Guyanese creoles express fears of being 'submerged' by a diverse population of other 'ethnic groups'. In reality, Guyane has been a country of immigration since the start of its colonial history, and further immigration would certainly be needed if the PSG's dream of internal conquest were ever to be realised. The very idea that Guyane's creole population might themselves constitute an 'ethnic group' only emerged fairly recently. It has been elaborated defensively, in response to the fear that Guyane-born creoles will soon find themselves in a minority position (Jolivet, 1990: 24-7; Jones & Stephenson, 1994: 118-20).

In recent years, the treatment in Guyane of Haitian and Surinamese asylum seekers has attracted criticism from the United Nations High Commission for Refugees. During the 1980s, it was clear that different regulations were being applied in the overseas departments from those in force in the metropolis (*Plein Droit*, August 1989: 34-7). Children who had been born in the overseas departments to Surinamese or Haitian parents were expelled, along with their parents. In the 1990s, forced expulsions of asylum seekers and refugees have taken place with the agreement of the Prefect.[2]

In the 1960s, a Guyanese deputy, Justin Catayée, recommended mass immigration from the francophone Antilles as indispensable for economic development in Guyane (*Equinoxe*, 1982: 50). Claude Silberzahn, Prefect in 1983, said that, without immigration, there would be no further economic growth or increase in production in the territory (Gorgeon, 1985: 70). The PSG, on the contrary, has not considered immigration a solution for Guyane's economic predicament. On the contrary, it proposes the construction of a stronger sense of national identity among creoles. Unfortunately for the plans of the PSG, experience suggests that immigrants are much more likely than local creoles to be involved in the 'productive' economy proper (in industry and agriculture). Guyanese prefer to work in secure office jobs in the public sector and in services (*Le Monde*, 19.4.1987).

Given immigration and emigration trends since 1946, the creole society is aware of its diminishing majority within the electorate and the population as a whole. This fear is expressed in exaggerated form by those who believe there is a deliberate policy on the part of central government to drown out any nascent independence movement (Drekonja-Kornat, 1984: 26-7). In 1982, Guyanese-born creoles composed 57 per cent of the population, compared with 68 per cent in 1974 (Gorgeon, 1985: 72-3). The proportion has probably declined since then (Aldrich & Connell, 1992: 104). Heightened concern in recent years with Guyanese identity has come in response to changes in the composition of the population and the electorate.

The conventional Left-Right divide has little relevance in the DOM, and even less in Guyane. Thus, it is quite consistent with its creolist position that the PSG is workerist and demands equal rights from the French state, but also highly exclusionary in relation to extending any of these basic rights, including the right of citizenship, to immigrant populations resident in Guyane. Their nationalist approach has opened up a space for the far Right to organise electorally in Guyane. In this respect, too, Guyane is unique among the over-seas departments. The *Front National* obtains between 5 and 10 per cent of the vote, whilst in the other DOM, Le Pen's party rarely manages to get more than 3 per cent Reunion (*Le Monde*, 10.5.1988). In the first round of the Presidential elections of 1995, the FN vote in Guyane was 8 per cent, compared with 1.7 per cent in Martinique, and 3 per cent in Guadeloupe and Reunion (*Le Monde Hebdomadaire*, 10.5.1995).

It does seem that French Guyane may have served as something of a testing ground for France, and for Western Europe as a whole, not only for space rockets, but also for restrictive and discriminatory immigration and asylum regulations. Some of the most significant changes introduced since May 1993, were first implemented in Guyane before becoming law in France (*Plein Droit*, August 1989: 34-7).

## The Best Laid Plans: Departmentalisation

Since the law of departmentalisation came into effect in 1946, the degree of central government control over local affairs in each of the DOM has been reinforced rather than weakened. This has undermined much of the already limited economic autonomy of the local creole elite. The insular mentality of the Caribbean creole society on the Guyane coast has been reinforced, as the population has moved out of agricultural districts and into the towns. This has also worked against any 'pioneering spirit' that might once have existed. Large sums of public and private funds have been invested in various income-generating schemes, but the key to public policy in Guyane is now more than ever political. In particular, Guyane is home to the largest commercial satellite launching site in the world, in Kourou. This is best understood as a prestige project for France, in the key area of defence and communications.  It is an important symbol of French grandeur and of Western Europe's relative independence from the United States in an area of sophisticated high technology.

The obstacles to cultivation of crops and raising of livestock in the Guyanese environment are constantly underestimated in official plans.  The most spectacular recent example was the much-trumpeted *Plan Vert* or Green Plan introduced in the mid-1970s.  Such 'still-born' forms of development planning undermine the credibility of any future plans for autonomous economic growth, in whatever form (Schwarzbeck, 1986: 177; Jones & Stephenson, 1994).  They leave behind "a wasteland of former livestock ranches and woodlands; no paper was ever produced from the pulp mill" (Aldrich & Connell, 1992: 163). Seasoned colonists, including Reunionnese who were formerly resettled in Madagascar, have despaired of ever making a living from farming in French Guyane (*Le Monde*, 29.4.1987).

Zebu cattle, introduced in the early 1980s, proved to be well adapted to the climate, and the number of beef cattle rose from 1700 in 1975 to 15 000 by 1984 (Tarche, 1985: 8).  Unfortunately for beef farmers, the meat of the zebu is considered inedible, and their meat has been refused by local supermarkets in favour of imported beef (*Le Monde*, 11.1.1986).  Outcomes of various plans to develop logging activities, and related paper and furniture manufacture, have also been consistently disappointing (Brasset, 1987: 3-5).  Wood production in 1985 was 95 000 cubic metres, less than a third of the target under the 9th Plan (Parant, 1985: 33).  Part of the reason for this is the high production costs, especially labour costs, in Guyane compared with neighbouring countries and other competitors.

A fundamental problem for agriculture is the sandy soil, which contains very little organic material and so is rapidly exhausted.  After a few years, even grass will not grow.  Producers have been obliged to convert to growing vegetables hydroponically, or to cultivating rice (*Le Monde*, 20.4.1987).  The imagined fabulous potential of the interior for agriculture may well prove illusory for ecological reasons.  In their book, Castor and Othily suggested that what was needed was a "pioneering spirit", but one that would incorporate "a sense of ecological and moral responsibility" (Castor & Othily, 1984: 302).  Growing awareness of the precarious balance that exists within tropical rainforests is likely to impede any further major settlement plans for Guyane's interior.

The French state's protective role vis-à-vis the tribal peoples within its jurisdiction has been reasserted since 1946.  Creole Guyanese society has been obliged to acknowledge that the Indians and the Bush Negroes are not 'primitive savages', but distinct peoples with cultures and a sense of civilisation of their own, which they should be allowed to maintain if they wish (Stephenson, 1978: 36). This 'politically correct' view sits uneasily with the PSG's political agenda, and their claim to represent the average creole citizen.

A special status, with local politicians and officials administering all internal economic and legal affairs, was first suggested for Guyane by Michel Debré in 1961 (*JORFAN*, 13.6.1961). Debré was in favour of the *mise en valeur* of the territory's resources and believed that this required some changes in legislation to allow more flexibility in commercial policy. The PSG also demanded autonomy as a means of ensuring cultural protection from the metropolitan French. Justin Catayée, who founded the party in 1956, was a Martinican settler in Guyane (*Equinoxe*, 1982: 48). The PSG is supported by significant sectors of the local commercial and business bourgeoisie as well as by the urban poor of Cayenne and Kourou (*National Hebdo*, 16.6.1988). The party is torn between the demand for greater autonomy from the French state and the concern to retain the welfare and other benefits of being part of France.

Departmentalisation has inevitably produced new posts in the public sector and in services. At the same time, there has been a drop in productive activity in the economy as a whole. In the mid-1980s, roughly 12 per cent of the workforce was employed in primary production, 14 per cent in industry, and 74 per cent in tertiary activities (*Europa Year Book*, 1988: 1082). To fill some of the more highly skilled posts, metropolitan French civil servants and technicians have been given generous incentives to come and work in Guyane. Most are located at the space centre in Kourou. Military personnel and business people have moved into French Guyane in significant numbers: there were an estimated eight thousand metropolitan French in Guyane in 1985 (Cherubini, 1985: 97). The whites are particularly resented because they compete in the public and commercial sectors, where qualified creoles have traditionally sought work. The PSG leadership attacks the privileges of this group and has also demanded that the right to vote be reserved for those with at least ten years' residence (*Le Monde*, 1.4.1982; Castor & Othily, 1984: 27). Distinctions between locals and outsiders are thus emphasised by the PSG, while those between indigenous Amerindians and creole settlers are ignored or denied.

Topless bathers, grant-hunting business people from mainland France, and the Foreign Legion are all equally unwelcome as far as the PSG is concerned. Metropolitan officials are seen as a parasitic group, siphoning off state development funds and public-sector salaries which, it is argued, should be paid to the Guyanese. Key sectors of the economy are controlled by Antillais (especially *békés* from Martinique) and metropolitan French (Stephenson, 1978: 33; Cherubini, 1985: 98). Not always without reason, the commercial and industrial elite is suspected of being in business primarily to pocket public funds rather than to boost the local economy and provide employment for the Guyanese (Castor & Othily, 1984: 229). Widespread fraud takes place in most sectors of the economy; indeed it is considered so prevalent that the banks are now unwilling to lend money to set up any logging or forestry businesses (*Tribune de l'Economie*, 14.1.1987).

Unemployment has reached chronic levels and more than ten thousand French Guyanese have left for mainland France since 1960, mainly to find work. Others have left to complete higher education or to rejoin members of their families already living in the mainland. Around half of these migrants were subsidised by BUMIDOM, the official agency responsible for promoting labour mobility out of the DOM from the 1960s until 1982.

The emergence of an 'ethnic' politics during the 1980s took place in a context of tensions between whites and non-whites. In 1983 there were riots in Cayenne when a 'European' (in fact a white creole man from Reunion) shot dead a Guyanese fisherman after a fight outside a restaurant (*Le Monde*, 6.11.1983). In 1985, legionnaires stormed a poor area in Kourou in revenge for the killing of a colleague during demonstrations demanding the Foreign Legion's removal (*Libération*, 19.8.1985).

Like their counterparts in Reunion and the Antilles, the Guyane electorate have high average abstention rates, averaging between 30 and 40 per cent. They show particularly little interest in European elections, with an abstention rate of 90 per cent in the elections of June 1989. But it is very interesting that the Indian abstention rate in that particular election was less than 10 per cent, suggesting that community mobilisation still operates effectively among this section of the population (*Le Monde*, 20.6.1989). At the regional and departmental level, the PSG has been much weakened by internal dissension between its leaders. In the legislative elections of March 1993, PSG candidates were beaten by one ex-independentist, and one RPR candidate, Léon Betrand, mayor of St Laurent and strongly anti-immigrant in outlook (*Caribbean Insight*, March 1993). In the Presidentials of 1988, Guyane distinguished itself by giving Chirac his highest vote in any of the overseas departments (*Le Monde*, 10.5.1988). No doubt the electorate will expect to be rewarded for this past show of faithfulness, now that Jacques Chirac has been elected President in April 1995. It is unusual for the electorate of the DOM not to vote with the existing government and thus 'play it safe'. That the electorate voted for the Right in 1988, and again in 1995, probably reflects the primacy of immigration over all other issues at the local level.

**Europe's Launching Pad: the Kourou Space Centre**

The satellite launching base at Kourou is one of the most important in the world. In the 1980s the French commercial satellite launching programme accounted for over half of the world total, and was competing with those of Japan and the United States. The existence of such an important and expensive facility in Guyane has required the construction of supporting infrastructure, in the form of roads, electricity networks and telecommunications facilities, as well as defensive police measures, trained personnel and unskilled workers. The base is a major source of income for the region of Guyane; for example, in 1990 the budget allocated for the base was 600 million French francs, compared with a total budget for the Guyanese monodepartmental region of 500 million French francs (*Le Monde*, 7.4.1990).

A series of rockets has been launched from Guyane under the auspices of the European Space Agency, the last Ariane rocket being launched in 1994. Like the nuclear and military bases that France maintains in the Pacific territories, the installations at Kourou are supposed to generate economic activity through 'knock-on' effects and 'linkages' with the rest of the Guyanese economy. This has hardly been the case, with "Kourou as isolated as a station in outer space, light years away" from the capital of Cayenne, where almost 70 per cent of Guyane's population lives (Drekonja-Kornat, 1984: 27; Aldrich & Connell, 1992: 154-5).

Because of its highly strategic role, French Guyane can be considered "a bridgehead in South America for France and the rest of the European Community" (Drekonja-Kornat, 1984: 26). Yet, within Guyane itself, the space centre at Kourou, and the recently constructed town which houses those who work there, remain outstanding an example of 'enclave development', primarily constructed for the purposes of prestige (Jolivet, 1982: 227). Relations between the white technicians and paratroopers and the local creole population are strained by the air of colonial aloofness. Kourou has also grown at the expense of other secondary towns in Guyane, attracting casual and skilled labour from as far away as Brazil. As Aldrich and Connell have observed, the retention of the base at Kourou represents an important strategic asset for France, as important for national defence and commercial interests as the nuclear testing base in Mururoa in the Pacific overseas territory of Tahiti (Aldrich & Connell, 1992: 262). This has created a strong dependency on the part of the Guyanese economy, which without the base would be seriously diminished even from its present slim basis (*Le Monde*, 7.4.1990). It could of course be argued that this skewed and 'artificial' type of economic development, is no more sustainable than ranching of Zebu cattle.

## Conclusion

Of all the French DOM, Guyane has the greatest autonomy in its status and in the legislation that applies there. Local regulations exist on land use, on agriculture, on housing, immigration, security and policing. This has been the case since at least 1961 with the introduction of the *Loi Debré* intended to take account of local specificities of the territory.[3]

Since 1981, local political configurations have again been altered by the deconcentration of some budgetary and planning powers to the Region of Guyane. Initially, regionalisation benefited the Left, and the PSG in particular. The hope of improved representation for small parties also led to the creation of a new pro-independence party, the PNPG (Le Parti Nationale Populaire Guyanais) in 1985 (*Le Monde*, 4.12.1985). Regional level government has also opened the French DOM up somewhat to their regional neighbours, but this has been less true in Guyane than elsewhere. The Region, as an autonomous administrative entity, has the power of signing conventions with the central authorities, and with partners in neighbouring countries. It is also responsible for the elaboration of plans to valorise the forest resources of Guyane (Castor & Othily, 1984: 212).

During the 1980s there were signs of a gradual upturn in the economy. Exports increased from 5 per cent of imports in 1982 to 10 per cent by 1985. The proportion of agricultural producers under 40 also increased, from 21 per cent in 1975 to 30 per cent in 1984 (Tarche, 1985: 12). Under present departmental structures, however, there is no reason why this marginally greater economic autonomy should be translated into any improvement in living conditions for people in Guyane.

Land remains the principal stake in economic development. So long as the French state retains almost exclusive control over the interior of the territory, no large-scale project of exploitation of Guyane's natural or human resources can take place without the state's full participation. Does this mean that independence will be necessary in order for Guyane's internal development problems to be settled? The impatience which is evident in (former British) Guyana with the special status of the Amerindians, in Guyane is directed at the French state's 'colonialist' protection of the interior. In the event of independence, however, it seems almost inevitable that the whole creole society would be agreed that special needs of the Amerindians could not be protected at the expense of Guyanese society as a whole. They would have to be sacrificed in the name of the common good and development. This explains why those who are the strongest advocates of greater autonomy or independence from France are sometimes the harshest in their denial of any similar right to independence or autonomy for the Amerindians. Arguably, Amerindians still have what the Creole nationalists want but seem unable to attain: a mode of existence and a culture which are not entirely dependent on external support.

It is likely that the government of an independent Guyane would have a much less tolerant policy on Indian land rights than the French state. As in Guyana and Surinam, cultural and economic 'integration' of the Indians would be pursued, and the probable result would be the virtual elimination of the Amerindians of the interior, along with their way of life and the rainforest environment on which their way of life depends. The position adopted by Forbes Burnham in Guyana was that "our hinterland is not a mere showcase for the passing admiration of curious anthropologists, archaeologists and tourists, but a vast place to be peopled and developed" (cited in Lowenthal, 1972: 183). Creole nationalists in French Guyane would be no less determined to make good the wealth of the forest.

It has been suggested that the key to understanding the complex interrelations between France and this overseas department is the unfinished and doubly 'unsettled' nature of the colonial project in French Guyane. In approaching the relationship between France and Guyane in this way, we have chosen to give less emphasis to the crucial strategic dimension of the French presence in Guyane.

## Notes

1. This spelling of Guyane will be used throughout.

2. Telegram from Ruanaldo Ronald Venetiaan (President of the Republic of Surinam) to François Mitterrand, 28 January 1993, text written 13.1.1993. The subject was the return of Surinamese refugees from French Guyane, according to UNHCR principles. The President objected: "But now the last phase of the project of the return of displaced persons is in danger of turning sour for both Surinam and France. We have learned that expulsion with the help of the police, of refugees who are intending to undertake a hunger strike, is being envisaged. This is against the principle that international repatriation should be voluntary and humanitarian..." I am indebted to Paris-based journalist, Greg Chamberlain, for a copy of this telegram.

3. "The project stipulates a special status for Guyane and the creation of a regional executive body...This body would enforce its decisions by administrative decrees in [health, social security, agriculture, industry, trade, tourism, public works, transport, housing, immigration, public finance, justice, security, police]", in Latortue, 1971: 188ff. In fact such an executive body was never created.

# 5  Franco-Algerian Relations: Immigration and Decolonisation

*As followers of a certain kind, social scientists often take political entities as natural units of analysis.*
Trouillot, 1988: 27.

*The orientalist discourse was based upon the problem of difference...Perhaps an alternative to orientalism is a discourse of sameness which would emphasise the cultural continuities between cultures rather than their antagonisms.*
Turner, 1989: 638.

## Introduction

So far in this study, the device has been used of standing the present world order on its head. By looking at its opposite, the study has tried to expose the peculiarity of the status quo, in spite of its taken-for-granted quality. We have looked at examples of post-colonial relations where, in Ernest Gellner's words, the colonised or underprivileged have indeed "...concentrated on a struggle to achieve full citizenship within the existing imperial units" (Gellner, 1964: 177). We cannot conclude that this has resulted in definitive and 'real' decolonisation, or in an end to the colonial relationship. Even with full citizenship, integration has not led to substantive equality between former colonisers and former colonised people at the level of inter-personal relations or material conditions.

The conceptual polarisation of post-colonial relations into independence and separation with unequal rights, on the one hand, and relations of integration with substantially equal rights, on the other, is too simple a dichotomy. The sheer scale and significance of emigration out of former colonial territories during the post-independence period can be viewed as evidence that both these strategies of post-colonial relations can be pursued simultaneously. Independence and separation may be the official decolonisation option at the collective or state level, whilst integration and a search for post-colonial inter-personal equality may be the strategy pursued at the individual or family level. The struggle of the underprivileged has sought to capitalise on the benefits of having a collective voice, while at the same time seeking to enter the citadel of the former colonial power and take a place within it (Mazrui, 1981: 62).

In 1962, Algeria's entry into the international system of states was accompanied by a massive departure of residents of French origin, as well as Algerians who had fought against the FLN (*Front de Libération National*) which was now in government. These initial movements were part and parcel of an inter-state policy of expulsion and repatriation which accompanied the granting of sovereignty to Algeria and of the consolidation of national state boundaries between the two countries. Similar mass movements of individuals at the time of independence occurred, for different reasons undoubtedly, into the former colonial metropolis from the British Caribbean and from Dutch Indonesia and Surinam. In these cases, such movements were voluntary and not part of the bilateral independence negotiations.

This chapter will look at the complex inter-state relations of Algeria and France concerning immigration issues in the years since 1962. For the most part, we refer to immigration of Algerians into France. Since Algerian independence, ever-increasing numbers of former Algerians and their children have settled in France and acquired French citizenship. By the late 1980s, there were more than two million foreign workers in France, including almost one million Algerian citizens. The total number of people of Algerian origin was around three million at this time, a figure which includes some half million *harkis* (those who fought on the French side in the Algerian war of independence) and their families (Etienne, 1989: 80-82). As this chapter will seek to demonstrate, the future position of second- and third-generation Franco-Algerians depends on the evolution of nationality law in France. Young Algerians born in France have already found themselves expelled to Algeria for minor criminal offences, even though they may have no entitlement to Algerian citizenship. They are now experiencing greater insecurity because of further changes in the French nationality laws to exclude those of Algerian origin born in France from automatic French citizenship at age eighteen. As one young *beur* put it, "*On va être un peu sans pays, quoi!*", which roughly translates as "we won't have our own country" (*Im'média*, May-June 1984).

By the 1980s, as the two states have drifted apart, the identity questions of these 'people in the middle' had come painfully to the fore (see Cartoon 2). However important such questions of identity might be, even more vital was the erosion of concrete legal and material rights to which French citizens and others resident in France are entitled. To a large extent, this access is dependent on negotiated immigration rights, and nationality status. These are elaborated partly in response to changing notions of national interests and identity in both France and Algeria. Table 5.1 highlights the range of coincidences and conflicts of interest which may arise in Franco-Algerian relations concerning the immigration issue. The table also identifies the impact of different types of inter-state collaboration and conflict on the rights of individual emigrants.

The concern here is to explore the interconnection, in matters of immigration and freedom of movement, between national rights to control borders and population movements, and rights that pertain to individuals. Of particular concern are the rights of Algerians living in France and their children to move and to settle in France, and to acquire French citizenship if they so wish. Reassertions of sovereignty over 'their people' by both states can (and do) restrict the rights of free movement and choice of nationality for people of Algerian origin. In a necessarily schematic way, Table 5.1 seeks to illustrate the way in which inter-state relations impinge on the room for manoeuvre of individual migrants.

During the post-colonial period, the freedom of movement of individuals has increasingly become conditional on inter-state negotiations and understandings. Increasingly, the flexibility of national laws depends on policies adopted at the EC level in relation to third country nationals. Yet cross-border movement remains vital to: "the fulfilment of basic human rights: marriage, family life, educational opportunities, reasonable employment" (Dowty, 1987: 16). In the case of refugees, cross-border freedom of movement may be necessary for maintaining life itself (Loescher, 1993: 12-15). Where the wealthy are concerned, such rights are more or less taken for granted: no-one seriously questions the right of the well-heeled to travel unimpeded throughout the world. For the poor, the consensus has emerged in the 1990s that tight controls and punitive treatment are needed to dissuade massive cross-border movement, and keep the needy 'in their place'.

In the case of Algerians' movement to France, there is an intransigent myth of 'labour rotation', according to which immigration is a cyclical, temporary phenomenon (Meissner *et al*, 1993: 41). In fact, since at least 1960, the tendency has been for Algerian immigrants into France to settle permanently, bringing their families in to join them, or marrying and bringing up their children in France. Until 1994, anyone born in French territory automatically acqui-red French citizenship at age eighteen. This included second-generation Algerians, who thus came to conceive of themselves as entitled to equal treatment under French law. Like the inhabitants of the DOM, they expected to have the same economic, social and political rights as any other French citizens. As so often when the underprivileged or formerly colonised try to escape poverty, unemployment, landlessness, family and state repression, and assert full citizenship rights, they have been confronted with an exclusionary and reactionary response. This applies both to the neo-colonial elite in the former colonies and to the former colonisers in the metropolis (Cohen, 1987; MacDonald, 1983).

It could be argued that the far right's challenge to the rights of immigrants and their families to French citizenship, is on a weak footing, given the strength of the republican tradition in France. On the other hand, the specific threat which the far Right poses comes at a time when long-term economic recession is calling into question the whole basis of French nationality, and the ability of the state to continue providing welfare benefits at established levels to the French population as a whole. Legislation introduced in mid-1993 removed the automatic right to French citizenship at eighteen for all those people born in France of foreign parents (*Guardian*, 17.8.1993). This reform brought the basic legal principle of *jus solis* into question, something which, since 1789, only the Vichy government had attempted (Silverman, 1992: 141-3; *Le Monde*, 12.4.1986). The change in law was delayed by the *Conseil Constitutionnel*, which considered parts of the legislation to be contrary to the national constitution, and asked for redrafting (JCWI, 1993a: 15). The provisions on nationality were introduced without any delay, and this reform removes the automatic right of eighteen-year-olds to French nationality. Unlike most of the other measures introduced by Pasqua, the citizenship amendment required a change in the provisions of the French nationality code before it could come into effect.

## A Tentative Model: Inter-state Relations and Immigration

The course of relations between France and Algeria since independence, concerning the immigration issue, appears to fall into a number of phases according to the degree of co-operation or conflict over the issue, as described in Table 5.1. On the left-hand side, the outcomes for individual and collective rights are specified. In the next column this is related to the nature of Franco-Algerian relations on the immigration issue, and the various possible forms of collaboration and conflict that could theoretically exist between them on the issue. The options open to the two governments are expressed in simplified terms regarding Algerian (A) emigrants to France (F) as: Letting in and Letting Out (LI (F), LO (A)) or Keeping In and Keeping Out (KI (A), KO (F)).

The often sharp contrast between rhetoric and practice needs to be kept in mind in any such model, since stated policies and actual policies tend to diverge in real life. Logically, as the table indicates, the maximum possible freedom of movement is when the two states, Algeria and France, place a differential value on the emigrants/immigrants themselves. Of the basic logical possibilities contained within the model, only the first form of inter-state collaboration tends to enhance rather than restrict the freedom of movement of individual Algerian migrants.

If policy is assumed to fit actual practice, then four logical possibilities contained within the model have been identified as the basic policy choices. It is helpful to describe these in detail, as they appear in Table 5.1.

(i) Algeria places a lower value on Algerian em/immigrants than France. The two governments will tend to collaborate to enable relatively free movement, or regulated but generous movement between Algeria and France. Emigrants will be LO and LI by the Algerian and French states, respectively. Collective, national rights and the individual right to of freedom of movement are most likely to converge in this policy context.

(ii) Algeria places a higher value on Algerian em/immigrants than France does. The two governments can collaborate to restrict the movement of Algerians, by agreeing to KO and KI in the case of France and Algeria, respectively. This will produce a clear and sharp conflict between individual human rights and state rights to control freedom of movement.

(iii) Both countries place a low value on Algerian em/immigrants. There may be conflict between the two, with Algeria Letting Out, and France trying to Keep Out. This is likely to produce or aggravate conflict between the two governments. It also limits individual freedom of movement. If border controls (KO) are not enforced by France, then illegal immigration is likely. Tolerance of this (LI) is likely if the economic value of Algerian migrant workers is high.

(iv) Both countries place a high value on em/immigrants from Algeria. This might happen in times of high growth and labour shortages. This may result in competition to attract and retain skilled workers. Algeria may try to KI such emigrants, contrary to international legal obligations to LO. If KI regulations fail to restrict emigration, however,

Table 5.1: *Conflict and Collaboration in Franco-Algerian relations over immigration*

| Degree & type of conflict or collaboration between F and A over Let In, Let Out, Keep In and Keep Out | Policy details of conflict and collaboration | LI/LO or KI/KO KI/KO |
|---|---|---|

SCENARIOS OF FRANCO-ALGERIAN COLLABORATION/CONFLICT
(Not in Chronological Order)

**(i)**

| Individual self-determination= state-defined national interest | A & F agree free movement Migrants lower value for A than F | e.g. 1962 LI (F); LO (A) |
|---|---|---|

**(ii)**

| Individual self-determination not = state-defined national interest | F & A agree on tighter quotas not uniformly enforced. Migrants higher value for A than F. Internal controls in F | e.g.1973-4 KO (F); KI (A) official policies only illegal migration (see vi) |
|---|---|---|

**(iii)**

| Individual self-determination limited by F state-defined national interest | F & A disagree over total migration. Shared low value of migrants for A & F | e.g. 1974-8 KO (F); LO (A) illegal emigration |
|---|---|---|

**(iv)**

| A migrants aim to take advantage of LI (F). A asserts state-defined national interest | A & F do not agree on need for migration. Shared high value of migrants for A & F | LI (F); KI (A) A wants quota F does not |
|---|---|---|

**(v)**

| Individual self-determination not = state-defined national interest | F & A agree quotas, but illegal movements in & out Migrants higher value for A than F | e.g.1963-8 LI quotas (F) LO quotas (A) |
|---|---|---|

**(vi)**

| Immigrants' demands for desire for integration and equal rights countered by high % with illegal status and internal controls | F & A each want the initiative in controlling numbers and asserting sovereignty | e.g. 1980s-90s LO/LI bypassed by citizenship question Legal changes in F |
|---|---|---|

LI=Let In  KI=Keep In  LO=Let Out  KO=Keep Out. A=Algerian Government/Algerian (migrants)  F=French Government there will be few KO restrictions from the French side. Franco-Algerian relations may be damaged by accusations of encouraging a brain- and skills-drain from a young, underdeveloped country. This is likely to be partly rhetorical, since the increased flow of emigrants would also, at least initially, increase remittances sent from France to Algeria.

Of course, this model cannot exhaust the possible range of policy positions. The table shows only two variations on the four basic logical possibilities. These are represented as (v) and (vi). One of the marked features of the late 1960s and 1970s was an apparently growing divergence of interests between the two regimes. Within France, there were, and remain, conflicting pressures on immigration policy. In particular, there has long been a tension between the perceived economic value of relatively lax immigration controls, and the perceived need to be seen to contain immigration movements for social and political reasons. The economic arguments in favour of immigration into France continue to be voiced even in a period of recession and unemployment. In practice the tension between economic and socio-political considerations has been resolved through the substitution, during the 1980s and 1990s, of officially-recruited workers (Algerians and others) with illegal immigrants.

The model presented here suggests that the optimum situation for the individual (i.e. free movement LO/LI) is only likely to be secured in a situation where the value which the two states place on Algerian em/immigrants diverges. It is unlikely when both states place the same low or high value on migrants. It is when the overall value placed on Algerian em/immigrants is higher in France than in Algeria, that free movement in both directions across the Franco-Algerian border is most likely. This may seem an obvious point, but it is worth making, since it is conventionally believed that the rights of international migrants are enhanced through close inter-state co-operation. States are just as likely to co-operate in order to restrict freedom of movement. International law obliges states to Let Out their citizens. However, it places no reciprocal obligation on any other state to Let In. The decision to KO/LI is therefore a question of perceived national interest, and making such a decision is simply regarded as part of the exercise of state sovereignty.

## 1962-73 Conflict and Collaboration over Immigration

The Algerian war of independence (1954-62) was both an anti-colonial and a civil war, and was fought on many fronts simultaneously. To those who fought on the French side, it is still a source of shame, hurt pride and frust-ration. Not without reason it was recently called the 'undeclared war' by the film-maker Bertrand Tavernier (BBC2 television, 18.4.1992; *Le Monde*, 18.3.1992). For those on both sides who believed in *Algérie française*, independence was a wound inflicted on the French family's psyche by an ungrateful offspring, in collaboration with the greatest traitor of all, General de Gaulle himself (Jones, 1991: 58; Harrison, 1983).

For those who opposed the French presence in Algeria, the war was a time of repression and brutalisation. It represented the splitting of a sense of 'self' on both sides, among parts of the population at least. This split had been almost unthinkable until the 1950s. As John Loughlin has argued, it later led regionalists and radicals in France itself to question the indivisibility of the Republic, and to assert the right of 'internal colonies' to separate self-determination and secession (Loughlin, 1989: 10-11). The impact was also directly felt in the remaining French DOM.

Throughout the French occupation and colonisation of Algeria, there had been a singular unwillingness to contemplate reform and the extension of the full range of civil, political and social rights to the mass of the Algerian population. This injustice contributed to the armed conflict, and meant the French state could not avoid feeling the consequences of the war 'at home'. The ambiguous relationship which persists between France and Algeria was illustrated in a recent Plantu cartoon in *Le Monde*, where an angry and fat Frenchman, carrying his baguette, shouts at a thin North African-looking man with a suitcase, "Rentrez chez nous; je veux dire chez vous!"[1] As Maxim Silverman has pointed out, such confusion over the nature of boundaries is a product of a continuing colonial mentality in France (Silverman, 1992: 34).

For the most part the army and the European settlers' attachment to Algeria was simply an attachment to their position of unquestionable dominance. As one writer of the time commented, "the Frenchman loves the Algerian like the cavalier loves his...horse" (Etcherelli, 1967: 226). Once the beast became rebellious and could not be subdued by force, the rider was forced to dismount, and love quickly turned to hatred. The difficulty for the French cavalier was that, if Algeria was a horse, it was one that would never be replaced.

The structural decline in the French population since the eighteenth century, and massive human losses in both world wars, are among the reasons why an assimilatory policy runs through modern French history with such consistency (Silverman, 1992: 28-31; Verbunt, 1985: 130-31). It also explains the largely favourable approach adopted by successive regimes to permanent settlement in France of non-nationals, and their full incorporation into the national labour force and citizenry. This demographic imperative served to give the egalitarian Jacobinism of the republican tradition extra material force.

Another response has been to urge French women to have more children; as Michel Debré has argued, "one cannot, at one and the same time, reduce the number of [French] children born, and keep out foreign workers" (Debré, 1972: 193). The purely demographic argument in favour of continued immigration still holds, since the French population has been declining steadily since 1974 (*Le Monde*, 10.10.1989). In terms of our model in Table 5.1, the value of immigrants from Algeria to French policy makers lies also in their demographic contribution to France.

At independence certain mutual obligations were recognised between France and Algeria: France retained access to oil reserves in the Sahara, and Algeria's citizens were granted virtually free access to live and work in the French Republic. The free movement of people between the two states was one of the key provisions of the Evian Agreements. Initially there was little or no perceived conflict between national self-determination and sovereignty for Algeria and the movement of individual Algerian citizens, as shown in Table 5.1 (i). This situation did not last very long and, starting in 1963, tighter controls were exercised over the departure of emigrants from Algeria. Officially, these restrictions came in response to a series of racist attacks and killings in France. The principle is quite well established under international law, by which "...the claimant state itself suffers a loss when one of its nationals is injured" (Akehurst, 1984: 87).

Since such attacks on Algerians living in France were not new, it would seem that the move to restrict emigration reflected the alarm of the new regime at the high rates of out-migration since independence. It also expressed the FLN government's desire to consolidate its own legitimacy, by encouraging its citizens to live and work within the country.

Much 'underdevelopment' theory depends on the assumption that whole units (states) exploit other whole units, for example through unequal trade relations. This approach was adopted by the Algerian trade unions, affiliated to the FLN. During the 1960s and 1970s they condemned the 'haemorrhage' of Algerian workers, who were seen as the bedrock of electoral support for the Party. The UGTA (*Union Générale des Travailleurs Algér-iens*), along with many 'radical' Algerian and French intellectuals, called on Algerians living in France to return and rebuild the country. Ben Bella asserted that "Algerians should be able to stay and live in their country. This would really be an achievement for independence" (Brandell, 1981: 109). According to the official position, the persistence of emigration was further evidence that the decolonisation process was still incomplete, and national liberation yet to be achieved.

As more and more Algerians settled permanently in France, the prospects of their ever returning became more and more unlikely (Hargreaves, 1990: 39).

Tacitly, the Algerian Government recognised from the start that the massive post-independence movement of Algerians to France would probably never be reversed, given the continuing economic difficulties facing Algeria. In an attempt to halt the departure of skilled people, the FLN soon committed itself to provide all graduates with employment in the public sector. Structures established during colonial rule could not be changed overnight, however. Algeria remained a low-wage economy, without adequate social or labour protection. Unemployment was estimated to affect two-thirds of the work force immediately after independence in 1962 (Himberg, 1978: 85). This in itself would have pushed large numbers of people to look for work outside the country.

There were also substantial 'pull' factors behind Algerian migration to France. Initially, pull factors included comparatively high wages, guaranteed employment and educational opportunities. Later, the presence of family members who were firmly established in France became a further reason to move. Indirectly, provisions which made it relatively easy for Algerians to acquire French citizenship and the attached economic and social, but also civil and political rights, may have influenced the decision of many immigrants to settle rather than to return to Algeria.

In 1964, the French and Algerian governments signed a protocol, agreeing to formally restrict Algerians' free movement into France. Loopholes in the law meant that massive emigration continued, mainly through the issuing of tourist visas. The following year, a strict clamp-down started to limit new emigration: in the first three months of 1965, only 11 745 people were officially allowed into France from Algeria, compared with 52 798 allowed in during the first three months of 1964. The total number of Algerian citizens in France had increased from 350 500 in 1962 to over 800 000 the following year (Brandell, 1981: 107).

Under the quarterly quota system introduced in 1964, both governments officially agreed to regulate Algerians' cross-border movement. On the French side, such quotas were simply based on the projected labour needs of the economy as a whole, and of a number of key heavy industries in particular (e.g. cars, steel and coal). More stringent medical examinations were introduced at the same time, eliminating around 5 per cent of applicants. Would-be emigrants also had to secure an offer of employment before arrival in France, and had to register at the *Office National Algérien de Main d'Oeuvre* before their departure from Algeria. In this way, both governments started to collaborate to restrict freedom of movement of citizens of the former colony into the metropolis of the former colonial power.

This policy of fairly loose quotas may suggest a variation on scenario (i) in Table 5.1 rather than a clear assertion by Algeria that its citizens were of higher value to the country than to France, as in (ii). The sheer complexity of unilateral and bilateral policies during the first few years after independence belies any such attempt to divide Franco-Algerian relations over the immigration issue into neat categories. During most of this time the structural labour needs of the French national economy were combined with the mutual concern of both governments to present the massive population movement after 1966 as primarily a temporary and cyclical phenomenon. Later on, attempts to control the physical movement of Algerian people were temporarily abandoned in favour of efforts to keep those working in France from fully integrating and acquiring French citizenship.

Paradoxically, the growing mutual suspicion of the two governments may have encouraged them to collaborate on migration control in order to prevent free population movement across the Franco-Algerian border, particularly of poor Arabs and of Berbers. In addition, official French policy seemed to be to hinder the cultural and legal integration of those Algerians already settled in France. This was a policy the two governments could agree on. Inga Brandell points out that there are solid material reasons why this collaboration was likely to be mutually advantageous. Permanent settlement meant an increase in family reunions, and this resulted in a damaging reduction of remittances sent back to Algeria. For the French economy, on the other hand, permanent settlement and family reunions reduced the purely economic benefits of Algerian immigration. Permanency created pressure on employers to pay a fair, family wage to Algerian workers, and increased the social costs to the state of supporting immigrant families. Settlement also resulted in Algerians becoming entitled to claim full French citizenship and a host of concomitant rights (Brandell, 1981: 35-6).

In an agreement of December 1968, the French and Algerian governments committed themselves to end the practice of allowing virtually unregulated population movement out of Algeria into France, and agreed to a quota of 35 000 per year (Silverman, 1992: 77). Both sides had their own economic interests in such a move at this time, and also invoked cultural and political reasons for imposing bi-lateral restrictions. But in spite of the appearance of officially agreed regulation and control of population movements out of Algeria and into France, there was in effect very little control until at least 1968. The years up to 1973 could be characterised as years of *laissez faire* on the French side, in part because demographic and economic justifications for allowing immigration from Algeria to continue did not yet clash irreconcilably (Verbunt, 1985; Silverman, 1992: 77-9).

In the first few years after independence, the authorities in Algiers in effect allowed virtually unimpeded movement out of the country. Critics were reassured that this 'temporary' movement would eventually enable more skilled Algerians to return after training and employment in France. It soon became apparent that this would not happen in most cases, and permanent settlement in France became the rule rather than the exception. Children born in France to Algerian parents automatically acquired French nationality at age eighteen.

The failure to stick to quotas on the Algerian side may be explained by the usefulness of emigration as a sort of 'safety valve' for the unemployed and politically disgruntled. Furthermore, remittances sent home were significant for many regions and for the country as a whole. There was greater concern at the loss of skilled people, technicians, graduates, mechanics and professionals, as their departure was seen to weaken the national infrastructure and restrict economic progress. Except for a brief period in 1973, however, there have been few restrictions by either side on the movement of skilled people. It seems that rhetoric and reality bear little relation to one another in the policies of both governments during this period.

At the same time, the Algerian state has undoubtedly made great efforts to discourage the cultural assimilation of Algerians living in France, and to preserve the myth of an eventual return to the 'home' country. The overall result has been that Algerians have been 'Let Out' of Algeria but the government has been reluctant to 'Let Go' of them once they are settled there. Concerning Franco-Algerians relations over the immigration issue during this period, we conclude with the observation from Himberg that, "throughout the first decade following Algerian independence, the two countries competed for control over the movement of workers" (Himberg, 1978: 13). The whole issue of emigration/immigration control has remained significant for subsequent Algerian regimes mainly for political and ideological rather than for purely economic reasons.

## Recession and the Tightening of Controls

Shortly after independence, one of the Algerian Government's main concerns was to keep up the level of remittances sent by emigrants living in France. This became a much less important consideration after 1973, when oil revenues largely displaced other sources of income, increasing from one-quarter of total export receipts to almost two-thirds between 1971 and 1974. Meanwhile, foreign remittances dropped from around one-eighth of total foreign exchange earnings to less than one-twentieth over the same period (Himberg, 1978: 248).

Unemployment, on the other hand, has remained a perennial economic and social concern; land reform has proved difficult and revenues from agriculture have continued to decline. Algeria's industrial development during the two decades following independence was highly capital-intensive, adding to the security of the regime, but doing nothing to reduce the shortage of reasonably paid and stable employment.

In 1973, the Algerian Government suddenly and unilaterally suspended all new emigration to France, showing that it was possible for the state to effectively control population movements out of the country, if it wished to do so. In terms of Table 5.1, this was temporarily a case of Algeria Keeping In at a time when France was still Letting In, corresponding to scenario (iv). As in 1964, the reason given was an increase in the number of racially motivated attacks on Algerian citizens living in France. On the other hand, the 1973 decision may have been to pre-empt an expected ban on entry from the French Government. This was duly imposed in the following year. No doubt, wishing to retain the initiative in policy making, the government in Algiers saw some advantage in being seen to make the first move, retaining the initiative rather than being dictated to. In terms of our model, therefore, the regime in Algiers would initiate a policy of 'Keep In' before the French authorities enforced a policy of 'Keep Out'. In some cases,

> The export of refugees [and emigrants] can...be used as a bargaining chip in inter-state negotiations over trade and bilateral political recognition. Typically in such situations, the sending state possesses considerable leverage in the bargaining process [by which]...the sending state can extract strategic and foreign policy concessions from the receiving state. (Loescher, 1993: 19-20)

This was not the case in 1973, when the benefits that the Algerian Government hoped to obtain by preventing emigration were not so much material, as prestige-related. In particular, the state was concerned to demonstrate its ability to undertake an independent line in its foreign policy.

As has already been mentioned, under international law the two responses, KI and KO, are not reciprocal (Carens, 1992; Dummett, 1992). States do not have the right to prevent their own citizens from leaving the national territory, even though other states may perfectly legally refuse entry to these same people. There is in effect a legal 'no-man's-land', where individuals can find themselves sandwiched between the right to leave and the lack of any corres-ponding duty on the part of any other state to allow them to enter. To be Let

Out of one country is obviously of little advantage to people unless they are Let In elsewhere.

The overall French attitude towards the economic implications of immigration has been largely favourable during the Post-War period. It is generally admitted that without the influx of labour from outside the country during the Post-War years, labour shortages would have seriously restricted economic revival and industrial growth, and would probably have made it impossible for France to achieve full employment (Verbunt, 1985: 162-3; Carchedi, 1983: 194, 206). This willingness to acknowledge the considerable economic benefits of mass immigration contrasts sharply with the tendency in Britain to stress the economic disadvantages, in spite of evidence that the benefits for Britain's economy have been considerable (Findlay, 1994). By 1973, the positive demographic impact was also already evident in France, with around 1.3 million people having acquired citizenship through naturalisation since 1960. Between 1968 and 1973, the population of France increased substantially for the first time since the late nineteenth century.

With the start of recession in the mid-1970s, the French Government's priorities and aims started to change. A joint ban on non-Common Market labour coming into the European Economic Community (EEC) in July 1974 was the first sign of the increasing importance of inter-EEC (now EU or European Union) collaboration. For the first time, the French government's bilateral negotiations with Algeria did not have priority over multilateral policies negotiated within the European Communities context. Algeria was simply included within the general provisions, which were intended to "regulate the arrival, residence and departure of foreign workers and their families" (Verbunt, 1985: 127).

In the mid-1970s, at a time when family settlement and permanent residence had become the norm for Algerians living in France, Paul Dijoud dusted off the idea of *rotation*, arguing that temporary employment for a strictly regulated number of overseas workers in France could play an important part in French 'development assistance' to 'sending' countries (Dijoud, 1976: 13-15). As with other neo-colonial policies, this was said to be of benefit both to the sending country and to France. There was assumed to be no conflict of interests between the collective, national interests of the states involved, such as France and Algeria, and the rights of individual migrants who would be the means of fulfilling such policies.

The end to legal immigration in 1974 was followed by the acceleration of illegal immigration. Under Charles Pasqua, Minister of the Interior, the police acquired wide powers of internal surveillance and control in 1977. They could immediately expel anyone found to have entered the country illegally, or working without authorisation. This procedure was combined with lax frontier controls, and did indeed result in a strange form of *rotation*, consisting of surveillance, expulsion and illegal return. Meanwhile, businesses benefited enormously from having a vulnerable and insecure workforce, who could be paid very low wages, were not able to protest, and could expect no protection from the authorities (Verbunt, 1985: 137).

By the mid-1970s, single male migration to France had been replaced by family reunification and the entry of wives, children and other family members. If anything, this family resettlement process was hastened by the coming of tighter controls, which made backward and forward movement more difficult for individual migrants. Permanent residents' rights had to be established to avoid being denied re-entry into France. The result of stricter internal controls and official restrictions at the borders was a sharpening of boundaries between France and Algeria: families and individuals were increasingly forced to choose to locate in one country or the other as movement back and forth was discouraged.

During the 1970s also, political pressure for immigration controls increased with the appearance of significant unemployment for the first time since the Second World War. French trade unions responded to the threat of redundancies by becoming more protective of national workers; the CGT (*Confédération Générale du Travail*) was inclined to define immigrant workers in France as part of the proletariat of their 'home' country, rather than as integral to the French working class (see Cartoon 3, and for a more in-depth discussion, see Chapter 6).

Official EC policy has consistently been to encourage member states to facilitate the integration of non-nationals already within the country, while taking steps to control the entry of any further primary immigrants (House of Lords, 1992: 6-8). Yet the very provisions of European Community legislation, by equalising working conditions, wages and other provisions, removed any strong incentives for workers to move from one member state to another. Indirectly, EC policies provided a further stimulus to non-EC immigration, by making it cheaper to employ such workers rather than inter-EC migrants (Straubhaar, 1988).

The status and activities of Algerian cultural and political organisations operating in France can be seen as a barometer of Franco-Algerian relations more generally. The *Amicale des Algériens en Europe* (AAE), which is the official FLN organisation for Algerians living in France, can be seen as part of the 'cultural' wing of the party, representing the policies of the Algerian government with respect to its citizens overseas (*Le Monde*, 23.6.1989). Until the late 1980s, the official position of the *Amicale* was that Algerian citizens living in France, and their families, should return to Algeria wherever possible. Until 1988 the AAE's official position, as stated by the President Chadli Benjedid, was that emigrants should return to rebuild their country. Yet no job was guaranteed to them, nor were they to be assisted in this task (Gaspard & Servan-Schreiber, 1985: 52-3). The French Government not only allowed the AAE to operate freely, but also accorded it official recognition. At the same time, the official policy was to be full integration of second-generation immigrants into France. This seemed somewhat contradictory, given that the AAE's activities have tended to delegitimise permanent settlement and full integration of Algerians in France.

The internal surveillance powers given to the French police have also played a major role in delegitimising the full integration of Algerian-born people and their children (Silverman, 1992: 142). Harassment has long been based on appearances. A North African, or anyone who looks vaguely North African, is more likely than anyone else to be stopped and asked for their papers, or to be treated in an abusive manner during questioning by the police.

Understandably, North Africans have also become easy prey for groups preaching political Islam. Such groups are opposed to the assimilation of Muslims living in the West to secular values. Bruno Etienne warned that by 'celebrating differences', the Left, which came to power in the early 1980s, perhaps unwittingly opened the door not only to the secret police of Algeria, but also to religious leaders and organisations funded by Saudi Arabia and elsewhere, who can now operate more or less freely among North African people (Etienne, 1989: 191; see review, *Le Monde*, 23.6.1989).

In 1989 the FLN (and therefore the AAE) finally accepted that French citizenship did not necessarily clash with fidelity to Algeria (*Le Monde*, 23.6.1989). This change in position came only after the recognition that, in the words of one scholar, the defence of an unchanging national cultural identity for all Algerians living in France placed the FLN in "a vicious circle of complicity with heterophobic racism" (Al Azmeh, in *Guardian*, 18.1.1994). Similar arguments to those made by the AAE were coming from the far-right *Front National*, who advised that people of Algerian origin should return home if they could not fully assimilate themselves to French culture and national 'ways of life'. Left and far right-wing political philosophies thus converged in the 1980s in denying the legitimacy of granting full citizenship to Algerian immigrants and their children (*Le Monde*, 29.11.1989). The question of how to disentangle these exclusionary practices and dialogues of the Left and Right is addressed in the last two chapters.

The tenor of the debate on immigration, assimilation and citizenship has changed since the early 1980s. In the first place, the Socialist Government, by allowing a large number of voluntary cultural associations to operate freely in France for the first time, appeared to endorse a 'multi-culturalism' of the British or North American type. Yet many 'immigrant' or *beur* associations which were created campaigned first and foremost for equal rights. Most spoke out in favour of a single citizenship, a secular republican political order and full equality under the law, irrespective of origin or status.

Some important issues remain to be agreed between France and Algeria; among these is the right of *harkis* to return to visit Algeria if they so wish. The forced marriage of young Algerian women, resident or born in France, has also caused controversy in the national media. Second- and third-generation French citizens of Algerian origin are more assertive than their parents or grandparents were in demanding equal treatment under the law, as well as the right to form their own autonomous cultural and political organisations outside official FLN structures (Withol de Wenden, 1991: 37).

For generations of Algerian origins born in France, the issue of citizenship, and the question of their cultural and political acceptance in France, have become their core concerns (Silverman, 1992: 129-31). Most have certainly opted to remain in France. Given the choice to perform military service in the Algerian or the French army, less than 5 per cent finally carried out their military service in Algeria (Etienne, 1989: 258-9).

## The Recession Revisited

Recessionary politics bolstered an exclusionary form of elite and working-class nationalism in France during the 1980s. The republican response to such xenophobic tendencies has also been strong. Leninist orthodoxy within the PCF (*Le Parti Communiste Français*) has proved an obstacle to any true solidarity between the communists and the Algerian workers and second-generation Algerians born in France, since the PCF view is that such people are properly part of the proletariat of their 'home' countries of origin. This approach had already outlived its usefulness in the 1960s, and yet persisted among French trade unions, echoing the position of the UGTA in Algeria throughout the 1970s and 1980s. Once again, only when they found their position dovetailing with that of the *Front National*, which favoured forcible repatriation, did the PCF and the French trade unions start to reconsider their approach. As one writer perceptively observed, "...the myth of return promoted by the homelands feeds the myth of return sustained by anti-immigration political forces" (Miller, 1986: 74).

The AAE and the *Front National* have in fact been attacking the same thing. As is often the case in post-colonial relations, particularly at the time of the independence negotiations, nationalists on all sides can 'agree to differ'. Both sides question the right of individuals to freedom of movement, residence and citizenship, and prefer to ascribe nationality to people on the basis of inherited criteria. Such similarities arise out of a common concern to place national, or collective, interests above the interests or rights of individual persons. In a different context, this occurred when Chief Buthelezi shook hands with the leader of the far right-wing Boer party, the AWB, in South Africa prior to the first general elections.

It is probably no coincidence that fundamentalist forms of political expression and action have grown in parallel on both sides of the Mediterranean. The rise of FIS (*Front Islamique de Salut* or Islamic Salvation Front) in Algeria has matched the rise of intolerant and xenophobic nationalism in France. Extremist political ideologies in both countries make perfect foils for each other, each side providing the justification needed for the vehemence of the other (Silverman, 1992: 112-3; *Independent*, 26.8.1994).

A combination of a nationalist trade union ideology and recession has prompted French governments to formulate repatriation proposals. Algerians have been the main target of such efforts, but not always the main participants. Their social and cultural integration is assumed to be more problematic than that of any other migrant 'group' (Meyer, 1987). It is worth noting that the participation in such schemes of Algerian nationals in France has been dependent on a high degree of inter-governmental collaboration between France and Algeria.

A first attempt to introduce a mass repatriation programme was in 1977. Under then Minister of the Interior, Charles Pasqua, emigrants were offered the sum of 10 000 French francs (FF), a sizeable sum at the time (Cohen, 1987: 159-60). The Algerian Government was totally opposed to this scheme, which was seen, not incorrectly, as a move aimed specifically at Algerians. The regime in Algiers also argued that it had not been consulted; that return migrants would be unable to find work, and refused to take any responsibility for reintegrating returnees. The result was a very low uptake by Algerians, who eventually accounted for less than one in twenty of those repatriated under the scheme (Miller, 1986: 73).

Repatriation proposals have worked better when preceded by official bilateral discussions and agreements, although there are strict limits on the extent to which inter-governmental agreement can determine the individual preferences of Algerians living in France. In December 1983, faced with massive job cuts in Talbot and Citroen factories, Algerian workers themselves demanded that they be given compensation and be assisted in the process of resettling in Algeria and starting businesses there. They demanded this as a condition of accepting redundancy offers, and with the support of the main trade unions (*Le Monde*, 24.10.1985). The following year, a voluntary repatriation scheme was introduced by the Socialist Government of François Mitterrand with the agreement of the Algerian Government. Franco-Algerian relations were much improved since the low-point of the mid-1970s, and the two regimes found themselves in basic agreement concerning the general aims of such repatriation schemes.

This second scheme was more generously funded than the first. Those who agreed to return to their 'home' country would receive up to 150 000 FF in compensation for the loss of earnings in France, as well as a grant of 20 000 FF paid on arrival. They were also entitled to a lump-sum payment equivalent to six months of social security entitlement. Between May 1984 and October 1985, there were 16 000 applications, and 95 per cent were accepted. In total, 45 000 people left for Algeria, and Algerian applicants accounted for more than half of all those who took part in the scheme, around 56 per cent (*Le Monde*, 24.10.1985). According to official sources, one year later almost half of the return migrants had bought their own businesses in Algeria; one-quarter were making a living from farming or fisheries, and one-eighth were employed in the transport and taxi business. After the first two years (1984-5), the success rate, measured in terms of the proportion of new businesses set up by return migrants which were still in operation, was estimated to be 80 per cent.

This is an unusual example of inter-state collaboration enhancing, rather than restricting, the freedom of movement of certain groups of people. In this case, state assistance was available from both sides for industrial workers who wished to return to their 'home' country of Algeria, and their families. In part, the scheme worked because it was consistent with individuals' strategies of seeking social promotion and improved living standards.

It is worth remembering that, in recent years, voluntary departures such as those described above have been the exception rather than the rule. In the two years following the election of a right-wing government in 1987, for example, an estimated 18 000 foreign residents were expelled from France under the second so-called *loi Pasqua* (*Guardian*, 30.5.1989). Furthermore, as the alteration of nationality law to exclude those with entitlements to residence and eventually to citizenship has become common practice in the European Union member states. Drawing on changes in British legislation, and the tightly ascriptive basis of German nationality law, this trend represents another, more invisible means of excluding those who have already apparently gained access to the benefits of membership in the polities of Western Europe.

**Negotiating Integration and Equal Rights in the 1990s**

The conflict between the goals of state policies and individuals' immigration and citizenship rights can be posed, first of all, in terms of a human right to mobility across international boundaries. But this right does not exist under international law; sovereignty of states over their borders has been given precedence in the crucial question of who is allowed entry into a country.

More complex problems arise when the boundaries are not purely geographical but social, legal and political as well. These boundaries may cut across and carve out identity, entitlement to state benefits, employment rights and other substantial citizenship rights. In this respect, there has been a steady erosion of the principle at the heart of French nationality law, known as *jus solis*, the right to nationality on the basis of place of birth, rather than according to blood or family ties, *jus sanguinis* (Silverman, 1992: 147). This erosion of access to nationality and citizenship, and the rights that such citizenship confers, has been justified with reference to *sécurité*, or what in Britain is termed 'law and order'. Already in 1986, the *loi Pasqua* authorised the police to deport any young person under eighteen years of age to their 'country of origin' (that is, to the country of birth of their parents) in cases where they were found guilty of petty criminal offences (*Economist*, 19.4.1988).

The existing basis for granting of French nationality at the age of eighteen to all those born in the country, the nationality code, a product of the constitution of the First Republic, has recently been reformed (JCWI, 1993a: 15). This change has been part of the agenda of the Right since the early 1980s or so (*Le Monde*, 23.3.1988). The aim of the reforms, according to the prime minister Edouard Balladur has been to oblige "those who wish to be French [to] clearly make a choice to that effect" (*Guardian*, 12.5.1993). The intention of the far right, however, is clearly to deprive immigrant populations and their children of the right to enjoy the same range of social and welfare provisions, and of civil and political rights by making permanent settlement difficult, "through the manipulation of nationality, citizenship and immigration laws..." (Cohen, 1987: 126).

For the young *beurs* living in France, the dilemma of mixed identity appears to be born of the clash between two titans: Muslim, Arab Algeria and secular republican France. But the cultural and political dilemma they face is not as simple as this image of 'Marianne versus the Veil' would suggest (see Cartoon 2). A study carried out in the 1980s found that second-generation North Africans did not perceive their choice as being between full assimilation and loss of cultural identity, on the one hand, and a return to tradition and withdrawal from French society, on the other (Muxel, 1988: 925-7).

They will in future nonetheless be obliged by law to demonstrate their allegiance to France and their 'worthiness' of citizenship. This will only apply to those born in France of Algerian (or other non-EC) parents, not those born in France of French parents. Although "[t]he social mores of young North Africans in France today are little different from those of their white counterparts", a discriminatory legal basis for citizenship has been introduced for the first time with the alterations to the French nationality code in 1993 (K. Malik, in *Independent*, 26.8.1994).

The questioning of the basis of nationality law seems to reflect a deep sense of crisis concerning the meaning of French national identity. Marceau Long, who was appointed France's first Minister for Integration in 1990, asked the perceptive question in a recent newspaper interview: "Why should immigrants' children be proud of their French citizenship if the children of the French bourgeoisie are not?" (*Le Monde*, 6.10.1992). During the 1980s, *beur* groups gradually become more vigilant regarding the political implications of the liberal, tolerant-sounding language of diversity and multi-culturalism. There was a growing realisation that the rhetoric of respect for difference could easily be misused. Discussing the policy of *droit à la différence* (the 'right to be different'), Farida Belghoul, a film-maker of Algerian origin living and working in France, once asked this important question:

Who exactly am I different from? I would suggest that the so-called right to be different can be a hidden way of excluding people. In the end, and whether you intend it or not, giving foreigners the right not to be like others prevents them from fully taking part in a democratic social and political life, on a par with French people. (*Im'média*, May-June 1984)

The same argument was made during the 'hijab' affair by those who opposed the exclusion from school of the girls concerned. This refusal to be cast as the 'problem' or the 'outsider' was also evident in a conference held in 1990 on the theme of *France and Algeria: Interacting Identities*, when one young second-generation Franco-Algerian, Nadia Amiri, denied that the *beurs* felt torn between two opposed identities. She preferred to express their double identity in a more positive way, saying, "We are equally at home in our trainers or our *babouches* (North African slippers)" (Stenhouse, 1990: 38). The importance of keeping open the integration is clearly articulated by groups like the *Nanas Beurs* (Silverman, 1992: 112). They argue that North African women in France face particular constraints on their personal freedom, both from French society and from their own families attempting to reassert community control over their sexuality and friendships (Etienne, 1989: 174).

Bryan Turner's observation that the dissolution of 'orientalism' might require a dialogue of similarity, or solidarity, seems relevant here (Turner, 1989). Michel Rocard distinguished between the integrationist and the pluralist models in this way:

> By integration we mean the protection of all ways of life; it is not the same thing as co-existence, where different groups rub along, blind to one another, or allow their so-called respect for each other's differences to become an excuse for the creation of what is effectively an apartheid society. (*Independent*, 9.1.1990)

A dialogue that emphasises differences and discontinuities also has much in common with colonial ideology, by tending to sanction inequalities. A post-colonial (or decolonised) understanding of human relations is more likely to emerge out of a discourse that emphasises similarities and cross-cutting connections that exist between people in spite of real differences. One outspoken advocate of *métissage* between French and North African identities is Bernard Stasi, former EC Commissioner. He has pointed out that when hard and fast distinctions are drawn between various discrete identities, it becomes much more difficult for people of mixed background to express their complex and multiple identity in positive ways.

The new culture which first- and second-generation emigrant groups create in the land in which they settle is identical neither to the original culture, nor to that of the indigenous population. Rather it is a hybrid, an admixture of elements. Caryl Phillips, writing about second-generation black people in Europe, observes that they "begin to develop at twice the speed of the home country...left behind. This virtually ensures that it will be impossible...to return, at least permanently" (Phillips, 1987: 123). To attempt to 'purify' the national and community cultures of emigrants/immigrants and their children is therefore a hopeless enterprise, since it denies the dynamism of their mixed experience and existence.

In 1989 a group of *beurs* visited Algeria to discuss their position as French citizens of Algerian origin, settled in France. Many of them could not speak Arabic; some were sons and daughters of *harkis*, whose relationship with Algeria was even more problematic. The visit was symbolically import-ant, since it indicated an acceptance by the regime in Algiers, that these second-generation Franco-Algerians were permanently integrated into French society. Nonetheless, the *beurs* also expressed their wish to have some sort of contin-uing link with Algerian society (*Le Monde*, 23.6.1989). In fact, for the most part, *beurs* over age eighteen continue to be considered French in France, and Algerian in Algeria (*Le Monde*, 6.2.1992).

The identity question for Algerians (and other North Africans) living in France is complicated by the existence of non-Arab minorities. Berbers are very numerous among Algerians settled in France and second-generation Franco-Algerians (Etienne, 1989: 177). They see the imposition of an Arab-language requirement in order to work in the public sector as a double imposition: not only is Arabic not their language, but they would be forced to learn classical Arabic, a literary rather than a spoken language.

With the rise of the FIS in Algeria, the legitimacy of the FLN Government is seriously in question. The party is still in place after having been voted out, and its right to govern is now questioned by virtually all sides, adding to the attraction of the FIS (*Le Monde*, 22.4.1990). Writing for *Le Monde*, André Fontaine warns against "adopting an attitude of exclusion towards the Algerians and throwing them into the arms of those who dream of avenging their defeat at the battle of Poitiers" (*Le Monde*, 5.4.1990). The French Government's decision to join the United States and Britain in the Gulf War rather than seek to act as intermediary alongside the Maghrebin countries further undermined the position of Algerian moderates (*Guardian*, 11.2.1991).

The assassination of reformist president Mohammed Boudiaf in 1992 did nothing to enhance the popularity of the FLN, whose conservatives were suspected of being behind the murder. Attempts to blame the killing on the FIS backfired (*Guardian*, 2.7.1992). The FIS agenda appears radical and anti-colonial in a certain, uncritical light, since what is proposed is no less than a 'second divorce' from France; the 'yolk' of full cultural, linguistic and religious decolonisation, rather than the purely formal 'shell' of independence (*Independent*, 19.1.1992; Assignment, BBC2, 19.11.1994).

The attraction of 'fundamentalist' political Islam may be a sign of the feelings of vulnerability of Algerians and other Muslim-born people in France and the rest of Europe. It is exaggerated to interpret such a move as an attempt to take over a secular, liberal social order, whether in France, Britain or Germany (Memmi, in *Le Monde Diplomatique*, March 1988; *Independent*, 7.8.1992; *Guardian*, 18.1.1994). As John Berger has put it, the 'return' to religion may be "a protest against the heartlessness of the materialist systems" (*Guardian*, 22.3.1990). On the other hand, the movement for the restoration of codes of practice supposedly in line with those in existence at the time of the Prophet Mohammed has potentially very repressive implications for many Algerians, and especially for women. Single women have been attacked and killed for the crime of behaving and living 'unislamically'. The anti-colonial reaction of the FIS thus appears to include in its aims an anti-liberatory strategy of repression of Algerian women. Undoubtedly, women themselves are "rebelling by wearing the veil", but this alone cannot account for its greatly increased use in Algeria and France among the Muslim community (*Guardian*, 18.1.1994).

The rise of essentialist political discourses in France and Algeria can be attributed to some common causes: economic and social upheaval in both countries, high unemployment and a loss of legitimacy on the part of the existing political elite. Co-operation between the two governments has only served to widen the perceived rift between the two monoliths of French and Algerian cultural identity. A shared opposition to Islamicist politics has brought the regimes in Algiers and Paris closer together. The FIS and other Islamic political movements can claim, with some justification, that there is a conspiracy against them. The French Government recently lobbied other G7 governments in order to obtain their agreement to provide some debt relief for Algeria (*Independent*, 9.7.1994; *Guardian*, 6.6.1994). The government in France has also made mass arrests and has detained suspected members of FIS and other radical Islamic groups resident in France, in response to pressure from the Algerian government (*Guardian*, 11.11.1993; *Independent*, 7.6. 1994).

Just as there is prejudice against French citizens with Algerian origins, there is also prejudice against Algerians with French origins. This form of prejudice is perhaps experienced most acutely by young francophone, western-oriented women. They are particularly vulnerable to the accusation that they have betrayed the (Algerian, or Muslim) community's 'honour' (*Le Monde Hebdomadaire*, 7-13.4.1994; *Guardian*, 7.7.1994). Particular problems arise for them because of their unwillingness to conform to strict neo-Islamic dress codes (which are not to be confused with traditional Algerian clothing codes for women). There is widespread ignorance among the francisised elite of written, and sometimes even spoken, Arabic. This makes them vulnerable in an increasingly arabised country.[2]

Table 5.1 showed that, among the possible range of policies and bilateral relations between France and Algeria concerning the immigration issue, nationality and citizenship for Algerians in France, only a few are likely to bring collective and individual rights into line. The acquisition of individual citizenship rights poses especial difficulties in the case of women, because of the role they are allocated as so-called guardians of their community's culture (Anthias & Yuval-Davis, 1992: 5). Conflicts at inter-community, and even international level, may be expressed in forms of subtle or overt social control of women and their exclusion from the political sphere, all in the guise of 'protecting' them from the enemy. As Eleanore Kofman has observed in regard to the political cosmology of the *Front National*, "[w]omen, as the guardians of the family, have to be protected against outside invaders. They risk being raped by foreign males" (Kofman, 1993: 5). Similarly distorted perceptions may well exist on the other side.

Women's integration poses a threat to the Algerian community, as a community. It is interesting that young Maghrebin women's attitudes have been found to be generally less family-oriented, and more left-wing, than those of young Maghrebin men (Muxel, 1988: 925-7). What was observed in the case of the French Caribbean communities and their integration into France can equally well be applied here to Algerians and the Algerian community in France. It seems that, "even when individuals are integrated, the community is not, precisely because the integration of individuals as such implies the disintegration of the community" (Etienne, 1989: 200).

## Conclusion

It seems that the 'new racism' of the 1980s and 1990s is really no different from the old, in that it seeks to exclude from the citizenry those who can be identified as 'alien' on the basis of appearance or dress, for example (Feuchtwang, 1990: 4). So long as 'home' is assumed to be the place where an individual's ancestors are buried, a zero-sum game between individual and community self-determination will persist. Wherever people's allegiances may lie, the acquisition of human rights remains conditional on access to residence and full citizenship of a state where the respect of such rights is at least the norm.

The 1990s mark the end of the Cold War, and for France this has meant the loss of its role as 'arbiter' and broker for the third world within the context of a bipolar world divided by the superpowers. France enjoyed considerable prestige during the 1980s among radical and non-aligned states opposed to doctrines of structural adjustment and free trade. This prestige has largely evaporated in the 1990s. At the very time when the prospects indicate that there will be a rising influx of Algerians seeking asylum from civil unrest in Algeria, the notion of France as a country of asylum, *France terre d'asile* is increasingly under threat (*Le Monde Hebdomadaire*, 7-13.4.1994; interview, F. Amrani, 14.4.1993). In the post-Cold War context, the foreign policy gains for France of adopting a liberal asylum policy seem to be outweighed by domestic considerations. For this reason, as pressures for admission increase in the years to come, restrictions on asylum seekers are more and more likely to be imposed which will lead to more people being kept out of France (Cels,

1989: 171). In any case, unified visa controls among EC states may prevent potential asylum seekers from reaching France at all. In early 1990, under the guise of inter-EC co-operation and national 'operating difficulties', the UK brought its visa policy into line with that of France, and for the first time introduced visas for Algerians, Moroccans and Tunisians (Home Office News Release, 23.2.1990).

Squeezed between two forms of intolerance and xenophobia which tend to mirror each other, the absolute priority of the second-generation and mixed Franco-Algerians becomes to secure their legal and substantial citizenship rights, but without abandoning their claim to be a distinctive part of the culturally diverse community of people living permanently in France. They must avoid the fate of being *sans patrie*, without a full citizenship, located in a bantustan like that of the Anguillans, Hong Kong Chinese, and formerly Bophuthatswanans and other bantustan 'citizens'. With continuing civil unrest in Algeria, it is also likely that increasing numbers of Algerians will be seeking asylum in France; this new movement of people will have serious repercussions for inter-state relations between the two countries (*Le Monde Hebdomadaire*, 7-13.4.1994).

## Notes

1. *Le Monde*, 18.3.1992. The cartoon means: "Go back to our country, I mean your country!" This indicates the French man's unwillingness to accept the loss of French Algeria, and a persistent hostility to anyone who has even the appearance of the enemy as it was perceived during the war: both part of the self (owned like a horse) and part of the indomitably alien other. This cartoon has not been reproduced, due to problems obtaining copyright. However, I was most grateful to the cartoonist Serguei, and his wife who acts as his agent, for allowing me the use of Cartoons 1 and 2. Cartoon 3 has no author, and I am grateful to *Le Monde* newspaper for allowing me to use it without requiring copyright permission.

2. There is still a great bitterness about the war in France, and it has not been swallowed. In Algeria, too, there is bitterness, and this has been expressed, for example, in the rapid arabisation of the administrative system. Using classical Arabic in official documents and routine administration has proved an effective way of discouraging further studies in France, and penalising Algerians who are highly assimilated to France and *francophonie*. As Caryl Phillips seems to suggest, however, the emigrants' culture develops in its own direction. French and Algerian identities, for example, have been reacting against each other since at least 1962, and probably far longer. Algerians living in France are caught between this polarisation, and sometimes feel themselves to be tugged painfully in two directions at once.

# 6 Propositions Concerning South-North Migration in a Post-Colonial Context

*It is in the specification of the circumstances under which citizenship...may be acquired by outsiders that all states confront the limits of their generosity and universalism.*
Freeman, 1986: 53.

## Introduction

Access to citizenship and citizenship rights has become the central object of struggle between immigrant populations and the state in Western Europe. This has become a covert form of a wider conflict between North and South, the terms of the debate reflecting judgements about the colonial past, about its significance and its consequences. Routine violations of the human rights of immigrants and asylum seekers and their children take place under left-wing as well as under right-wing governments in Western Europe. This is not to suggest a heroic role for immigrant families or asylum seekers. They simply find themselves at the centre of a post-colonial (or neo-colonial) debate concerning entitlement to citizenship and to political and civil rights as well as to basic welfare provisions. Moreover, where 'immigrants' are being deprived of basic human rights, the rights of the 'indigenous' population are likely to be under attack as well.

Ten common arguments used on the Left and Right about former colonial subjects seeking access to the metropolis are identified in this chapter. In many cases these themes have a long history (Balibar, 1991: 101). Each one is examined in turn and some internal inconsistencies are revealed. The underlying question is whether it is possible to argue for a position where, whenever collective and individual rights come into conflict, individual rights are given precedence. It emerges that, where there are severe restrictions on immigration and on the extension of rights to first- and second-generation non-nationals, this is almost invariably the result of rights of collectivities having been given priority over those of individuals. Nor is this critique confined to the far right. As Silverman has noted, "The structural nature of racism within the nation-state...creates problems for the Left's opposition to racism, as the nationalist tradition is also a fundamental part of its own ideology" (Silverman, 1992: 119).

## First Proposition: Immigrants should return home to develop their own countries

This particular proposition seems to be based on the belief that states have proprietorial rights over those who are born within their boundaries. Those who 'belong' to a state owe their first duty to it, irrespective of where they live or any subsequent allegiances formed (Dummett, 1992: 172). Everyone born as a citizen of a particular country is seen to have duties which they must fulfil for the remainder of their lifetime. For men, these may include the bearing of arms in the event of war, and in military service. For women, they may include the bearing and rearing of children or perhaps, as in China, refraining from bearing them. It is as though people are the territory of government, and may be used as the government sees fit in the national interest. Trade unionists and left-wing 'radicals' are just as likely to take this position as those on the Right (for an example, see proposition seven).

Regimes seeking to escape underdevelopment can exert pressure, especially on skilled emigrants, to return 'home'. Those who seek to acquire another citizenship are seen as virtual traitors. Some states such as Algeria have made efforts to persuade their nationals not to seek citizenship of the state of immigration, even when they are fully entitled to do so. In the case of Algerian emigrants, many have become trapped by a combination of the exclusionary response of the 'host' population and government, and the unwillingness of the 'home' government to let go (Hargreaves, 1990: 39). We saw in the last chapter that governmental elites may collaborate to restrict individuals' freedom of movement across their borders (Dummett, 1992: 178). Such forces combine to make what Robin Cohen describes as the 'helot' status of immigrants all the more inescapable (Cohen, 1989: 165). Even UN bodies like UNCTAD adopt the official position that skilled emigrants from third world countries should return home in order to assist with their own country's national development. Medical and technical personnel have come under particular pressure to return (Mazrui, 1981; Dowty, 1986: 159-60).

Academic writers tend to believe that most, if not all, emigrants are deeply homesick (Cohen, 1987: 34). There seems to be an implicit assumption that this homesickness is compounded by the guilt of having betrayed one's motherland and trying to settle in a country that is not one's own. There have been numerous studies focusing on emigrants' sense of displacement and iso-lation. Only a few deal with their integration, and with successful strategies of circular migration and settlement (for example, Philpott, 1973). Dispro-portionate concern with return migration has thus contributed to creating a 'myth of a myth of return'. The idea that feelings of malaise and alienation are quasi-universal among immigrants and their children also ignores the fact that most 'home' countries have neither the means nor any intention of reintegrating return migrants in the future (Gaspard & Servan-Schreiber, 1985: 53).

The acquisition of a new citizenship is sometimes assumed to be only a temporary and partial solution to the 'helot' status of immigrants and their families. If this assumption is made, then even 'radicals' on the Left can conclude that immigrants are somehow to blame for the problems they face in their adopted countries. This arises from the view that such people are stub-bornly refusing to do the right thing. In this nationalistic understanding, they should go back to their country of origin and contribute to its national develop-ment by working there, in whatever way they can. Their imperfect integration into the social and political structures of the country of immigration can thus be attributed to their own voluntary exile, rather than being seen as the out-come of discrimination in the 'host' country.

In this view, cosmopolitanism, which involves physical and social movement across cultural and national boundaries, creates new hybrid and mixed forms of culture that simply do not have the same legitimacy or historical authenticity as the national or ethnic culture. The dangers of ethnic nationalism being taken as a natural rather than a politically designed phenom-enon are clear for all to see in contemporary Europe and elsewhere. In former Yugoslavia, for example, each bout of ethnic self-assertion has involved trampling on existing cosmopolitan communities and dividing them. This kind of classification of people seems no less virulent than classical racism. It may even be more dangerous, because it seeks to make racism respectable (Guillaumin, 1991: 13). As one commentator on anti-racist strategies has recently observed:

> Categorisation of human populations by culture or ethnic origin is no different from racial categorisations (when the ascription of origin assumes a fixed cultural essence in the individuals categorised)...It just sorts people into cultures and cultures into places. Place may be a division of labour or of territory or of both. (Feuchtwang, 1990: 4)

The assumption that objectively identifiable geographical and ethnic communities exist, and that people belong to them from birth till death, is surprisingly resilient, and survives considerable intermixing and high levels of social and territorial mobility. In most states in the world, moreover, even if citizens fulfil their obligations to the state, they will not be granted concomitant rights. States' persecution of their own citizens is a world-wide reality, and to argue that the country of origin or birth will always be someone's homeland, irrespective of that person's wishes, is to consign many to the Gulag. This is sometimes masked by an apparent concern for third world development (House of Lords, 1992: 8-12).

The idea that every citizen has lifelong and unavoidable obligations to their state of 'origin' is used to justify repatriation proposals, whether coercive or not. Taken to extremes, the assertion that all people have a lifelong duty to their state of origin could lead to support for compulsory deportations in the presumed interests of developing countries! It is in any case notoriously difficult to ensure that repatriation is genuinely voluntary. Violations of human rights in this context are especially likely in the present climate of high unemployment and with no Cold War to justify a tolerant refugee policy (Carens, 1992). The fear of being 'invaded' is invoked in defence of ever more repressive and unjust exclusionary measures, even though evidence is emerging that a demographic gap is likely to create labour shortages in several West European countries, including France, within the next ten years or so (*Independent*, 27.10.1991).

As with any authoritarian politics, ordinary third world people are still being asked, after thirty or more years of independence, to sacrifice their immediate personal interests and rights, including their freedom of movement, for the greater good of the state. In exchange, they are promised a new political and international economic order in which they will eventually achieve their full liberation (Ait-Ahmed, 1980: 23). Nationalist arguments have been used in forums such as the UN to claim that ideas of individual human rights are alien to African or Asian people. In his study of 'Afrofascism', Ait-Ahmed reminds us that indigenous ideas of human rights existed in a wide range of non-western cultures: among the Incas; among Arab and Bengali poets and mystics; within African proverbs; as well as with Cicero, Locke and Rousseau (ibid.: 29). Speaking of the Algerian experience, where human rights are attacked from all sides as a 'Western' notion, one author comments:

> These rights are universal and inherent in all human beings. The fact that one culture, historically speaking, first became aware of these rights in no sense implies that such rights are only compatible with that particular culture. (Lahouari, 1994: 150)

Punitive schemes designed to oblige third world nationals to return to their countries of origin are largely ineffective. Imposing penalties on graduates and others who have not returned to their home countries may well dissuade them from returning at all, further hastening the "reverse transfer of technology" (Dowty, 1986: 162-3).

The benefits of emigration for 'sending' countries, are often considerable, particularly for smaller states dependent on remittances. Remittances are often still a vital source of foreign exchange and capital. According to one report, the recent large-scale movement out of the Francophone countries of the Sahel of mainly single men has led to such remittances from migrants overseas "replacing a state which is virtually bankrupt" (*EuroReporter*, April 1992: 39-40). The money sent home finances the building of schools, clinics, houses, and the provision of basic services which governments were once responsible for. In this context, emigration is a symptom of the rigours imposed by structural adjustment policies, and by privatisation and public expenditure cuts in particular.

## Second Proposition: Immigrants who settle permanently and become citizens must be culturally alienated

This is particularly often said of emigrants from former colonies who want to settle in the former colonial metropolis. It is also said, for example, of Muslims living in non-Muslim societies, or exiles who have been outside their country of origin for many decades. After all the damage the coloniser has done, so goes the argument, how can individuals who were formerly colonised, or whose parents were subjugated, agree to settle in the former colonial metropolis? Very often they are destined to carry out menial tasks and receive very poor wages.

In the French context, the idea that all North Africans should return home eventually is reinforced by the constant use of the term *immigrés*, even when referring to second- and third-generation children of North Africans, who have acquired full French citizenship. Since *immigré* denotes impermanence, its constant use undermines the permanency and legitimacy of the *beurs* and *harkis* presence in France. For the *harkis*, who fought on the French side during the Algerian war of independence, and their children, to be placed on the same footing as recent and illegal immigrants is especially insulting. All the more so, since their prospects of ever returning to Algeria are almost non-existent.

The evidence for the rest of the EC also suggests that the so-called 'immigrant population' and their descendants are settling permanently and may never return to their original country of emigration. According to a survey carried out in France in 1983, 43 per cent of 'immigrants' said they would prefer to remain even if they were offered work at 'home'; by 1990 over 60 per cent said they would wish to remain under these circumstances (*EuroReporter*, April 1992: 36). Unfortunately, this growing desire to remain has coincided with growing intolerance towards 'immigrants' on the part of the indigenous population of Western Europe. Whereas the immigration issue was of serious concern to only 8 per cent of those questioned in France in 1983, by 1991 the figure was 41 per cent (ibid.).

The idea that assimilation involves obliteration of one culture by another has its origins in the apparent failure of the 'melting pot' of United States society. In this context, "assimilationism was a sinister policy of 'ethnocide' and the state should give full recognition to ethnic and racial sentiments" (Van den Berghe, 1981: 4; see Memmi, 1991: 32). In Britain cultural assimilation has similarly been seen as ill-advised. In France the term has come into severe disrepute since the Algerian war, and 'assimilation' has gradually been replaced by the more neutral-sounding 'integration'. Some have argued that the greater attraction of ideas of assimilation in France compared with Britain is due to different notions of national identity. The British (or more precisely the English) identity tends to be seen as given in terms of roots and origins, whereas French identity can be constructed through adherence to republican values and institutions.

At the end of the Second World War, both British and French nationality were extended to include, at least notionally, all overseas colonial subjects. This spirit of universalism did not survive independence in the 1960s, when the automatic rights of freedom of movement and settlement of former colonial people started to be dismantled. Those who were to be excluded were once again said to be too 'culturally different' to be able to fit in. In Britain more than in France, there was emphasis on colour differences. According to the principle of *jus sanguinis*, which now runs both through British immigration and British nationality law, it is the ancestry of a person that determines their legal status, rather than their place of birth or upbringing (Dummett & Nicol, 1990; Carens, 1992: 44).

'Cultural alienation' is a term sometimes used by sociologists and other intellectuals in referring to those they feel sorry for. Settlers who want to fit in culturally are thought not to be aware of their own best interests, which lie in going back 'home', or at least maintaining their home culture and refusing assimilation. This inverts rather than subverts colonial values, which asserted the primacy of Western values over those of the rest of the world. The formula now reads: Third world - good; Western world - bad, but the reversal of hierarchies does not prevent the sacrificing of individuals' rights in the interests of a collectivity. It also gives Western people much more freedom in cultural terms: whilst it is thought highly cultured and sophisticated for a Westerner to be interested in Indian dance, film or music, in African art or in Caribbean fiction, the same does not apply to the Indian, African or Caribbean person interested in Western culture, fiction, film and dance. The whole notion of a 'right to be different', or *droit à la différence* in French, can lead individuals to assert points of difference from others, and to neglect commonalities that may also exist between themselves and those around them (Memmi, 1991).

### Third Proposition: Immigrants and their children will always appear 'different', leading to conflict and misery

This proposal again rests on the assumption that it is somehow natural, biologically or culturally, for people of the same colour and genetic stock to remain together and intermix. It also assumes that it is somehow not natural for mixing to take place between different colour groups (or 'races'). Ultimately, such mixing is said to cause conflict, both within the offspring of mixed relationships, who will not be able to clearly define their roots, and for a mixed society, which will be equally lost and alienated. Ultimately, intermixing is said to produce tensions that cannot be reconciled, and can thus result in civil unrest, riots and criminality. Subconsciously, this fatalistic argument is powerfully backed by the experience of Nazism, itself propelled forward by the mobilising capacity of such ideas in times of economic and national crisis. A central preoccupation of the Nazi regime was to reverse the centuries of mixing between those identified as of Germanic 'race' and those Germans whose origins, according to the racial theories, lay elsewhere.

The same excuse (that there exists a natural, unalterable state of affairs) is used by governments everywhere, including in France and Britain today, to justify opposition to an egalitarian and cosmopolitan social and political order (Berger, 1975: 140). The far right wants to return to the (entirely mythical) primordial national entity. Roger Scruton, speaking of citizenship, for example, argues that "the bond which ties the citizen to society is...not a voluntary but a kind of natural bond" (Scruton, 1980: 31). This kind of argument seems to have greater resonance among public opinion and official outlooks in Britain (and Germany) than in France. As already suggested, the inclusion of a 'patrial' clause to exclude people with no British-born grandparents from British nationality and immigration rights was an example of this (Bevan, 1986; Carens, 1992: 44).

In a counter-intuitive way, this whole critique of a multi-cultural society is perceptive and well-directed. Widespread cultural and sexual mixing of people regarded as coming from different communities or groups does indeed pose a serious challenge to any idea of fixed and permanent boundaries between ethnic, religious or other groups of people. When boundaries of identity and nationality become more flexible and porous, it becomes more apparent that they are politically and socially rather than 'naturally' defined. The very idea of mixing or *métissage* between 'cultures' makes it clear that cultures are inorganic, are made by human beings, and cannot be traced back to some primordial ancestral gene pool. The New Right intellectuals express disgust and horror at the cosmopolitanism of contemporary Western European societies. Along with left-wing intellectuals, immigrants and second-genera-tion settlers do not fit comfortably into the construct of a natural or 'historic' nation (Siedel, 1986).

Those who yearn for predictability and neatness, and wish to avoid all mess and confusion, find disconcerting parallels between the rootless, unsettled and mobile peoples of the present and those of the past. Contem-porary hostility towards physically and cross-culturally mobile groups of people, such as gypsies, travellers and migrant workers, echoes hostility to Jewish people in the past, as depicted in the image of the 'wandering Jew'.

Integral to this discourse of exclusion and closure is the positioning of women. In all forms of fundamentalism, including ethnic chauvinist nationalism, 'our' women are exclusively for 'us' and should not mix with men from other groups. The opposite does not usually apply, since 'their' women can also be 'ours', if they are the spoils of war, or are described as wanton enough. In a context where men's out-mixing is acceptable but that of women is not, women are especially vulnerable to accusations of being culturally alienated and having sold out to the enemy. Women who take the same liberties as men in their choice of sexual partners, for example, or in employment, can more easily be branded traitors to the nation. Individual women's rights to freedom of movement and association are thus liable to be trampled where they come in the way of a male elite-defined general community interest (Kofman, 1993). Yet there are tensions created by this mixing of gender and ethnic or cultural hierarchies. If those who want 'foreigners out' also want women back in the kitchen, sooner or later there is likely to be a shortage of workers (Gaspard & Servan-Schreiber, 1985: 11).

In Britain, the *Salisbury Review* is a semi-respectable forum for the expression of views hostile to multiculturalism. In France, similar arguments can be found in the writings of GRECE (*Groupement de Recherche et d'Etude pour une Civilisation Européenne*). This group finds itself confronted by the logic of voluntarism that lies at the heart of the republican ideal type of French nationality. The GRECE state the following as if it were damning:

> If France is merely a concept, totally removed from the realities of soul and blood, then patriotism becomes ideological and contains within itself all the germs of universalism; he who wishes to be French is French. (Cited in Siedel, 1986: 128)

In a different light, this criticism is a compliment, since it gives credence to the idea that republican ideals are in fact being translated into reality in matters of nationality and citizenship law. In this voluntarist conception of membership of the nation, and of allegiance to the state, rather than being determined on the basis of ethnicity, religion, colour, place of birth or some other variable over which people have no control, French citizenship is simply granted on the basis of subjective allegiance. As Michel Debré puts it, you are asked whether "you have the feeling of belonging to the national community" (Debré, 1972: 212-3). This model must be regarded as close to a legal and ethical ideal, since it minimises the conflict that can arise between the interests of the individual citizen and the collective national interest. While this is certainly an ideal, it is not possible to find examples of nationality being granted simply on the basis of such allegiance, quite irrespective of place of birth, period of residence, service in the national forces or other tangible proofs of allegiance.

To justify the introduction of ever harsher immigration laws, rules and regulations, often implemented by the police in association with immigration officers, the former British Home Secretary, Kenneth Clark, has reiterated received wisdom, also current in France, according to which: "[g]ood race relations are heavily dependent on strict immigration control" (Spencer, 1994: 307). Strict control has included the forcible expulsion of supposed overstayers, one case of which led to the death in 1993 of Joy Gardiner, subsequently condemned by the courts as manslaughter. Commenting on the logic of official policy, Sarah Spencer observes that such restrictions affect the relatives of non-white people already resident in the UK, and are totally inconsistent with efforts to counter discrimination within Britain.

> The perception that black and Asian people (in particular) are undesirable members of British society is endorsed, while members of existing minority communities have been made to feel unwelcome and insecure. (Spencer, 1994: 339)

**Fourth Proposition: Immigrants are visitors and, if they are not happy, they should go back home**

This theme connects closely to the first three, but asserts more explicitly that the state's responsibility for upholding human rights is limited to upholding the rights of its own citizens, and not those of non-nationals living within the country. Aliens do have fewer rights than nationals, and in practice tend to have even fewer the poorer and less influential their country of origin. The treatment of Bangladeshis in the UK is much harsher than the treatment of Japanese people, for example, and this is mainly because Japan is a wealthier and more influential country than Bangladesh. Colour does of course play a role, as is clear from some exceptional cases, such as the arrest of a black American citizen at Heathrow during the time of the riots in Los Angeles following the Rodney King case.

That some people have few civil, political, economic or social rights in their country of origin seems, by some perverse logic, to justify according them similarly few rights in the country of immigration or asylum. There has been a hardening of attitudes towards all incomers from countries affected by indebtedness, war, drought and economic and political collapse (Muntarbhom, 1989: 192). Attacks against refugees have increased dramatically in many West European countries in recent years. One study on global asylum policies concluded that:

> ...political leaders in the West have a special responsibility to speak out forcefully against racism and against violent attacks against asylum seekers and foreigners. If political leaders do not speak out for tolerance and integration, they implicitly offer support to the forces of intolerance and violence. (Loescher, 1993: 200)

Migrants and asylum seekers from former colonies will tend to be treated the most harshly, particularly if the metropolitan population resented the independence of the former colony in the first place (interviews, JCWI, August

1992). Algerians in France experience sharp hostility and resentment partly for this historical reason, given the complex feelings of betrayal experienced by part of the French population in relation to the war of independence (Andrew, 1984: 340-41). If they complain that they are subjected to racist abuse and brutality, second-generation North Africans in France, like young Asian or Caribbean British youth, are liable to be told, 'If you don't like it here, why don't you go back home where you came from?'

Examples of mistreatment being condoned by the authorities are manifold. In one case in France, residents of a hostel were subjected to arbitrary and corrupt practices and, when they complained of this treatment to the local police, the response was to arrest three of the migrant workers. No charges were brought against the warden of the hostel (Castles, 1970: 11). More recently, North Africans arrested as suspected 'terrorists' have been incarcerated in prison-camp conditions (*Independent*, 26.8.1994). In Britain, suspected illegal immigrants and asylum applicants are detained in prisons and privately run remand centres. There has been nothing in Britain that quite resembled the shanty towns of Nanterre and other Paris suburbs in the 1960s and 1970s, but living conditions for many recently arrived migrants are grim. They may be housed in bed and breakfasts, poor quality council housing, or even imprisoned for months without any charges being brought against them.

Increasingly, immigrants and asylum seekers tend to be seen as the lowest rung on the social ladder; the last in the pecking order. It may be that a country's treatment of its immigrant populations can reveal something about the notions of social hierarchy that exist in that country more generally. The more anti-egalitarian is the dominant ideology, the harsher the treatment of people at the bottom of the social order is likely to be. In this context:

> The principle of equality is the revolutionary principle, not only because it challenges hierarchies, but because it asserts that all men (and women) are equally whole. And the converse is also true: to accept inequality as natural is to become fragmented, is to see oneself as no more than the sum of a set of capacities and needs. (Berger, 1975: 141)

Efforts to restrict the rights of asylum seekers, immigrants or settled minorities may well have a 'boomerang effect' on the whole population.

Continuity with the colonial past reinforces the tendency to consider it normal to abuse the civil liberties of immigrants and citizens of non-European, third world origin. However, such abuse undermines the moral and legal ground for protecting the rights of all citizens, irrespective of their origin. An attack on immigrants' rights and refugees' rights, and those of their children, has contributed to the general erosion of the contents of citizenship in Western European states in the past few decades. As one leading UK immigration lawyer insists, "...the unwillingness to accept [that] the process of granting citizenship has implications for civil liberties" has already facilitated the erosion of human rights for all British citizens in such areas as *habeas corpus* (Bevan, 1986: 139). This is a view shared by other legal authorities in the field of immigration and nationality law (MacDonald, 1983: 6).

The problem becomes particularly serious during a period when most Western governments actively undermine the previously agreed distinction between economic migrants and refugees. The United States and the United Kingdom and other EC states have reclassified most asylum seekers from the South as environmental or economic migrants, thereby denying that receiving countries have any obligations to treat asylum seekers justly. From the point of view of international law, terms such as 'economic migrant' are used to legitimise routine violation of the principle of *non-refoulement*, the right not to be turned away (Dummett & Nicol, 1990: 280-82). It is worth remembering that the 'economic' qualifier was first used to describe, and discredit, the demands for asylum of Jews and others fleeing persecution in Nazi Germany in the 1930s (Loescher, 1993: 17).

Western definitions of human rights, with their emphasis on civil and political rather than economic and social rights, have tended to favour the granting of 'asylum' status to those individuals who sought to leave the former communist countries, where the problems were seen to be political rather than economic. For those applying for asylum from the South, and especially from poorer countries, the chances of being granted asylum were much less, since even serious violations of these people's economic and social right were not seen as grounds for asylum under existing law. They were often classified as migrants. During the Cold War, the only significant exceptions were refugees from Vietnam or Cuba, both socialist countries aligned with the former Soviet Union.

## Fifth Proposition: Immigrants have a lot of dependants, and expect to be supported by the welfare state

The supposed tendency of third world people to come to West European countries specifically in order to exploit the comparatively generous welfare policies is much publicised by the press and the media generally. Supposedly, such incomers seek to gain maximum advantage by legally and illegally making the greatest possible use of social security, public health care, low-cost housing, state education and other forms of state-provided services. This is sometimes used as an argument in favour of tight immigration controls

(Goodin, 1992: 11). It becomes convenient in times of crises of provision of such services to blame shortages on 'scroungers', at home and from overseas, including *bona fide* refugees. Fiscal deficits are blamed on bogus businesses hiring illegal immigrant workers and paying no tax or national insurance. Frequent raids on Ghanaian, Turkish and other foreign-owned businesses in Britain have been made with the aim of detecting tax and social security fraud as well as illegal immigrants (JCWI, 2.3.1990).

This belief in the dishonesty and laziness of poor incomers has a long history. Under legislation introduced in 1905, any alien who became a burden on public funds within twelve months of arriving in Britain could be summarily expelled (Bevan, 1986: 73). Similar provisions apply today to foreign residents in the UK and in France. They need to demonstrate their ability to support visitors financially without recourse to public funds, before their families are allowed to enter the country (*Marxism Today*, January 1988). Indeed, even legitimate recourse to public funds or services has become risky since the point of contact with a welfare office is also, increasingly, a point of internal control. Social services now routinely share information with the police and the immigration services (House of Lords, 1992: 28). As noted in a recent report of the Joint Council for the Welfare of Immigrants,

> The government has increased the connections between immigration status and benefit entitlement. From 2 August 1993, income support is no longer available to anyone applying for leave to remain [in the UK], except asylum-seekers. This causes hardship to some, particularly vulnerable people, but also provides a further excuse for Benefit Agency officials to check immigration status of applicants and intensify their liaison with the Home Office. (JCWI, 1993a: 12)

In France, too, local authorities have wide-ranging powers to formulate local regulations which can deny access to housing, employment and social services (Silverman, 1992: 131-2). We should also note the heightened significance of internal controls for non-nationals generally, in the context of the European Union and the creation of a single common frontier (Owers, 1994: 264-81).

In fact, because of the stigma and penalties attached to claiming of benefits during the first few years of a foreigner's residence in the UK, there is some evidence that the fear of being penalised may lead to the significant under-claiming of benefits which immigrants are by rights entitled to (Cohen, 1987: 127; Rex & Tomlinson, 1979: 62). Evidence of institutionalised discrimination on the part of Social Security staff was uncovered in a recent Citizens Advice Bureau report (*Guardian*, 5.2.1991).

The arbitrary and secretive way in which administrative authorities tend to operate is familiar to anyone who has ever been in prison, or has spent some time dependent on social security or unemployment benefit. Discretionary decisions are favoured over statements of entitlement. The burden of proof lies with the claimant, and there is a general presumption of guilt rather than innocence. In response to a request some years ago from immigration lawyers to publish full instructions as issued to Immigration Officers, the Immigration and Nationality Department of the Home Office replied that they could not do so, since "...publication of the instructions as a whole would impair the effectiveness of the immigration control by assisting those who would circumvent it" (IND Notice No. 13/90, 1.5.1990). The Immigration Service Union (ISU) forms a powerful lobby and was largely behind the successful campaign for the removal of the right of MPs to defend particular applicants for immigration or asylum.

Delays and postponements are endemic. All this applies even more to applicants to enter UK from abroad; sometimes they have to wait several years before even obtaining an interview to see if they are eligible to visit their family in the UK, even if only for a holiday (JCWI Bulletin, Spring 1994). On the other hand, surprise 'village visits' are made by overseas Embassy staff in countries such as Bangladesh and Pakistan in order to assess the veracity of information provided by those applying to visit or settle in the UK (JCWI files).

During the 1960s and 1970s, women of West Indian and Indian origin were more likely than caucasian women to be employed outside the home. They were therefore likely to be claiming less benefit. The proportions of women working outside the home in the late 1970s were 88.5 per cent for Caribbean women; 60 per cent for Indian women, compared with 48.5 per cent on average for the whole of the UK (Cohen, 1987: 115). One would be wary of making this point too loudly, however; it is only women's supposed dependence on their spouses' income that has led to them being treated as less of 'immigration problem' than men. Equal opportunities campaigning can backfire, as in the case of the 'primary purpose' rule, which covers marriage of non-nationals with people resident in the UK. These rules were challenged in the European Court of Human Rights, and the British government found guilty of sexual discrimination. The outcome was unexpected: the British government simply brought men and women's rights into line through a levelling-down process (Sachdeva, 1993).

The argument that the larger families of immigrant people impose an unacceptably heavy burden on the welfare, health and education systems of Western countries may work in the short term if numbers are significant. In the long run, however, this does not hold, since those same children will later become part of the economically active population, contributing to national wealth and revenue.

A racist culture, which believes all immigrants to be 'on the make' find its expression in jokes in the popular press and in the media about Muslim men keeping their four wives in style on social security, or illegal immigrant-owned businesses employing relatives without paying national insurance. Such current jokes encourage a feeling among the body of the 'tax payers' that they are supporting a parasitic class of people of foreign origin. Humour of this kind is not new, and was used very effectively to stir up anti-Semitic feelings in Nazi Germany (Gaspard & Servan-Schreiber, 1985: 665-7).

In the British case, a recent study suggested that immigrants are perceived as competing with the indigenous population for housing and welfare provisions. Not only are such conclusions based on confusion between the categories of 'immigrants' and 'ethnic minorities', but most of the accommodation occupied by non-white people is not wanted by the 'indigenous' population in any case, because it is in poor condition or in unattractive slum areas (Silverman, 1992: 101).

> The fact that certain ethnic minorities are geographically concentrated in certain places in Britain has served to heighten the popular misconception that the descendants of former immigrant groups occupy jobs or housing stock to the disadvantage of the rest of the population. (Spencer, 1994: 161)

In fact, resentment may be caused by the way in which central government tends, both in France and Britain, to pass on the cost of supporting the welfare needs of immigrant families to Left-controlled, and generally poorer, local authorities (MacMaster, 1991: 20).

The purpose of the welfare states, since its origins, has been to provide "material protection from contingencies that are beyond [the citizens'] privately organised capacity to avoid" (King, 1986: 165). In Western Europe the state may pay for education and health and generally provides a basic income during periods of sickness, maternity or unemployment. The costs of provision are for the most part recouped from taxation on individuals and businesses. To neglect education, care for the sick or provide national insurance cover for such unforeseeable contingencies as involuntary unemployment would be politically unpopular. It would also allow some people to become needlessly unproductive (in some cases through death). Investment in human resources is a strategy recommended for the countries of the South, where it is recognised that such investment is expensive but bears fruit in the long run. The same could equally be said of the North.

An attack on the principle of universal welfare access has taken place in the 1980s, during a decade of recession, illustrating some of the points made in discussing proposition four above. In the UK many formerly universal benefits have now become means-tested. This has been legitimised by the shift in popular perceptions of benefit recipients as profligate, dishonest, lazy and even criminal. The list includes single mothers, dole scroungers, homeless people, travellers, black youth, and so on. The strategy of eroding universal rights, and depriving all British citizens of certain previously accorded entitlements, has been based on a scapegoating of pockets of supposed 'free riders', who are seen as the wreckers of each system of public provision because they take from the system but are not prepared to contribute. Means-tested benefits are introduced under the guise of helping the 'truly needy'. Because they are targeted towards vulnerable and marginalised groups in society, such benefits are easier to remove altogether than universally provided services (King, 1986: 171). In the context of Britain in the 1980s and 1990s, blaming immigrants for abuse of tax and benefit systems has become a popular way of preparing the public for the tightening of access to benefits as well as the further restriction of immigration and free movement in and out of the country.

Cuts in welfare entitlements generally are related to monetarist beliefs, which are based on the notion of the perfectibility of the free market, an idea approaching anarchy at the economic level. This dovetails neatly with the less economistic arguments of the New Right against universal welfare provisions: namely that the 'nanny state' stifles the initiative and sense of responsibility of individuals and local communities. This argument encourages states to drop their previous responsibilities for citizens' health, employment, welfare and education. All this is done in the name of 'empowering' those who are abandoned to their fate. This drastic reduction in the scope of the modern state's responsibilities towards its citizens is reminiscent of the late Victorian morality of the liberal state, which concerned itself only with extreme and 'deserving' cases of poverty.

The same principles have been put forward as justification for exclusion of immigrants from any welfare entitlements. One of Britain's leading economists looks back nostalgically to the late nineteenth century, when: "the nation [and the state]...did not consider itself responsible for economic deprivations endured by the immigrant" (Mishan, 1988: 24). Precisely! At that time the state did not consider itself responsible for the welfare of the vast majority of British people either. Most were not even citizens themselves. Indirectly, Mishan provides further evidence for the argument that human rights are indivisible. Economic liberalism in the nineteenth century also meant:

...no protection whatsoever for workers (including children), no limit on the number of working hours, no right to strike, no vote for 90 per cent of the population, and unbridled corruption among the political and economic establishment. (*Le Monde Diplomatique*, April 1986)

Attempts to exclude potential beneficiaries, especially those easily identifiable as recent settlers or immigrants and their families, based on the assumption that such people abuse existing welfare systems, will finally tend to impinge on the whole population of a country by facilitating an erosion in welfare entitlements for everyone. This tendency to blame outsiders for all the flaws and weaknesses in government-provided security systems of various kinds, while the government attacks basic minimum standards of welfare cover for everyone, is particularly obvious in the UK. Statutory minimum wage legislation has been removed, trade union powers have been severely restricted, welfare benefits for 16 to 18-year olds have been removed, and others reduced. All this has happened at a time when stories of scroungers, many of them non-UK citizens, have appeared with increased regularity in the daily newspapers. With the exception of Germany, it does appear that those West European states with generous welfare provisions are generally also those with the least restrictive policies towards immigration and asylum issues (the Netherlands and Denmark are just two examples).

## Sixth Proposition: Many immigrants are criminals, and do not deserve protection under the law

This proposition clearly relates closely to the last one. Criminality or the presumption of illegality led the 'TREVI' Expulsion Committee set up an Ad Hoc Group of EC officials on Immigration, primarily to discuss inter-governmental co-operation on drug-related crime and terrorism (*Guardian*, 27.5.1993; JCWI, 1993a: 11-12). The Ad Hoc Group's remit also covered freedom of movement, asylum and family union issues within the EC. The Group worked closely with national immigration officials and ministries responsible for immigration control, but took no advice from pressure groups representing migrants' interests, from legal experts or from advice and support organisations. The information they received was thus bound to be biased, and based on hysterical fears of 'invasion' by illegal immigrants and 'economic migrants' claiming to be refugees (*Independent*, 27.10.1991). The Expulsion Committee's remit is highly problematic to start with, since it groups together asylum seekers with suspected terrorists, drug smugglers and other criminals (Silverman, 1992: 155).

A similar association between immigration and illegality is made in the training provided to immigration officers. The idea of identifiable ethnic 'communities' is used to create the impression of widespread illegality, fraud and drug trafficking among people of different nationalities. A former officer with the Immigration Service reported that, during his training, he was taught, for example, that Muslims do not consider it a sin to lie to non-Muslims, that most Nigerians smuggle drugs, that Irish people are all drawing welfare illegally and are frequently connected to terrorist organisations, that all Sri Lankans and Zairians are cowards, who come to Britain for an easier life, and that almost all Sikhs and Iraqis will engage in subversive politics (*New Statesman*, 26.10.1984; Dummett & Nicol, 1990: 235). The introduction of a single EC border has not changed the situation for these 'undesirables', not even if they are resident in one EC country and travelling to another. A sort of informal apartheid system exists, with rejection rates far higher for non-Caucasians than for those from third world countries (Dummett, 1994: 137-158; *Economist*, 8.1.1993). Immigration officers have based annual pay claims on their efficiency at refusing entry to non-EC arrivals in the UK.

Part of the Ad Hoc Group's remit has been to facilitate the exchange of information on alleged illegal immigrants, social security fraud and drug-related crimes committed by non-EC nationals. Immigration officers and police have shared information and collaborated in early morning raids on colleges, businesses and hotels in attempts to arrest, and ultimately to deport, any illegal immigrants. At the same time,

> ...the British economy continues to rely on unauthorised low-paid workers doing jobs which settled people cannot be persuaded to undertake because of the low wages and bad conditions. (JCWI, 1993a: 12)

The same is true, broadly speaking, of France, where the police have virtually unrestricted rights to stop, search and detain suspected illegal immigrants (Silverman, 1992: 64).

In France, the link between criminality and immigration has been made explicitly and openly since the mid-1970s, the start of the recession. A series of tough deportation measures were introduced under internal minister Charles Pasqua in 1977 and again in 1986, the latter resulting in a doubling in deportation numbers. The justification for such harsh measures was a supposed breakdown in law and order, known as *l'insécurité*, which was attributed to high levels of criminality among young North Africans in particular. The brutality of the French police in daily dealings with the non-white population living in France, and the relative neglect of much racially-motivated crime against the immigrant and non-white population, can be traced to an assumption that immigrant groups and their children have some sort of 'natural predisposition' to violent crime and illegal activities. A popular fear of foreigners' criminality is used by politicians, including Jacques Chirac and others on the moderate Right, as an explanation for the rise in xenophobia.

The tendency to be more concerned with law and order than with issues of employment or social justice is typical of voters of the right and far right. According to a study carried out by SOFRES in 1986, only 12 per cent of PCF voters thought law and order related to the immigration issue, compared with 73 per cent of *Front National* voters, who felt law and order should be the central concern in any immigration policy (Schain, 1986: 12). The association made in the media, and by the *Front National* between a rising crime rate and the Socialists' supposedly liberal policy towards immigration, contributed to the election of a right-wing government in 1987 and 1993, and the election of Jacques Chirac in 1995.

As well as being directed specifically at immigrants, foreign and non-white people, the fear of criminality can be associated with the belief that there exists a generalised and mixed criminal underclass of sorts. Criminals of all origins are seen to form a sort of sub-species of human being who, like illegal immigrants, should not be extended "the liberties of free Englishmen", or indeed of free Frenchmen (Gilroy, 1987: 77). This resembles arguments used in France and Britain in the nineteenth century concerning the lumpen 'under-class' of unemployed and itinerant workers, who were seen as dangerous and constitutionally unfit (Silverman, 1992: 102). 'Blaming the victims' has also been useful in explaining the prevalence of inner city riots in poor areas of Western Europe. In this account, which is generally favoured by the police, the media and politicians, the term 'inner city' becomes a euphemism for the poorest parts of major cities where people of Asian, African and West Indian origin are predominantly concentrated. Yet riots also take place in 'white' areas, as has become apparent with rising unemployment on outlying estates of major and secondary cities during the 1980s and 1990s in both France and Britain.

In his important work, *There Ain't No Black in the Union Jack*, Paul Gilroy demonstrates the way in which during the 1970s and 1980s, the British popular press, the media, the courts, the police and politicians have contributed to the idea of a 'black pathology' of crime. Similar perceptions of North Africans have been created by the media in France. Unflattering pictures are constructed for other groups as well, by tying them in with crime: skinheads, cockneys, punks, travellers, drug addicts. As with any other victim-blaming strategies, such stereotypes make it possible for the more privileged in society to continue believing that the social system is fundamentally fair. Flaws are seen as arising out of the deviant behaviour of specific 'problem' groups of people, who simply need to be brought into line in order for balance to be restored.

Yet the major problem of violence affecting the non-white and immigrant populations in Western Europe is an alarming increase in 'racially' motivated attacks against asylum seekers, settled foreigners and nationals of non-European extraction alike. There are daily reports of such violent attacks, which in the UK have been growing more rapidly than almost any other category of reported crime (*Times*, 2.4.1994). An official report on the living conditions of Bangladeshis living in London's borough of Tower Hamlets in the mid-1980s found that already:

> ...it is not uncommon for windows to be broken, dogs unleashed on victims, racist graffiti to appear on people's homes...verbal abuse seems to have become an everyday part of Bangladeshi life in the borough. (Race Relations & Immigration Sub-Committee, 3.2.1986: 7)

Since then the situation has deteriorated, with asylum seekers and refugees being killed and subjected to death threats in London and other major European cities. In both France and Britain there is oppressive police surveillance of the non-white population, including those who are full citizens of non-European origin or parentage. In some cases non-nationals born in Britain or France have been deported to a country they may never even have visited because they have committed a minor crime, such as burglary (JCWI, 1993a: 19).

Detention without trial for many months of those suspected of being illegal immigrants has become routine, although it constitutes a serious violation of these people's basic human rights. Expulsions and refusals to allow entry are also carried out almost routinely, violating the principle of *non-refoulement* "which establishes an obligation on the part of the receiving state not to send [a person] back to the state where he [or she] may be persecuted" (Muntarbhom, 1989: 192). Studies on the rights of refugees generally concur that the term 'asylum' needs to be broadened to include victims of war and environmental devastation as well as those subjected to individual persecution on account of their beliefs (Loescher, 1993; Gurtov, 1991: 485).

As has already been suggested, where human rights are concerned, what starts as a price paid by a few may end up being paid by everyone. The authors of a recent study show that both the Special Branch and MI5, which now police 'subversive' British citizens, were originally created to monitor and control aliens (Charlton *et al*, 1988: 26). From the start, however, their remit included the policing of 'enemies within' in the form of communist subversives, Irish and Jews (Dummet & Nicol, 1990: 153).


## Seventh Proposition: Immigrants undermine trade union solidarity, and worsen unemployment

This is a more important feature of the whole debate on immigration in France than in Britain. Immigrant groups on the continent have themselves been more likely to define themselves in economic and class terms, as part of the working class and part of the industrial workforce, rather than in cultural or national terms. Most commonly, observers on the Left, whether academic or activists in trade unions and political parties, define immigrants as part of the 'super-exploited' section of the working class. Alternatively there may be reference to neo-colonial relations and the importation of surplus labour into the impe-rialist core from the dependent peripheries of the former colonies (Brown, 1992).

There is a strong nationalist strand in orthodox communist politics in France. Even in 1992, the PCF continued to view non-French workers as part of the working class of their 'home' country. This was shown in the dialogue of solidarity used, with references to solidarity between foreign and French workers being the norm, and in illustrations which also show immigrant and French workers as being divided and ruled by the capitalist class (Cartoon 3). This led to a false sense that Algerians' and other foreign workers' presence in France was temporary and cyclical, an idea shared by both the Left and Right. By adopting the ideology that French and immigrant workers should take up the struggle against capitalist exploitation as two separate but united forces, 'side by side', the PCF and its trade union, the CGT, implicitly accepted the idea discussed under propositions one and three that immigrant workers will not settle, but will eventually return to their countries of origin. As we saw in the last chapter, there has been almost no 'rotation' of the non-French population in France since the 1960s. This idea has outgrown whatever usefulness it may once have had (Verbunt, 1985: 159). It is particularly irrele-vant to the second generation of 'beurs', who acquire French citizenship at age eighteen and are almost certainly going to remain permanently settled in France.

Berger noted that French trade unions in the 1970s "appealed for improved living conditions for migrants. But [had] never been able to think beyond the proposition that the migrant worker belongs to the country he [*sic*] has left, and therefore does not belong" in France (Berger, 1975: 144).  Such attitudes are not confined to periods of unemployment but were already prevalent in the trade union movement in the 1960s, when the economy was expanding rapidly and new job opportunities were being created (Castles, 1970: 13; Withol de Wenden, 1991: 120; Brown, 1992: 135).

By the 1980s, the PCF actively favoured the repatriation of foreign workers to save French workers' jobs.  It became apparent, not for the first time, that such positions dovetailed uncomfortably with those of Le Pen.[1]  The Left, including the Socialist Party which came to power in 1981, reiterated the idea that immigrants seeking to settle permanently were suffering from cultural alienation.  Added to this was the perception that such *assimilés* were suffering from a stunted sense of class and anti-colonial consciousness.

Gary Freeman complains that, after 1945, large-scale immigration and permanent settlement of former colonial subjects was the last thing the West European Left needed (Freeman, 1986).  The implication is clear: French, British and other West European trade unionists had enough worries without being obliged to also take up the defence of foreign workers, whose position complicated the fairly clear-cut class divisions and Left-Right politics of the early Post-War era.  This is an essentially static view of class conflict, as a national rather than an international phenomenon, and neglects the positive contribution that immigrant workers could make to trade unions' overall activities.  Such fears that migrant workers would undermine indigenous working-class gains are not new; they occurred during recessions of the nineteenth century as well (Balibar, 1991: 102).

In fact, it would be quite logical to argue that it was precisely the sharp restriction in the numbers of immigrant workers coming into the UK during the past two decades that caused the chronic weakening of the British trade union movement during the 1980s, and its lack of solidarity faced with a repressive government.  This has made it possible to force down wages, and to impose worsened working conditions and declining health and safety provisions on all workers, regardless of their origins.  After all, more immigrant workers could have meant that national workers could protect their own benefits and wages by claiming that cheap labour should be limited to non-nationals.  It may be no coincidence that repressive anti-union legislation was introduced in Britain in the 1980s, at the same time that "old protective practices, like closed shops and demarcation agreements were used to freeze out migrant labour" (Cohen, 1989: 155).

As I observed in the last chapter, the economic benefits of immigration are often emphasised in France (Silverman, 1992: 42-8; *Plein Droit*, 1991: 41). By contrast, a recent study by Sarah Spencer assessing the economic impact of immigration in the UK noted the tendency of decision-makers to underestimate the benefits for business and for the country's economy as a whole (Spencer, 1994: 195-201). She concludes that part of the problem in Britain is the lack of accurate statistical measurement. The problem can be remedied, but little is being done to collect the more accurate data required.

> Immigration flow statistics present a very different and much more favourable picture of the potential economic benefits of migration than do statistics for the least well assimilated ethnic minority populations...Systematic and detailed information of this kind on the economics of immigration does not exist in Britain. (ibid: 162-3)

In both Britain and France, certain industries, notably the clothing trade, the construction industry and some parts of agriculture, depend heavily on illegal and vulnerable workers who receive very low pay for casual work. The alternative to such labour practices would not be to employ nationals on acceptable wages, but for such businesses to go bankrupt (*EuroReporter*, April 1992: 30-31).

In recent years, with rising unemployment, this picture has changed, with politicians in both countries eager to absolve themselves of responsibility for rising jobless figures by any means possible. A document produced by the then newly elected Socialist Government in 1982, which stated that the French economy could not survive without the estimated four million foreign workers in the country, was apparently never released (Gaspard & Servan-Schreiber, 1985: 90). In spite of the apparent benefits of cheap, flexible immigrant labour, a connection has increasingly been made, by politicians, trade unions and others, between unemployment and immigration, especially illegal immigration (Verbunt, 1985: 154). The argument is not one-sided, however. In France, if surveys are to be believed, the proportion of those questioned who believed that sending migrant workers home would relieve unemployment among the rest of the population declined from 34 per cent in 1981 to 20 per cent in 1988 (*EuroReporter*, April 1992: 37). Since 1945, it seems that

> ...the presence of foreign labour [was] a condition for full employment of the indigenous labour power in times of high conjuncture and of reduced unemployment in times of low conjuncture. (Carchedi, 1983: 201)

Elsewhere, Freeman acknowledges that labour migration has made a positive contribution to Post-War economic growth in Western Europe. It played a role "in cushioning indigenous workers against the effects of unemployment and recession" (Freeman, 1987: 192). Others have claimed that the use of immigrant workers is anti-inflationary and has allowed for considerable social mobility of nationals (Layton-Henry, 1992: 67). The tendency for trade unions to exclude immigrant workers from skilled and highly-paid sectors of employment is comprehensible from this perspective (Brown, 1992: 135).

These purely economic benefits of foreign labour are likely to diminish as migrants and their families settle permanently (Cohen, 1987: 123-6). Eventually such settlers are absorbed into the national population. Their permanence tends to raise their expectations of equal treatment and reduces their vulnerability to very low pay, even if they remain marginalised and poorly integrated. This settlement process has been hastened in all West European states by legislation that has sought to 'tighten up' immigration controls. Such laws have encouraged permanent settlement and family reunions, and positively discouraged temporary, cyclical labour movements between North and South.

If access to citizenship is denied, even for the second generation born in the country of in-migration, or if prospects for social mobility in the metropolis are poorer than they would be in the country of origin, then first generation emigrants and their families may wish to return. Repatriation, as we saw in the last chapter, has occasionally been demanded by foreign workers within the trade union movements. Such schemes can undermine the morale of those who wish to remain, and may weaken trade unions by 'buying off' some of their members working in key industries. French trade unions showed little opposition to repatriation policies, even though these undermined any attempt to oppose redundancies more generally.

In Britain, a small repatriation scheme has been in operation since 1971, mainly to send 'home' foreign nationals on welfare, the long-term unemployed or mentally ill. The only reference made to the fund until recently was by Conservative MPs on the Right of the party, seeking to cash in on the electoral popularity of 'immigration control'. In recent years, however, voluntary repatriation has come to be demanded by some people living in Britain, particularly those from Caribbean countries, who may still not feel 'at home' in the mother country. Bernie Grant MP is among those who feel that a scheme of voluntary repatriation for those who wish to return to their countries of origin should be publicly funded.

### Eighth Proposition: Immigrants' integration is neo-colonial and stunts their revolutionary potential

This statement is close to the second and seventh propositions, and comes mainly from the Left. This particular approach rests less on a class analysis of the position of migrant workers and their families, than on a third-worldist understanding of post-colonial relations. Such a view was popularised by Frantz Fanon, and also by Herbert Marcuse and Jean-Paul Sartre. The resultant form of anti-colonialism has already been discussed in Chapters 1 and 2, when I questioned the general assumption that sovereign statehood is a necessary condition for liberation from colonial relations (Taylor, 1989: 67-8).

A starting point in assessing this particular objection to permanent immigration and settlement of former colonial people is to explore what likelihood there is of the people concerned achieving substantive citizenship rights through revolutionary struggle within their state, the former colony. To argue that immigrants should simply struggle for liberation in their countries of origin is to ignore the often harsh realities they face. It is cynical to condemn some people to unremitting hardship in the place they were born, or where their parents come from. Idealistic depictions of third world states as 'human-scale' and 'communal' can rub along comfortably with a total disregard for the suffering of people living in poverty and daily abuses of power. Such images of heroic struggles for development can also become excuses to neglect the importance of achieving equal rights for immigrants and non-nationals living in Western Europe.

The thankless task of defending individual migrants' rights has been left to lawyers, social workers and other professionals, with comparatively little trade union or left-wing mass action. Another surprising conclusion arising out of this proposition is that the former colonial powers (France and Britain, for example) have no responsibility whatsoever to assist regions and peoples they exploited under colonialism, thus enabling them to reach a standard of living comparable to their own. This question of obligations of the North to the South has been discussed in the case of the DOM, and is returned to in the last chapter (see Gosling, 1991).

We can reiterate a question asked at the start of the book: why should it be considered more radical to try and obtain full rights within the newly independent state, or 'home' country, than to try and obtain them within the colonial metropolis or 'host' country? As Robin Cohen has argued, the latter strategy can certainly be seen as a refusal to accept a second-class citizenship, a 'helot' status, floating somewhere between full citizenship and colonial or slave subjecthood, deprived of any significant material and civil rights (Cohen, 1987: 138-9). Within the range of options that may be open to the former colonised person, the most attractive from the material and human rights point of view may be to try and obtain full citizenship for himself or herself and their children, within Western Europe (or North America).

Demands for equal treatment for immigrants, and their full and equal incorporation into the formal legal and institutional arrangements of the country of immigration, pose a challenge to the Left, equivalent to that posed to the monarchy by the storming of the Bastille in 1789. Only this time, the Bastille is being stormed from inside.

The parallels which exist between the strategies adopted by the political elites in the French overseas departments and the discourse of equal rights adopted by many immigrant associations within the EC context now become somewhat clearer. In both cases, there is a deep challenge to the colonial and neo-colonial order; the demand being not for withdrawal and remote assistance, but for admission and incorporation of the formerly excluded colonial subjects as if they were already full citizens. As was extensively argued in the last chapter, in looking at Franco-Algerian relations over the immigration question, to see the foreign worker (and the family of such workers) as simply building blocks of national development of the post-colonial state is to sacrifice their individual human rights and welfare to the supposed greater good of the entire national collectivity.

**Ninth Proposition: Many immigrants' religion is different, and so they cannot fit in with the host society**

This is really a variation on proposition three, with the difference that religion rather than colour or 'race' is the supposedly unavoidable cause of conflict in this case. This particular argument has most frequently been used in relation to Islam, and to a much lesser extent to other religions such as Hinduism and Rastafarianism. A recent report to the Trilateral Commission explains the problem in the following terms as it affects France and Germany: "For both, Islamic immigrants are about one-third of their foreign populations and are seen to pose major dilemmas where integration issues are concerned" (Meissner *et al.*, 1993: 41-3). Yet formerly, as colonial subjects, Algerians, Moroccans and Tunisians shared a single (if mythical) French nationality, and the colonial rulers did not consider it problematic that separate regulations covered the religious lives of Muslims and Christians (Dummet & Nicol, 1990: 82).

The way in which West European states define their own identities in relation to Islam varies with the context: at times the stress is placed on the difference between an essentially secular understanding of law and public life and any religiously-based political order. At other times, Christianity is seen as a unifying cultural influence, distinguishing the EC and its potential members from predominantly Muslim countries such as Turkey and the Maghreb, with whom association is seem as possible, but not full integration. One reason religion has become a dominant theme in the debate on the place of immigrant and second-generation nationals in Britain and France, for example, is the rise of a discourse of cultural racism. This is sometimes called the 'new racism' which does not stress biological differences alone, but hides its xenophobia under the mantle of respect for others' cultural distinctiveness (*Le Monde*, 27.10.1989). Supposedly incompatible world-views, such as that of Islam and that of Christianity, or that of a theocracy and that of a secular democracy, are often contrasted. Conflicts which this dualism creates are seen as its cause. This was the case even with the Gulf war, where the conflicts involved were economic and political in nature, but were presented in crudely black-and-white religious terms.

Both Christians and secularists, for different reasons, may claim that the settlement and absorption into the institutions of the 'host' society of large numbers of people with a different religion threatens to dilute and undermine the stability of the existing social order, which is based on respect either for secularism or Christianity. The problem of coexistence is seen to arise out of the fact that Muslims consider Islam a world religion and the only true faith, in the same way that Christians do Christianity. In a sense it is this similarity, rather than any differences, that can be said to cause the conflict. The problem of competition is aggravated when there is a strong political and community basis for the Muslim faith, as there is in the immigrant experience of social exclusion in Western Europe.

A recent and dramatic example of such a conflict between religious values (both Christian and Muslim) and secularism was the 'hijab affair' in France. A strong reaction against the wearing of the headscarf in schools by young girls was seen as partly responsible for the rising vote for the *Front National* (Brechon, 1991: 62). The Right claimed to see in this incident an attempt to culturally colonise and 'conquer' France and impose an alien culture through attempting to proselytise Christians (Brechon, 1991: 64, 72). The young women's bodies were the territory on which a politicised form of the inter-religious conflict was played out. For some of the Muslim families, the hijab was a defensive mechanism, a "communal boundary-expressing symbol" (Rozario, 1991: 30). Debates in France concerned whether or not the girls should be excluded from school for wearing the hijab. Arguments raged between those who advocated no compromise with the forces of 'obscurantism' and recommended that the girls be excluded from school, and those who argued that it was vital not to exclude the girls, since only their inclusion could ensure that they were given a chance to escape the 'obscurantism' of their parents (Silverman, 1992: 112-3). In the latter case there was no doubt a concern to avoid segregation, but both sides betrayed an overestimation of how genuinely secular, enlightened and integrationist the French education system actually can be.

It is not uncommon for the far Right to claim to be in favour of 'respect' for immigrants' distinct religions as well as their 'different' cultures. The only party in France to extend its recognition to the FIS (*Front Islamique de Salut*) when it was elected in 1992 was the *Front National*. By the same token, the claim to want to preserve separate cultural identities is made by those who see themselves as protecting some notion of an authentic French (or British) identity, religion or culture. Such policies can oblige people to preserve some particular and often externally defined shell of their culture, often in a ghettoised form (Gaspard & Servan-Schreiber, 1985: 78-80).

On the other hand, the gradual fragmentation, intermixing and incorporation of communities of Muslim foreigners and their children would tend to suggest that religious belief would gradually become a matter of individual conviction rather than a collective or community concern. This is the hope of such writers as Bruno Etienne, for example, who argues that the integration of individual immigrants and their children into French society necessarily implies the disintegration of their communities (Etienne, 1989: 198-200).

Problems with this process of privatising religious belief and practice will arise where the gradual individualisation that integration implies cannot take place, or is being reversed by sharpening political divisions between host and immigrant people. Such a reversal can be seen to have taken place in France, where new forms of political Islam have been asserted by Algerian community leaders and have been expressed through an emphasis, for example, on the veiling of women of Algerian origin or parentage living in France. There has been a strong response from the media and the intelligentsia asserting the need for immigrant communities to respect the neutrality and secularism of the public sphere and the laical political culture of the French Republic.

The reassertion of Islam as a parameter for identity formation among parts of the immigrant population is in part a response to worsening economic conditions in the 'home' countries, and the search for new forms of identification outside the parameters of the classic republican Left-Right divide (*Le Monde*, 20.10.1994). It also expresses a reaction against the reassertion, within Western Europe, of a certain sense of pan-Christian solidarity and a harking back to ancient conflicts with the Muslims in the wake of the first and second Gulf Wars. In other words, like the assertion of ethnic identity, there is nothing natural or inherent to either Islam or Christianity that leads them into conflict. Rather, there are specifically political forces that have led religion to occupy a more central position in the 1980s and 1990s on the world stage than for several decades previously. Among second-generation Algerians in France, the return of some to religion results from a feeling of not being accepted, and is part and parcel of the so-called search for roots (Memmi, 1991). The conditions for ethnic politics are in part created by mass-immigration, but also by the prevalence of economic recession and its effects on both the indigenous and the immigrant populations. This trend of 'return to one's origins' is discussed more fully in the last chapter.

Efforts to reassert the community basis of and control over religious belief and practice have also taken place as an effort to counter the ongoing, and probably irreversible, process of individualisation of former immigrant communities (Etienne, 1989: 200). One image that comes to mind is that of two women, perhaps sisters, pushing a pram. One may be wearing a hijab or full chador, the other may have short hair and be wearing jeans, as depicted on the cover of the book, *Here For Good*, by Stephen Castles and Heather Booth. This picture is not uncommon in most British and French cities. The existence of hundreds, if not thousands, of converts to Islam among the indigenous population of France, Britain and other EC countries is further evidence of the individualisation of Islamic religious belief in the West European context. There is conflict; but it is less between the monolithic forces of religious world-views than between the legally codified autonomy of the individual, and their right to freedom of worship, as ensured by the state, and the claims of religious authorities in general to exercise rights over the collectivity on the other hand.

For Franco-Algerians the choice of religious practice or secularism overlaps with the apparent conflict between an Arab and French identity. The Arabisation of Algeria, with the resulting valorisation of all that is not French, has left some *beurs* torn between two polarised (and increasingly mutually hostile) political ideologies of cultural identity (*Le Monde*, 20.10.1994). The experience of being torn between such polarised identities can be depicted in cartoon form (see Cartoon 2). Yet the simple, bounded image of the cartoon is belied by the innovative ways in which individual people juggle and combine multiple identities in their daily lives without necessarily feeling any discomfort in doing so.

Liberalism and the defence of human rights are not the exclusive preserve of the secular state. The leader of the Muslim community in Paris recently declared that "Islam, too, holds dear the notion that France should remain a land of liberty, equality and fraternity for all" (*Independent*, 6.6.1993). With raids on supposed Islamicist activists and sympathisers becoming more frequent, and their detention without trial routine, there is a growing feeling that the French government is singling out North Africans and "sending a message that Muslims do not belong in France" (*Independent*, 26.8.1994). Even among liberals there is a growing insistence that the secularism of French public life be respected.   A recent study by Julia Kristeva expressed concern at the notion that integration implied respect only for the cultural values of those coming into France.   She insisted that this respect for difference should be applied equally to French national culture (Kristeva, 1993: 60-4).

Islam's supposed incompatibility with French secular culture has been used to justify removing automatic French nationality for people of North African origin.   This will makes it easier in future to exclude such people from the citizenry and to remove their basic civil rights (Etienne, 1989: 257).


**Tenth Proposition: There are already too many foreigners and, if any more come, indigenous people will be swamped**

This particular objection to free movement is generally backed up by a pseudo-scientific notion known in French as *seuil de tolérance*, or the tolerance threshold, of the indigenous society towards foreign people.   The analogy is a medical one, with the 'foreign bodies' being regarded as a virus which, in large enough numbers, will automatically bring about a defensive attack from the 'host' community.   Such notions have wide appeal because of their apparent objectivity.   They draw on work by sociologists of the so-called Chicago school in the United States, who examined the notion of a critical mass of black inhabitants (MacMaster, 1991).   When this critical ratio of white to black was reached, it was claimed, the area would 'naturally' start to be abandoned by non-blacks (Silverman, 1992: 74-5).   In fact, there were much more complex reasons why some inner city areas became predominantly black, most notably the better employment opportunities and the more rapid upward social mobility of whites.   Real-estate companies also put pressure on people to move so that they could benefit from low property prices to but up inner city areas cheaply (Terkel, 1993).

The French experience is quite different in the sense that the cost of supporting the newly immigrant populations and their families fell mainly on suburban areas of the major cities rather than inner city areas.   In these poorer, working-class districts, the burden of providing affordable housing and welfare allowances for the families of immigrants was shouldered by left-wing municipalities with low budgets.   The concept of *seuil de tolérance* thus found some echo among local PCF officials who found themselves faced with impossible demands (MacMaster, 1991: 14-20).

In biologistic language, immigrant communities are described as 'mushrooming' in inner city areas; foreign migrants may 'swarm' or come in 'hordes' rather than simply travel (Bevan, 1986: 28). There are also military metaphors that might be employed in describing the impact of incomers on resident populations: the idea of invasion may be used, or of infiltration and take-over. Sexual fears may also be expressed through worries concerning the number of children that foreign incomers are likely to have, and whether they are likely to intermarry and intermix with 'our women', and so on (Balibar, 1991: 76; Etienne, 1989: 184). The idea that there exists some objective and identifiable limit to the proportion of non-nationals that can be tolerated (say 10 or 15 per cent of the total) cannot be dissociated from the understanding of the foreign or immigrant population as somehow inherently problematic.

In Britain, where the proportion of immigrants and their families is around 5 per cent (compared with 8 to 9 per cent in France), any 'imbalance' which may emerge is due to continuously high levels of out-migration, as much as immigration. Net out-migration from the UK for the period 1955 to 1968 has been estimated at 669 640, and at half a million for the years 1971 to 1983 (Castles & Kossack, 1973: 31; *Economist*, 19.4.1986). According to one of the UK's foremost immigration lawyers "[s]ince 1968, primary immigration from the New Commonwealth and Pakistan has been clearly under control" (Bevan, 1986: 36). Most demands for entry from the New Commonwealth are made by family members of people already resident in the UK. Tighter measures are sometimes introduced simply for publicity purposes: one example was the stricter controls imposed after 1988 on Bangladeshi women wishing to join their husbands in the UK, at a time when the 'queue' of applicants had shrunk from 26 600 in 1978 to 8200 in 1987 (*Marxism Today*, January 1988). In the early 1980s, there were still only 61 Bangladeshi women for every 100 men, compared with a ratio of 83 for Pakistanis, 98 for Indians and 106 for West Indians (Castles *et al.*, 1984: 114).

The Numbers Game, as Vaughan Bevan calls it, has been played by both Left and Right in most EC countries. In Britain, politicians outbid each other in wild speculation on what would happen if such and such a piece of control legislation was not introduced or properly enforced. The same game is also played by some economists, who generate estimates of the numbers of people who would 'flood' into Britain if there were no controls on entry. It is the ultimate argument against free movement, since no government wishes to lose the goodwill of its electorate by exceeding their 'tolerance threshold'. In the Numbers Game, the fear is created that any loosening of immigration (or asylum) controls would result in a whole catalogue of political and social ills in the 'host' country. Immigration officers, for example, come to internalise dominant perceptions of the need for tight controls at the point of entry.

> As you do the job, day after day, your conception of what you are doing changes. The very purpose becomes to keep out Moroccans, Indians or hippies...I never met a single immigration officer who did not feel we were 'letting in too many foreigners'. (*New Statesman*, 26.10.1984)

It is this perception of 'letting in too many foreigners' that prompts politicians of the right wing of the Conservative Party to demand tighter immigration controls, as well as official support for repatriation. Harvey Proctor, in a question to the Overseas Development Minister in 1992, asked whether part of the aid budget could not be devoted to "immigrants who take advantage of the Government's voluntary repatriation scheme" (*Hansard*, 19.7.1992, Cols 15-16). His question referred only to those of New Commonwealth origin, specifically mentioning India and Pakistan.

The fear is obviously that immigrant people and their descendants would not only take over the jobs and businesses of indigenous people, but that they would also start to do better than them, and would increasingly compete for resources and income. This ties in with the fifth and seventh propositions. There is the additional argument that criminality and violence would be likely, as the indigenous population perceived their own position to be deteriorating in comparison to that of the foreign population (an inversion of proposition three). One thing which assists in the perpetuation of this myth is inadequate statistics on departures, where the gross figures are not broken down into nationalities, so that there is no way of knowing, besides national census material, how many people of different nationalities remain in the UK.

J.K. Galbraith comments wryly on the British post-colonial obsession with keeping out former colonial subjects, and the rapid turnabout in the early post-independence years. "Only one generation divides the Tories who defended the Empire from those who defended the home island from the erstwhile Empire. God must smile" (Galbraith, 1979: 103).

The Numbers Game has the advantage of appearing to be solely concerned with objective cost-benefit considerations of a numerical order, which can be estimated in an impartial manner. In fact, talk of numbers, quotas and limits evokes in the public perception a host of other, more qualitative and moralistic objections to immigration. By virtue of its apparent innocuousness, the notion of a tolerance threshold is especially popular with politicians and media commentators. In France, the term *seuil de tolérance* has been used without apology by Jacques Chirac, former leader of the RPR (*Le Monde*, 22.6.1991).

The most alarming form of the Numbers Game has been in relation to asylum seekers. For those from Eastern Europe and the former Yugoslav Republic, as one iron curtain was lifted, another was erected in the form of tight controls on asylum seekers and emigrants from the East (Storey, 1991: 8-12).[2]  By evoking the spectre of mass movement into Western European countries, and the disaster that might cause for the existing inhabitants, the governments of Britain, France and other EC member states seek to justify their non-respect of international norms governing the treatment of asylum applicants.  The Dublin Convention of 1991, which was ratified by Britain, Denmark, Greece, Italy and Portugal, was "an agreement to reject asylum applications from any refugees who passed through a supposedly safe third country on their way to seek sanctuary" (Storey, 1991; *Guardian*, 27.5.1993). The Convention thus removes the obligation on governments of second countries of asylum to even consider asylum seekers' applications (Loescher, 1993: 125).  Generally, asylum applicants from countries considered low-risk (and many from countries considered high-risk) are returned to the country they first set foot in, under the terms of the Dublin Convention.  In other cases an application for asylum can be rejected out of hand on the grounds that the claim to be a refugee is 'manifestly unfounded' (Randall, 1994: 203-4).

## Conclusion

One of the features of the current period is a crisis of belief in Western Europe in the value of a centralised, unitary state with a democratic multi-party system.  What Balibar calls the "national and cultural identity crises" of European states are hastening a process of scapegoating, taking the form of racism (Balibar, 1991: 79).  Accompanying this there has been a delegiti- mation of the concept of assimilation, which Memmi has described as a "terrible word, a very difficult word" (Memmi, 1991: 32).  In the wake of European-wide integration a revitalised and more egalitarian understanding of integration and assimilation policy is urgently needed.  Any such policy should aim to promote equality in all dimensions of human rights.  It should not mean the obliteration of any one way of life by another, nor a uniformity which is intolerant of differences.  Yet there is always a danger that, in the context of hierarchical relationships, the celebration of differences can be turned around and used as a basis for exclusion (Memmi, 1991: 33).  If the 'new Europe' cannot be based on respect for human rights of all people living within its borders, it is hard to see how it will be able to improve the lives of its citizens.

Ideally, mixed, hybrid forms of identity could find expression in new types of education, cultural expression and living conditions. These would represent a mix of imported and indigenous elements, combined into something altogether new. This fertile mixed offspring could contribute towards a less staid, more lively notion of 'Europe' as EC member states move closer together. One example is found in the French Caribbean in the form of *créolité*, and is discussed further in Chapter 7. But in France, cultural assimilation and civic integration are still conceived as the only possible alternatives to a fragmentation of the fabric of the society.

> Many fear the splitting of common 'universalist' principles into a myriad of particularisms...not without reason, for down this road lies the possible rise of new 'fundamentalists' (cultural, religious, class-based, gender-based, ethnic-based and so on) who might usurp the new power vacuums and claim to speak politically for 'the group'. (Silverman, 1992: 148)

In the past, of course, assimilationist policies were almost always tied in with colonial conquest, with missionary coercion and manipulation and with the creation of a small and privileged elite of the colonised, who were cut off from the rest of their own society. In today's context, anti-assimilationist policies are often also neo-colonial, in that they emphasise difference at the expense of any possibility of building solidarities or cross-cutting connections across boundaries of 'race' and nationality (and often class and gender as well). On the whole, the term 'integration' may seem preferable to 'assimilation' since the former seems to denote a more complex, many-sided process. Integration is supposed to be rooted in respect for the equal worth of all parties involved, whether these are states, groups or individuals, and unlike assimilation, integration implies an acceptance of cultural variations, and a search for similarities and solidarities among people. This is the official view as expressed by the French President of the High Commission of Integration, Marceau Long (*EuroReporter*, April 1992: 4-5). Where integration takes place at the individual level, it implies a neutral public space, and the separation of civic rights and responsibilities from private ones (*Le Monde*, 6.10.1992). A recent study of anti-racist strategies in France has stressed the need for activists, intellectuals, politicians and others to reassert the basic republican principles established by the French revolution (Taguieff, 1992). One reviewer of the study commented:

> If the most effective form this 'new' anti-racism can take is to drag out and dust down the principles of 1789, Jules Ferry, the Enlightenment and *laïcité* and build a republican consensus around them in a revitalised Jacobin state, then so be it. (O'Shaugnessy, 1993: 60)

In practice there may be great difficulties in the process of cultural assimilation and mixing, since livelihoods and identities may be under attack. Although "international migration is not the solution to the North South gap" (Castles & Miller, 1993: 268), the option of physically and legally moving across boundaries is a choice that most people in the world would like to have. It is at present much easier for the rich and educated to achieve than for those whose lives may be more precarious. For the poor and the rich alike, such movement may at some time become essential if they are to secure even the most basic level of human rights (including their basic material and security needs). It is all too easy for academics, intellectuals and relatively privileged politicians to argue that poor people from the former colonies should remain where they are, hoping for better conditions at home. All the signs point to a continued deterioration in economic prosperity and political peace in most of the countries of emigration (Gurtov, 1991; Seabrook, 1993)).

There is a final, historical reason for accepting the increasing movement of people across the globe, whether as refugees or as migrants, and that is the precedent of the European states' own period of state consolidation and what is sometimes still called 'nation-building'. Throughout this period, the boundaries of the state system were determined by the colonising designs of the European powers. Although they fled persecution, those who left Europe were not barred from entry elsewhere. From the seventeenth century to the early twentieth century,

> Europeans who feared persecution [or wanted a better life] could move to one of the many immigrant countries in the New World still eager for an increased labor force and for settlers to fill empty territories [*sic*]...Consequently, before the twentieth century there were no hordes of homeless Europeans cast adrift in a world that rejected them. (Loescher, 1993: 34)

Present policies towards those 'cast adrift' from the former colonies and the peripheries of Europe reflect in microcosm the wider inequities of the world order: migrants and refugees alike are treated as mere conveniences or liabilities, and integrated or expelled, legally and illegally, more or less at will. They are the 'helots' of the present system of internal and international stratification between different categories of people, including stratification among legally settled inhabitants of Western Europe (Cohen, 1989: 163).

Faced with daily violations of basic human rights by the so-called 'advanced industrial democracies', there is very little that any international organisation or any international legal body can do. International law is not binding on states, and little could be expected to result from any international court cases taken out against any states that constrain and remove individuals' citizenship rights in these ways.

An emphasis on the need to 'respect differences' and distinct identities within a multicultural society is common to both relativist post-modernists and the new far right. It has been argued here that such a position can undermine the reaffirmation of shared and common basic human rights at the political and civic levels. In the Jacobin model of the state, the basis for membership of the nation state's citizenry is individual allegiance to the republican consensus. Interaction is based on direct communication between the state and the citizen, without the intermediary of community or distinct cultural groups. This may go against the current of much 'politically correct' thinking, particularly in Britain and the United States, but is not without its advocates there as well (for some examples, see the recent work of Paul Gilroy and Stuart Hall). Within a strict Jacobin form of integration it may just be possible to avoid the routine violation of individual persons' rights in the name of a greater, collective good. In an era of chronic recession and post-modern cultural relativity, such violations continue to be a distinct danger. It would be naive to assume that any international convention or legislation could prevent states from mistreating their own citizens or those of other states who seek entry, residence and citizenship, but the establishment of international ethical norms remains perhaps the only alternative to the rule of the power of the strongest.

## Notes

1. In 1989, asked whether sending immigrants home was a way of resolving the unemployment problem, 15 per cent of Socialist voters agreed; 23 per cent of RPR voters; 24 per cent of UDF voters; but 26 per cent of PCF voters and 65 per cent of FN voters (figures from SOFRES, 1989: 129). This may well reflect what Robin Cohen has remarked; namely a significant increase in working-class racism during periods of high unemployment (Cohen, 1989: 155).

2. East European governments were very unhappy at this state of affairs, confirmed at the Conference on the Movement of Persons held in Vienna in January 1991, at which "...the communique-and the conference-disabused officials from Eastern Europe of any notion that Western governments would welcome the lifting of the iron curtain by throwing open its borders" (*Financial Times*, 12.2.1991). Yet in the future, the picture does not look as bleak for the Eastern Europeans as for the New Commonwealth, Maghrebian, Turkish and other migrants and asylum seekers from the 'South'. As Andy Storey points out "It is now likely that unemployment and poverty in Eastern Europe, rather than population growth in Africa and elsewhere in the Third World, will provide the solution to Western Europe's labour shortages of the twenty-first century" (Storey, 1991: 17).

# 7 Post-Colonial Liberation and Human Rights: a Feminist-Humanist Perspective

*I thought the Brown decision and the civil-rights movement would liberate the whites as well. But if they were liberated, you'd have to liberate blacks too. They didn't want that sort of liberation.*
Kenneth Clark (psychologist) in Terkel, 1992: 337.

*I don't trust no man to change things, because I look back over the history of the times, I hear them talking about revolution. If they keep having revolutions, why haven't things changed? Every time the ones who fight for the revolution win, they become the oppressors. That is not the way it's supposed to be.*
Little Dovie Thurman (born again, former Black Power advocate) in Terkel, 1992: 63.

*...'roots' is fine as a banner in protests against dominance, but it must not be allowed to become an all-purpose slogan. If you dig down deeper you find that roots can be very tangled things.*
Memmi, 1991: 31

## Introduction

So far we have adopted a comparative approach to European relations with former colonial subjects. We have sought to explore some small corners of a much broader and under-researched area, what Holland defines as "the interaction between the crises of decolonisation and metropolitan transition" (Holland, 1991: 84). In Western Europe itself the imperial mentality is far from dead. Domestically it is directed against the 'underclass', which includes, but is not confined to, those distinguished by an 'ethnic' tag, who may also be permanently disenfranchised because of their origins. As John Berger remarks, by accepting the existence of this immigrant underclass, "the [indigenous] working class comes to accept the basic bourgeois claim that social inequality is finally an expression of natural inequality" (Berger, 1975: 140). In the last chapter it was argued that, once such arguments about the 'natural' inferiority of whole groups of people are accepted, claims to basic levels of welfare and justice are undermined for all members of society. Each person's claim can be made conditional on fulfilling criteria of status, income, origin, sex or other ascriptions.

The case studies selected were of interest because they diverged from the post-colonial norm of separation and state sovereignty. It has been argued that both immigration and integration can challenge the colonial hierarchy. In this final chapter, however, we hope to shed some light on some more general questions of post-colonial relations, focusing on what human liberation might mean in this context. The hope is that it will be possible to say something new about well-worn questions asked about emancipation from both feminist and humanist standpoints. In the humanist tradition of 'liberating narrative', the question is whether it is possible "...to represent the quest for freedom in history?" (Taylor, 1989: 19). According to Patrick Taylor, "[i]t is possible to do so only on the basis of an open-ended narrative that offers a critique of the myths imposing finite closure on human possibility" (ibid.).

From within feminism comes the salient question, "do we yet have any idea of what the word revolutionary may mean outside the normal dimension of the hero?" (Leclerc, 1981: 85). The answer of humanists like John Berger or Eric Fromm would be that the equality of all people is the overriding revolutionary principle. "Equality has nothing to do with capacity or function: it is the recognition of being" (Berger, 1975: 141).

Refusal to recognise inter-personal equality at this basic level of being and entitlement arises out of what Eric Fromm has called 'the escape from freedom' (Fromm, 1960). Fearing isolation and meaninglessness, a person may offer up their individual autonomy to some greater collectivity, seen as capable of giving them security and protection in exchange. The urge is to "fuse oneself with somebody or something outside oneself", for example the community or nation, or even a class or gender "in order to acquire the strength which the individual self is lacking" (Fromm, 1960: 122). This can be seen as the personal root of collective authoritarianism (Kristeva, 1993: 2-3). In this chapter, we consider the implications for human rights and self-determination in post-colonial relations of fusing personal identity with that of a greater entity in the search for 'national liberation'.

Boundary construction and reproduction, both literal and metaphorical, are a problem for any liberatory discourse that takes the 'community', the 'people' or the 'nation' as its subject. This is likely to affect women particularly, since "the control of female sexuality is...of utmost importance in maintaining group boundaries and social hierarchy" (Rozario, 1991: 15). Colonial rule did not work through a simple binary of colonised: coloniser. It created and exacerbated other social divisions, including those of class, ethnicity and gender (Asad, 1973; Leacock, 1981; Amadiume, 1987). We will look at gender relations, and particularly at what might be the conceptual relationship between decolonisation and the transformation of power relations based on gender oppression. The anti-colonial writing of Frantz Fanon will be examined in some detail in relation to gendered constructions of the hero.

Does post-colonial liberation imply that some groups of people must wait until after a decolonised political order has been achieved before their own marginality is addressed? In the South African context, one woman describes this approach: "Let's get political liberation first...then the women can start their thing later" (Mpumlwana, 1992: 20). She contrasts this with her own understanding of liberation: "true liberation meant liberation from all forms of oppression, political, gender, economic, class, religious, ethnic or racial..." (ibid.: 19). We also consider in this chapter what rationale there might be for such a broad conception of liberation.

The aim is to use a wide variety of sources in order to elucidate these questions at different levels: individual, collective, national and in inter-state relations. The chapter concludes with some individual profiles of people who in some way challenge conventional notions of bounded identity. Two volumes of recent interviews carried out on the 'race' question in the United States and the UK have proved especially valuable sources of interview material, which has been used throughout (Alibhai-Brown & Montague, 1992; Terkel, 1992).

## A Brief Note on Post-colonial Theory

It may be surprising that we have so far avoided discussion of what is known as 'post-colonial theory'. The basic reason is the tendency for this broad school of thought to direct its energies towards deconstructing the Enlightenment notion of universal human rights. As Robert Young noted recently, there is considerable resistance to post-colonial theory among African and Asian intellectuals working in those continents. He suggests that this may be because the theory "tends to neglect the universality of human rights as a basic requirement for a decent life" (Young, 1994: 78). Almost invariably, the critique made in post-colonial theory is not that such rights are not respected by authoritarian regimes around the world, but that the very concept of human rights is invalid, as well as 'bourgeois'. This fashionably world-weary post-modern conclusion coincides with that of oppressive third world governments who claim that human rights are an alien Western concept. There is a strong case for arguing, on the contrary, that the notion of human rights is universal, but that in the past it was appropriated by Western thinkers and colonisers as if it was their own invention (Ait Ahmed, 1980: 22, 29). Without a basic commitment to defending human rights, deconstruction as a social science practice all too often seems to be confined to rather obfuscatory debunking and critiquing (Kobayashi & Peake, 1994, for a recent example). Such analysis also has an inhibiting quality, as noted by Bryan Turner, which "tends to make one nervous about definite stand points" (Turner, 1989: 636). One example where it was vital to take a 'definite stand point' is presented later, in the form of Michel Foucault's 1984 declaration in defence of the Vietnamese boat people.

Some of the tools and insights of deconstruction are undoubtedly useful for exploring post-colonial relations. One is the insight that no one single cause can be identified as primordial in explaining social and political phenomena. This insight is hardly new, however. As Stanley Hoffman remarked as long ago as 1965, "...the nature of causal relations in the social sciences is such that it is impossible to reach valid generalisations about the effects of a single factor" without risking "platitude" (Hoffman, 1965: 125). Another important insight of post-modern and post-colonial theory that can be taken on board is the need "to think about phenomena in flexible and open-ended ways, relationally", and the need to avoid thinking in terms of "solid, bounded, homogeneous entities" (Wolf, 1988: 759). Yet here, too, we should not neglect the hard realities of state policies, borders, laws and institutions which continue to determine the life opportunities of people, particularly those who find themselves 'on the margins', not through choice but by being structurally placed there. These people are the most vulnerable to exclusion and violence from the state and the collectivity (Memmi, 1991: 39).

We have decided to locate this last chapter within a broadly humanist-feminist perspective in order to distance our position from that of post-modern theories of post-colonialism, which appear to be neither humanist nor feminist in their implications. The conclusions reached in this chapter should of course be seen as limited in their scope: it would be ridiculous to try and produce any comprehensive account of something as wide and diverse as post-colonial human liberation.

## Beyond Entry and Exit in Post-colonial Relations

For convenience, political demands of newly independent states on the world stage may be classified into two types: what Ali Mazrui calls the 'knock of entry' and the 'knock of exit' (Mazrui, 1981: 62). On the one hand, as outsiders, third world states demand the right to full and equal participation; on the other hand, there is the urge to leave the system altogether and attempt to establish a different order that is more just and equitable. Independence, as it took place in the former European colonial empires, generally pre-empted any moves towards a comprehensive transformation of the economic, social and political structures inherited from colonialism. National sovereignty became a goal in itself and this served to obscure the indivisibility of human rights, both internally and internationally between the former colonial powers and the former colonies.

The majority of third world states have now lost all but the most nominal sovereignty in domestic economic affairs, having been forced to agree to far-reaching 'restructurings' in order to repay debts incurred two decades ago (Seabrook, 1993). In the Caribbean, welfare provisions and basic living conditions have deteriorated in many countries since independence, and external economic dependence has been reinforced. In a lecture to mark his eightieth birthday, C.L.R. James was talking about Barbuda, an island state of two thousand people which had recently obtained its sovereignty: "What is all this independence? It's a lot of words" (James, 1984: 19). Remembering himself he added that he believed in independence, but later commented that, whilst sovereignty brought "a national flag...an anthem...a prime minister", it brought little else (ibid.: 53).

Regimes in many post-independence states face political challenges domestically from minority groups who feel themselves to be marginalised. Such groups may demand 'exit' from the post-colonial state and seek separate statehood themselves; as Tony Smith explains "[t]he civil war lurks in the heart of every movement of national liberation" (Smith, 1978: 90). By the 1990s, this is becoming all too obvious, with civil wars outnumbering inter-state wars, and being particularly prevalent in countries which gained their independence at considerable cost, after a period of violent conflict.

Similar mechanisms of exit and entry exist at the personal level as well. Yet, whereas the 'knock of entry' is seen as appropriate for post-colonial states when they demand their right to equal participation and fair treatment in the international economic and political system, it is rarely given the same legitimacy when it is the individual who is 'knocking at the door' demanding equal rights. To allow people freely to search for the most generous 'rights of access' (Faber, 1984: 373) available internationally is seen as incompatible with the goals of national economic development and political sovereignty for third world states. The right of all people to take part fully in the economic, social and political life of the country where they settle is said to conflict with the rights of all states to equal treatment in the international system.

The case of Puerto Rico is an interesting one, and somewhat similar to the French overseas departments in terms of the parameters of local political debate. The majority of Puerto Rico's electorate either support the existing 'compact' association agreement with the United States or are in favour of full statehood and integration into the US Federal system. Pro-independence parties usually receive around one-tenth of the vote, and find more support among Puerto Ricans in the United States than from those in the island. Nationalist commentators typically argue that the willingness of Puerto Ricans to accept "prosperity in subordination" (Landes, 1969; 12) and remain dependent on the United States in order to maximise their welfare opportunities and emigration rights is "not a heroic mentality, but a colonial one" (Levine, 1980: xxv).

Pro-independentists claim that Puerto Ricans have been 'bought by welfare' and no longer know what is good for them. They have been seduced and emasculated politically (Martinez, 1977: 577-8). One pro-independentist argues, for example, that any acceptable post-colonial status must be "premised on the principle of equality of peoples" (Rivera-Ramose, 1991: 125). Integration and statehood, even though they would result in greater formal equality and probably in higher incomes as well, are seen as worse than association. Entry of the Puerto Rican 'people' into the international arena is therefore demanded in the name of national self-determination and against all evidence. Exit of Puerto Rican people living in the US is also expected in efforts to rebuild the homeland.

This rather simplistic dichotomy between strategies of entry and exit in identity politics and North-South relations echoes debates between liberal and radical feminist writers concerning the possibility of 'making it' within the patriarchal system, or leaving it and constructing an alternative reality. In either case what is being challenged is the premise that women's "specific social status is immutable" and somehow 'natural' (Eriksen, 1993: 155). Both strategies of entry and exit seek to alter the nature of relationships and make them more equal: entry on the basis of membership of a collectivity; exit on the basis of the creation of a new, more equal collectivity. What they have in common is a belief in the ability of a collectivity to bring about human liberation. Materialist and environmental radical feminists have devoted considerable energy to deconstructing dualistic divisions of the entry/exit type. Their avowed aim is to overcome the splits imposed by patriarchal thinking and behaviour between members and outsiders, public and private, as well as between nature and culture, male and female, mind and body.

"[S]eparatism is patriarchy's favourite way of thought and action" (Shiva, 1992: 6). It is therefore in a process of *rapprochement*, and in healing the rift between opposites, which are not really opposites at all, that personal and collective liberation are sought (Hermann, 1981: 171). Essentially this is a humanist insight; as Alison Jaggar expresses it, "Feminism is about reintegration in an holistic mode of being and doing" (Jaggar, 1983: 269). The ideal is integration based on mutual respect for differences. However, before this is possible, the concept of difference needs to be separated from the "patriarchal paradigm of sameness" according to which difference denotes subordination and dualism (Shiva, 1992: 10). Emancipation, as reintegration between different categories split by dualistic thinking and freedom from possession, needs to apply equally to all categories of people, but also to people's relationship with nature and work (Oakley, 1981: 12; Daly, 1984: 409).

In practice, people, like governments or states, can "invoke aspects of cultural equity and difference situationally when it serves their interests" (Eriksen, 1993: 138). Economic decolonisation of the third world is seen as requiring "liberation from past patterns of economic domination", simultaneous with improved access to markets, to capital, to technology, and in some cases allowance for labour mobility between South and North (*Third World Quarterly*, 1979: 118). These demands for exit and (re)entry on a more equal basis are only apparently contradictory.

Similarly, in the French overseas *départements*, local politicians combine exit and entry strategies quite effectively in relations with the central institutions of the French state. Demands for identical treatment (entry), as for instance in welfare provisions or minimum wage levels, coexist without difficulty with requests that the DOM's 'special features' be taken into account in policy-making (exit), for instance with regard to language, unemployment or trade policy. In fact the use of the two strategies in combination is one means that local politicians use to try and maximise resources available for local distribution.

The same transcendence of the dualistic categories of entry and exit can be found in local cultural politics. *Créolité* is an Antillais invention that has complicated the black/white dichotomy of *négritude*, and better represents the complex reality of mixed cultures and colour in the Caribbean DOM (and in Reunion as well). Edouard Glissant's work has been instrumental in extending the idea of *créolité* to the wider Caribbean context through what he calls *antillanité* (Burton, 1994: 133-6, 140-47). Martinican and Guadeloupean intellectuals like Daniel Maximin, Patrick Chamoiseau and Raphael Confiant have taken these notions further (*Le Monde*, 19.5.1990; *Libération*, 24.7.1989). Such writers express confidence in the assimilatory capacity of creole culture, and in its dynamism. The mixture of 'races', known in French as *brassage des races*, is presented as a source of pride rather than as something negative or 'unnatural', as is so often the case. In 1989, nine-year-old Samantha Laval had a hit song entitled *L'Avenir est au Métissage* (Mixing is the Future). The song warns all conservatives, who resist change, to become more accepting, since such mixing will inevitably continue.[1] *Créolité* as a culture of synthesis, incorporation and the refusal of exclusion presents an alternative to the backward-looking and defensive nationalism of the New Right in France. It seems, on the other hand, to have much in common with traditional Gaullist and Jacobin French nationalism, which is also self-professedly assimilationist.

Second-generation French Algerians have the same ability to make the most of living 'in two cultures', and have produced the synthesis of *beur* identity. "There is no clear evidence" that such complex or compound cultural identity is "inherently problematic, but such ambiguous situations can certainly be difficult to handle in an environment where one is *expected* to have a clear, delineated identity" (Eriksen, 1993: 138). This also applies to people of so-called 'mixed race', for whom hard and fast notions of cultural and community boundaries can create identity problems rather than resolving them. Some personal experiences of this are presented in the last section of this chapter.

According to post-colonial theory, neither exit nor entry can result in human liberation, since people cannot escape their contingency and incoherence through such strategies (Eriksen, 1993: 151-52). The notion of liberation would be equated with human rights, and seen as one which "needs to be dismantled from the inside" (Balibar, 1991: 77). It could be observed in passing that many post-colonial theorists themselves, such as Homi Babha, Gayatri Spivak and Edward Saïd, are products of assimilation to Western academic establishments. In the process of their integration into these institutions, they have found themselves segregated in various ways as 'black' or 'oriental' intellectuals. They have responded by deconstructing the bounded identities they have found themselves thrust into by others.

Marginalised people generally may be forced to take on group identities because of the prevalence of exclusion and segregation rather than through choice. The question therefore is not really whether groups or individuals exit or enter, but under what terms they do so: whether voluntarily or through coercion, and with what results. Boundary-creating and maintaining devices may be imposed from outside: announcing one's ethnic identity may simply result from making a virtue of necessity. The collective 'self' will come to be perceived as besieged by enemies from outside and from within (Balibar, 1991: 76). "Presented with the choice between being an underclass or an ethnic minority, many groups opt for the latter" (Eriksen, 1993: 125). In such a system, the temptation will arise for group leaders to start asserting forms of authoritarian control over those perceived as 'members' of their own ethnic group.

As Balibar notes, the sexual dimension is often very important in fuelling moves to establish and harden inter-group ethnic and national distinctions; "racial hostility is nourished particularly by myths about sexual attacks, interbreeding, women of one race being stolen by men from another" (Balibar, 1991: 76). Like racial antagonism and fear, the myth of sexually predatory males from other communities is a means of justifying predatory behaviour in relation to other communities' women. As such it has the quality of a self-fulfilling prophecy.

## Binding Women to Communal Boundaries

One means of asserting control over the process of group boundary creation and reproduction will be to tighten patriarchal control over women, by linking their sexuality to their allegiance to in-group solidarity: "[a]n Englishman's home may be his castle, but it is his wife's prison" (Jaggar, 1983: 131). Internal policing of the sexuality of both sexes may be increased, but it is likely in a patriarchal and patrilinear system that women, regarded as the 'weak underbelly' of the group, will come under particularly close scrutiny. "Control of motherhood is a totalitarian impulse", comments the novelist Emily Prager; to dominate society "you go through the women and try to gain control over how and with whom they are breeding" (*Independent*, 25.1.1992).

The control of women's sexuality and mobility can be seen as a distinctly 'colonial' as well as a communitarian and patriarchal impulse. Frantz Fanon saw French strategy for undermining native culture in Algeria in these terms:

> If we want to destroy the structure of Algerian society, its capacity for resistance, we
> must first of all conquer the women: we must go and find them behind the veil...and in
> the houses where the men keep them out of sight. (Fanon, 1970b: 23)

If unveiling women was the colonial policy, then decolonisation implied a
reversal in this policy, and women's reveiling (ibid.: 28-9). Both these
strategies denied the Algerian woman any role in the process of social and
political change. In Fanon's writing generally, she is not regarded as an actor
or a self-determining human being. Rather she is the passive territory over
which a battle rages between two 'species of men': the coloniser and the
colonised, the settler and the native (Irigaray, 1981: 105).

This phenomenon of competition for patriarchal control of women's bodies
is referred to by materialist feminists as 'sexual colonisation' (Jaggar, 1983:
269; Mies *et al.*, 1988). It could be argued that this makes a false analogy
between women and colonised people, since, whereas "[e]thnic minorities may
be expelled, exterminated or ignored, women cannot be treated in the same
way" if continuity of the community is to be assured (Eriksen, 1993: 155).
This is a valid point, but it does not mean that women are treated as free and
equal members of the community. On the contrary, because the metaphorical
and literal boundaries reside in women's bodies, their reproduction will be
closely guarded in any system of separatism and 'authoritarian closure'
(Etienne, 1989: 184). Like Memmi's portrait of the colonised person in
relation to the coloniser, the woman cannot be an autonomous person in
relation to the man, since he needs her to act as his 'other half' to gain a sense
of his own superiority (Mies, 1989: 53). The next section explores further the
notion that the liberation of some categories of human beings is necessarily
based on the subjugation of other categories.

A good example of the way in which the control of community boundaries
requires control of women's sexuality comes from Martinique, in the case of
the economically dominant white *béké* minority. There are sharp internal class
divisions between the wealthiest *Grands Békés*, the middle-ranking *Moyen
Békés* and the poor *petits blancs* (Kovats-Beaudoux, 1973: 245-50). A
detailed anthropological study carried out in the 1960s revealed the importance
of marriage for maintaining these sub-group categories (Kovats-Beaudoux,
1973). Whilst *béké* men did marry women from outside the white community,
this was much less common for *béké* women, who were closely chaperoned
and secluded to prevent such an occurrence (ibid.: 265). Intermixing across
the three sub-groups, or with non-whites, was considered less serious for *béké*
men as it did not involve mixing the 'line' (ibid.: 254). However, for a woman
to marry or have children outside the prescribed social group was for family
inheritance to be lost to people of another name (ibid.: 264). Those who

decide to marry across social or colour boundaries may even be disinherited. But whilst *béké* men frequently have coloured mistresses, for a *béké* woman to have a coloured lover would be a disgrace and would dishonour her whole family line. The cost for the woman of the community's boundary maintenance and 'self-repro-duction' is thus higher than the cost for the man.

Actual people live vulnerable lives, and perhaps the most vulnerable of all to abuses of their human rights are poor third world women (Shiva, 1992: 3; Mies *et al.*, 1988). "These women may depend on others but lack the supp-osed securities of dependence. They are impoverished, but are often provid-ers" (O'Neill, 1992: 51). Interdependence and symbiosis are essential parts of such women's life experience which are not taken into account in the liberal conception of the atomised, autonomous and 'self-determining' individual who appears to live without dependence (ibid.: 51). Often such women also carry the invisible burden of the collective honour of their communities on their shoulders. If they seek to exercise their human rights in terms of choice of a spouse, reproductive control or free movement and cultural mixture, they may easily be accused of being 'untrue to their culture' (Rozario, 1991: 15-22). The same applies to migrant women in the West, whose freedom of physical and social movement is usually more restricted than that of their male counterparts (for an example, see Fawzi El-Solh, 1993).

The delegitimising of inter-'racial' sexual relations has been noted in the black community in both Britain and the United States. It seems that black men and women carry out a certain degree of internal sexual policing, particularly of women. Thus black women who choose white men as lovers risk being "severely chastised...for selling out the 'race', or they are accused of being like prostitutes..." (Collins, 1990: 191). Several interviewees in both volumes used in this chapter report this double standard which operates between men and women in 'mixed' relationships (Terkel, 1992: 50, 68; Alibhai-Brown & Montague, 1992: 17, 32, 285, 290).

From another angle, the same process can be expressed as something more positive. In the US context, Herbert Klein has remarked that "...the new pro-Afro-American ideologies...gave a legitimacy to mass opposition to the 'whitening' process and helped reduce the high cultural cost of integration into the dominant society" (Klein, 1986: 270). Communitarian policing of sexuality applies to both sexes, and to both blacks and whites. For the white man, the sexual union of the black male and white female is the "horror taboo", in the words of one psychologist interviewed in Terkel's study (Terkel, 1992: 336). Such relationships may provoke a violent response from those white men who see themselves as vulnerable faced with the supposedly greater sexual prowess of black men.

## Self-Determination: States and People

Terms such as 'independence', 'self-determination', 'autonomy' and 'human rights' are used to describe processes and conditions at various different levels: at the individual level of the person; within and between communities; for states and 'nations'; and at the international, or inter-state, level. These terms also have legal, political, economic and psychological meanings which are sometimes conflated and confused. A false analogy has long been made between the coming to autonomy, and psychological maturity, or 'self-determination' of the individual human being, and the economic and political 'self-determination' of whole states and communities of people (Feuchtwang, 1990: 10-11; Stagner, 1987: 7-16). It will be argued here that this equation is false and misleading, and that it often lies at the heart of abuses of human rights in the name of collective developmental and political goals.

This tendency to collapse the members of a group or community into one amorphous whole lies at the heart of many forms of extreme nationalist and fundamentalist politics. At the same time, it is an impulse which emanates 'from below', as it were; from individuals seeking the security that appears to derive from complete identification with the greater body of 'the people', whether in terms of class, gender, nation, religion or culture (Fromm, 1960: 122). Yet to talk of the state's identity or personality, as one would of an individual person, is, as Bikhu Parekh notes, "to introduce a risky and misleading concept...[which] reifies and homogenises what is distinctive to a society and suppresses diversity and fluidity" (Parekh, 1994: 102).

The attribution of 'personality' to communities or territories as if they were living beings is very obvious in the case of the French overseas departments. We may have been guilty of it in this study, in attempting to described the 'development' and degree of 'autonomy' or 'integration' of each of the Antilles, Reunion and Guyane. The islands in particular are often referred to as female beings; the 'orphans', 'sisters' or 'dancing girls' of 'Mother France'. Their inhabitants may not be entirely satisfied with the relationship, but that is normal in any family (Hintjens, 1992a; Burton, 1993). Out of such analogies arises the implication that the Antilles and Reunion are somehow 'natural' parts of the French *ensemble*. In descriptions of slave emancipation and later of the transformation of the former *anciennes colonies* into French departments, the analogy of the family has often been used, as in the following account:

> She [i.e. France] grants reparation to those unfortunates for the crime that long ago tore them from their parents and the land of their birth, by giving them France as a fatherland (*patrie*) and, as their inheritance, all the rights of the French citizen. (Sablé, 1955: 72, cited in Burton, 1993: 78)

The Republican defence of the emancipatory core of French national culture is well known. In this view, French national culture is described as "open to others, without losing its soul" (C. Khaznadar, *Le Monde*, 12.5.1987; see Kristeva, 1993). The problem with this is its oversimplification, as Parekh noted above. This description makes French national culture sound like a 'being'; in fact like the healthy, well-balanced adult of Eric Fromm's description, for example, who can have a "spontaneous relationship to man and nature, a relationship that connects the individual with the world without eliminating his individuality" (Fromm, 1960: 24). At the individual level, one may be able to accept that the healthy, open-minded person is one who is able to 'meet the other' without feeling threatened; who is able to avoid what Bruno Etienne calls 'self-bantustanisation' (Etienne, 1989: 187). But what can this mean when it is extended to a whole state system and a national society? It creates expectations of good behaviour that are bound to be disappointed. Those who believe in this vision of France as a healthy, liberated personality may expect to find their own identity within this greater being. But the loss of personal independence that this implies is ultimately likely to lead to frustration and resentment (Fromm, 1960: 24; Memmi, 1979: 56). This sense of disillusion is evident in political life in the French overseas departments, where the projection of a benevolent personality was particularly strong during the colonial period, and was extended by de Gaulle in the 1960s.

There is some basis in reality for the assertion that French political culture has in many respects a stronger liberatory tradition than its equivalent 'national' political culture in the UK. The contrast between them was explored in relation to immigration and nationality policies. It is also worth remembering that anti-colonialism too is not new; Western anti-colonialism has existed for a long time alongside imperialistic cultural notions within both Britain and French 'national' culture (Young, 1994: 78). By the same token, even the most ardent critics of French colonialism, such as Frantz Fanon, have agreed that French Republican ideology contains a strong humanitarian thread (Carew, 1988: 37-8; Spillman, 1981: 273). In his novel, *God's Bits of Wood*, Sembene Ousmane has the most radical rail workers' strike leader declare, "We know what France represents, and we respect it. We are in no sense anti-French" (Ousmane, 1986: 182). He thus succeeds in depicting the strike as first and foremost a bread-and-butter issue.

The false analogy of states' emancipation and development with that of individual human 'selves' has led to a markedly nationalist definition of human rights in international law. In effect, the universality of such rights is contradicted by the terms of inter-state agreements: "when boundaries are taken wholly seriously...international justice is not just played down, but wiped off the ethical map" (O'Neill, 1992: 56). The position of international migrants in the present world system can be taken as an example of this.

The treatment of asylum seekers in Western Europe and North America is today among the most harsh in the world. It involves expulsion; *refoulement* of those who have not yet arrived by sea or air, imprisonment without trial, and removal of the right to appeal (Randall, 1994). Yet these governments are the most able to bear the costs of liberal refugee policies. Asylum seekers are increasingly being equated with illegal 'economic migrants' fleeing poor conditions in their home countries. Furthermore, these conditions are seen as the responsibility of the people or countries themselves, and not of colonial or neo-colonial policies of the West (Gosling, 1991: 51). In *Victims of Development*, Jeremy Seabrook comments that the major causes of economic migration from the South are in any case the misapplied and inappropriate policies of the West. Such policies are transmitted through various international 'development' institutions, and often leave people worse off than before (Seabrook, 1993: 150). Western governments justify the expulsion and further persecution of asylum applicants by claiming that:

> They are bogus, phoney, they employ a catalogue of ruses, tell falsehoods and lies; thereby demonstrating that the moral character of those we once ruled over has not improved since we 'gave' them independence. (Ibid.: 148)

This fiction acts in the same way that racism, class prejudice and sexism do within the state: "for the benefit of the accuser, and to the detriment of his victim, in order to justify aggression or privileges" (Memmi, 1991: 29). As social scientists working in areas of research and practice related to development issues, there is little doubt that we "inherit the colonizer's path" (Trouillot, 1988: 27).

Ever-tighter restrictions, claimed to be needed to prevent 'hordes' and 'floods' of new migrants from the East and the South, have also cost the third world a great deal in lost revenue. In the 1992 UNDP Human Development Report it was estimated that restrictions on freedom of movement of persons comprise fully "half the $500 billion annual costs to developing countries of closed global markets" (*Guardian*, 24.4.1992). The same report calculated that the cost to the North of restricting labour mobility from the South would also be considerable - some $1000 billion by the year 2000 (ibid.).

It was observed in Chapter 5 that international law recognises the right to free emigration under Article 13, but accords individuals no matching right to immigrate. Respect for national sovereignty precludes making any such provision (Storey, 1994: 111-12). Yet the right of exit is not realisable unless there exists a corresponding right of entry somewhere else. In effect, those who have somewhere to go are at present free to leave, whereas those who are not accepted as immigrants or refugees elsewhere have no effective right to leave. Any human right, if it is to be known as such, must be universal. "If there is a universal right to emigrate, it belongs to Haitians, Turks and Sri Lankans" as well as to British, French and United States citizens (Dummett, 1992: 174). It follows that there is a need to establish in international law some sort of provision covering the right to freedom of movement across international borders.

The Universal Declaration of Human Rights includes the following articles which express the contradiction between universally attributed human rights, and human rights subject to state policies. Article 28 reads: "Everyone is entitled to a social and international order in which the rights and freedoms set forth in this Declaration can be fully realised." Article 29 appears to qualify this in stating that "Everyone has duties to the community in which alone the free and full development of his [sic] personality is possible." Article 28 implies some obligation on the part of all governments to ensure that the economic, social, civil and political human rights laid down in other articles can be implemented and extended internationally. Article 29 appears to reverse the emphasis, by making the individual accountable to the 'community' (presumably the state) in which he or she resides, or from which he or she originates.

The person remains the possession of his or her country of birth, rather than a sovereign individual, possessed of human rights including the right of freedom of movement. In this system, citizenship is "assigned at birth", and generally "not subject to change by the individual's will and effort" and has "a major impact upon that person's life chances" (Carens, 1992: 26). Recognising states' rights over their citizens is a means of sanctioning a very high degree of international inequality in the substantial rights to which people have access. Like feudal serfs, Dummett sees the world's poor as "chained to their countries of origin because nobody wants them as immigrants" (Dummett, 1992: 172). It is hard to imagine that the Universal Declaration of Human Rights could have altered this situation in any way, given that its wording had to be agreed inter-governmentally.

Article 28 suggests the universality of human rights, irrespective of circumstance and accidents of birth. As Eric Fromm argues in a different context, this can only be asserted if "ethical principles" are given priority over and above survival of the national community itself (Fromm, 1960: 182). Only then could an individual belong to a community in which his or her individual liberties and freedoms could never be overridden in the name of the collective good. An example of such universalistic thinking comes from Michel

Foucault, who in 1984 published a statement in response to the plight of the Vietnamese boat people. It contained the following clause, on which he based his claim to defend the rights of these refugees:

> There exists an international citizenry, which has its rights, which has its duties, and which promises to rise up against every abuse of power, no matter who the author or the victims. After all, we are all governed and, to that extent, in solidarity. (Translated from *Libération*, June 1984 by Keenan, 1987)

Foucault cites the emergence of such groups as Amnesty International and other human rights organisations as evidence that governments can no longer claim to have a monopoly to "intervene in the order of politics and international strategies" (ibid.). This statement reads like a statement of the ideal form of post-colonial relations based on equality of the international 'citizenry'. Foucault upholds the notion that human rights, if they exist at all, should be global in scope. This places him close to the camp of so-called human rights 'enthusiasts' who believe that "rights of residence, work and welfare, as well as burdens of taxation, should be global" (O'Neill, 1992: 56).

Whereas the right to freedom of movement (whether within states or across international borders) is widely acknowledged as a natural right (Dummett, 1992), the same is not true of national self-determination. In fact it is often not regarded as a right at all. There is no logical end to the potential for upheaval through the exercise of the so-called national self-determination principle (Cobban, 1945: 139; Thurer, 1987; Kedourie, 1984: 348-9). Several arguments can be made in defence of the argument that national self-determination is not a human right but a political principle. The first is that, unlike freedom of movement, the right of national self-determination is too complex to be a part of natural law (Thürer, 1987: 22). The second is that 'nations' cannot be identified objectively, since they are always defined politically. Unidentifiable entities cannot be given 'rights' (Cobban, 1945: 28). The most pragmatic and powerful argument is that, in practice, the 'right' of national self-determination has been misused in the past. The assertion of such a right "...in practice has led to a practical denial of individual rights and the enthronement of the principle that might is right" (ibid.: 47). The realist claim is that might is indeed right (Gosling, 1991: 59). This is certainly a point of view, but it is hardly a point of view that can be raised into a moral principle.

We would therefore concur with Cobban's point of view that "rights are rights for individual, though not isolated, men and women, or they are not rights at all" (Cobban, 1945: 47). Foucault's statement ties in with this, and also comes close to the position taken by 'natural law' theorists. The removal of rights to asylum for Vietnamese people in Hong Kong, for example, and their detention in centres resembling prison camps, is from this perspective "blatantly unjust"; in the natural law tradition "it is from the fact of being human, not the fact of being a citizen, that rights arise" (Dummett, 1992: 172). It is interesting to see natural law converge so closely with the position taken by Marxist humanists such as John Berger and Eric Fromm, not to mention feminists like Alison Jaggar and Vandana Shiva.

## Righting Wrongs

In contrast with such universalistic notions of emancipation, most current definitions of human freedom seem to imply that the freedom of some (men, whites, the rich) can be gained only at the expense of others (women, blacks, the poor). Thus the rise of the West is seen as having depended on the impoverishment of the former colonies. The implication of this is that the transformation of living conditions in the West cannot be achieved universally. In this vein, Maria Mies argues: "the rise of man was based on the descent of woman, Europe's progress was based on the regress of colonies..." (Mies, 1989: 53). J.K. Galbraith sees the same mechanism at work in the economic sphere, where "The servant role of women is critical for the expansion of consumption" (Galbraith, 1979: 41). Of course, Marxism is the classic example of a belief system that sees the wealth and freedom of the few as dependent on the exploitation of the poor majority and their economic, or even literal, enslavement.

Such approaches imply that what is needed is a reversal in the existing order, a sort of turning of the tables. At the international level, this takes the form of restitution for colonialism. At this level, the fact of profiting from the colonial past, and continuing to profit from a neo-colonial world system, "places some responsibility on [Northern states] to compensate those nations who have been the victims" of such exploitation (Gosling, 1991: 66; see also Carens, 1992). This cannot ensure that the compensation provided would be properly distributed or invested to improve current living conditions for the poor in those countries. In a similar way, it has been suggested that individuals who are prevented from moving to the West and improving their living standards should be personally compensated (Goodin, 1992: 8-9). Again, this would be difficult to implement in practice.

In the last section the idea of restitution was used to describe the policies of France in the overseas departments. In the French Antilles, Guyane and Reunion there has been a rapid *rapprochement* to metropolitan standards of longevity and health, with a dramatically rapid demographic transition. In financial terms, there has been a sizeable and sustained net transfer of resources from the metropolis to the DOM, mainly through state institutions in the form of salaries, grants, social welfare provisions and infrastructure. Integration into the European Communities has added another channel of transfer.

What is important here is that all these net financial outflows are acknowledged to take the form of entitlements rather than 'aid' or 'charity'. This is not because responsibility is accepted for past wrongs (Gosling, 1991: 61-3). The state is simply seen as having a duty to intervene in order to ensure at least a proximate degree of equality between its citizens overseas and in the metropolis. Kenneth Robinson, a seasoned commentator on decolonisation, concluded early on that "'[d]epartmentalisation' is not a means of maintaining a disguised form of colonial government" (Robinson, 1954: 195). Some thirty years later, however, he observed that the colonial problem in the DOM was not resolved for all that (Robinson, 1984: 34). The distinctiveness of territories many thousands of miles from mainland France, where most people speak creole rather than French in daily exchanges, and where there are still strong historical resonances from the times of slavery, means that the colonial question is unlikely to disappear altogether as a bone of contention in local politics (Souquet-Basiège, 1979: 494).

Independence in the rest of the Caribbean has all too often resulted in a transfer of responsibility to the new state without any concomitant transfer in effective power or capacity. Sovereign governments are held responsible for the outcomes of domestic policies even when they are completely at the mercy of international donors, international trade regimes and policy conditionalities. Economic, political and cultural power have shifted from Britain to new partners, including the United States, Canada and the EC. It has certainly not shifted significantly to the local elite or capitalist class. The former colonisers and current trading partners deny any responsbility for the deteriorating economic and social conditions in many independent Caribbean countries. Power without reponsibility is the essence of the neo-colonial relationship.

In the anglophone Caribbean, material living conditions have actually deteriorated for most people, and particularly for women and children, since independence. Infant and maternal mortality levels in particular have increased quite sharply in the past two decades (Massiah, 1987: 965). The former colonisers have denied any responsibility for these conditions, and have introduced new laws sanctioning international segregation through tighter nationality and immigration legislation imposed on the citizens of the former colonies. Thus the granting of collective 'freedom' was accompanied by the removal of the individual right of free movement. Since such changes were seen as matters of 'national interest', they were never discussed with the states whose citizens would be most affected, nor even within the Commonwealth forum (Layton-Henry, 1992: 75). As Hugh Tinker noted,

> ...by a painful paradox, within twelve months of South Africa's departure [from the Commonwealth], Britain introduced the first law entailing the exclusion of Commonwealth citizens, aimed unequivocally at black and brown Commonwealth people from the Caribbean and South Asia. (Tinker, 1977: 68)

Formal emancipation cannot of course guarantee substantial equality for individuals any more than for states. The comparison with slave emancipation crops up in much writing on decolonisation in the Caribbean context, and highlights the danger of focusing on formal rights without taking stock of material living conditions. As one Caribbean journalist comments: "[t]here is no point in telling a man he is free, then allowing him to starve on your doorstep" (cited in Lowenthal & Clark, 1980: 300). In Antigua in the 1830s slaves were forcibly 'emancipated' so that plantation owners could avoid the tax burden. Once transformed into 'free labourers', former slaves were obliged to work in order to feed themselves, and the planters found that this made them work harder (Richardson, 1983: 77). Interest in the theme of slave emancipation can also be related to the nationalist preoccupation with what Hegel called the "coming to history" of formerly colonised peoples through overturning the old social and political order (Taylor, 1989: 46).

This is not even subconsciously to argue in favour of slavery or colon-ialism, even under conditions of material plenty. But to formally 'liberate', with no regard as to whether the conditions exist to make that freedom substantial, can result in a new and more subtle form of subordination: one which may be all the more lasting for being less easily identifiable. The illusory nature of such formal 'freedoms' was frequently expressed by exiles from communist bloc countries, prior to the end of the Cold War. In Terkel, a South African man, Mark Mathabane, makes this point about life in the US:

> At least in South Africa, I knew what I was fighting against...Here I am told I am free, I'm the equal of everyone, fair play is the name of the game. Yet, try as many of us do, we seem to get nowhere. (Terkel, 1992: 321)

Among anti-colonial discourses, that of Frantz Fanon most clearly advocates a decolonisation of reversal. He does not argue that reversal per se can result in decolonisation, but he sees the turning of the tables of the coloniser on himself as a necessary part of the cathartic violence of a liberation struggle. He claims that in the colonial context violence can act as a detoxicant. In particular, he sees it as useful in breaking down the mystification that colonialism creates in the colonised's mind (Taylor, 1989: 7-46; Fanon, 1970b: 52). We will attempt to deconstruct Fanon's notion of liberation from a humanist-feminist perspective and will dwell on his work at some length, since it is widely read and remains highly influential.

This tendency to justify violence of the hero in a noble cause is characteristic of the French Left as a whole, and has been criticised by several French feminists. Annie Leclerc criticises the tendency to glorify violence, including violence against women, as somehow 'liberatory'. "Heroism is played out in the face of death...It is death that raises the hero's temperature. Not life; that leaves him cold", she complains (Leclerc, 1981: 82). Claudine Hermann comments that in such heroic discourses the victim is often depicted as 'deserving' the violence they are dealt (Hermann, 1981: 77). There is a more serious point to be made, which is that the tendency to see violence as an effective psychological and political weapon is common to colonialism, patriarchy and the liberatory current exemplified by Fanon. The legacy of Freudian psychiatry is clear in Fanon's work, and particularly Freud's anti-humanist conclusion that the human condition is essentially characterised by hatred, fear and neurosis (Jaggar, 1983: 127). More importantly, there is a singular risk in the violent anti-colonial war of reproducing the process by which domination was asserted in the past (Mies *et al.*, 1988: 88-9).

Violence, in Fanon's writing, as Patrick Taylor has pointed out, is not an end in itself. It creates a *tabula rasa* on which the former colonised people can build a new nation (Taylor, 1989: 61). Decolonisation thus starts out as "a programme of complete disorder" (Fanon, 1963: 29); the idea of revenge is the first impulse of the colonised, since he (and it is he, not she) has been deprived of everything that is his by rights: his land, property, identity and a history of his own. He wants to take, and to possess, what the coloniser has: "to sit at the settler's table, to sleep in the settler's bed, with his wife if possible...there is no native who does not dream at least once a day of setting himself up in the settler's place" (Fanon, 1963: 32).

This powerful descriptive passage evokes images from Orwell's *Animal Farm*. It is a theme that recurs in more recent post-colonial fiction. In the novel *Heroes of the Day*, the main character says, "if somebody just walks into your house and takes your food and eats it...even sleeps with your woman...I would kill for that...What's mine is mine" (White, 1990: 130). Such (re)possessive visions strangely echo the beliefs of racialist politicians of Western Europe, including Enoch Powell and Jean-Marie Le Pen, when they claim that white womanhood is vulnerable and threatened by immigrants' 'rampant sexuality'.

Fanon uses the veil as a metaphor for the relation of competition between the (male) native and the (male) settler. Women, he suggests, can be divided into those who wear the veil and those who do not. He takes this as an unambiguous indicator of "her overall attitude with respect to foreign occupation" (Fanon, 1970b: 33). Fanon seems to extend the Freudian theory of seduction to the Algerian 'nation', by using a mythical analogy of women's body with the body politic. Yes, veiled women carried bombs, but so no doubt did unveiled women (Fanon, 1970a: 43). The possibility that women might choose not to wear traditional dress, and yet be anti-colonial, does not seem to occur, since women are regarded as the embodiment of community (or of its disintegration). Fanon points out no comparable external boundary marker for men, who are therefore more able to take complex positions in the war. When an Algerian bought the mainland French newspaper, *Le Monde*, at a news-stand, for example, this came to be regarded by the French authorities as a subversive act (Fanon, 1970a: 64-5). Such was the complexity of the colonial/anti-colonial divide in this war.

At the level of individual post-colonial relations also, Fanon's work has been immensely influential. He was one of the few writers who early on dealt explicitly with sexual relations between 'black' and 'white' men and women. His two chapters on this theme in *Black Skin White Masks* have been widely discussed and applied. In his own words, Fanon's concern in this book is with the "liberation of the man of colour", who needs to be freed from "the arsenal of complexes that has been developed by the colonial environment" (Fanon, 1968: 10, 30). He does mean man, and not colonised coloured people in general. Fanon explains the difference between male and female sexuality in the following way: when the white woman accepts a black man, "there is automatically a romantic element. It is a giving not a seizing" (ibid.: 46). The white man, on the other hand, is the one who seizes; he is seen as the active party. Yet the coloured woman, Mayotte Capécia, a fictional character whom he analyses, is said to have sold out to the colonial values by falling in love with a white man with blue eyes (Fanon, 1968: 42-7). She is very much the victim in the novel, having been abandoned by her white lover, who has not even acknowledged her existence publicly. She seeks, but cannot find, love and economic security. Instead of sympathising with the woman's vulnerability in a racist society, Fanon concludes in stern tones that this book is a "sermon in praise of corruption" (ibid.: 42). For good measure he adds: "...it is legitimate to say that Mayotte Capécia has definitively turned her back on her country" (ibid.: 53). Fanon is much more understanding of the black man who seeks to have sexual relations with a white woman, even though in the end he agrees that this relationship, too, is doomed.

In reviewing the plays of Aimé Césaire, Clement Mbou makes the observation that women are not recognised as having any active or political role in his drama. "She [i.e. woman] forms part of the weight of the past" (Mbou, 1979: 98). Here too the hero is depicted as killing in order to usher in a new social and political order, and the act of killing is depicted as brave and heroic (ibid.: 99). Césaire sees colonisation as akin to 'thingification' of the colonised person (Césaire, 1972: 21). Yet he appears not to notice the parallels with his own 'thingification' of women.

For both Fanon and Césaire, then "[w]oman is never anything more than the scene of more less rival exchange between men, even when they are competing for mother-earth" (Irigaray, 1981: 105). Fanon deplores the rape of Algerian women, not because of the pain and suffering it causes them, but because of the humiliation it causes their husbands and male relatives (Fanon, 1970a: 182). There is a strange socio-biologistic quality to both Césaire and Fanon's anti-colonial writing, which sits uneasily with their self-professed humanist universalism. Taylor locates their work within a "European tradition of liberating narrative" (Taylor, 1989: 19). It would seem equally, if not more, convincing to locate it within a patriarchal tradition of masculinist heroics, peculiar to no locational culture in particular.

Two feminist researchers based in Guadeloupe have responded to the implied accusation from Fanon and Césaire that women are less nationalist than men. Their study of women's condition in the French Antilles was based largely on interviews and life histories, and strongly defended Martinican and Guadeloupean women against any such accusations (Alibar & Lembeye-Boy, 1981: 19-53). They ask why black men's sexual relationships with white women are not seen as 'whitening the race' in the same way as those of black women with white men (Alibar & Lembeye-Boy, 1981: 50-1). They add that accusations of 'selling out' to the enemy may have the hidden purpose of justifying and excusing continued male aggression and violence against women in the present (ibid.: 51; Jaggar, 1983: 263).

When the freedom of men and women, black and white, rich and poor is seen as irreconcilable and antagonistic, any change comes to be seen as threatening by those in power. On the other hand, those who are excluded from the benefits of society may look for a means to overturn the social order, and may hope one day to be in a position of ascendancy themselves. Marginalised groups themselves are likely to be divided into those who believe reform is possible, those who believe it is impossible, but accept their position, (having internalised their own inferiority) and those who believe it is possible to overhaul the existing social order, transforming it. In Terkel's book, Timuel Black, a teacher, distinguishes those black American intellectuals who "have a devotion to the buried democratic spirit of the country" from those who say "it's never going to work" and advocate opting out: what was earlier termed 'exit' (Terkel, 1992: 202). At the inter-personal level, there is the belief that a post-colonial order will result in displacement of the former oppressors. One white man tells us that: "...the blacks have the future...They're telling us: move over, dude. It's our turn now" (Terkel, 1992: 309).

At the level of collective imagination, immigrants may serve just this function; they may act as an enemy outside, yet conveniently close. Their presence may be perceived by the (supposedly beleaguered) dominant group as a form of revenge by those they have oppressed. This fear of the 'Empire striking back' may explain the ferocity with which deportations, border controls and rejections of requests for visas are currently being implemented in Western Europe, for example.

Writers as diverse as Enoch Powell and Ali Mazrui share this under-standing of immigration as a reversal of the old colonial order. Powell sees a 'systematic (and reversed) colonisation' taking place, with indigenous British people's "towns being changed, their native places turned into foreign lands, and themselves displaced" (Powell, 1968: 202-3). As one recent study on altruistic and selfish behaviour concluded, "[t]here is evidence...that people's expectations of others are based on how they themselves have behaved" (Caporeal *et al.*, 1989: 691). Mazrui has argued that since economic and cultural 'penetration' was forced on the colonies, it is now the turn of the former colonial powers to experience counter-penetration (Mazrui, 1981: 72-3). In *Hand on the Sun*, a novel that depicts the lives of young Asian men in Britain, one character's political position is described as follows:

> He felt that black people had a right to come to this country by virtue of their history, the colonisation of their lands and enslavement of their peoples by Britain, and to live here free of restraint or harassment. (Mahmood, 1983: 128)

As the first two quotations at the start of this chapter suggest, to see liberation in terms of guilt and revenge can act as a self-fulfilling prophecy (Bigo, 1991: 3). If the consequences of change are feared, then there will be resistance to any change whatsoever that may upset the existing order. Something akin to fear appears to operate where immigration is concerned, and can be detected in the quotation from Powell above. The long-term decline of Britain's social structures and political life is often attributed by the Right to a dilution of the national character through immigration. In this context, we can understand Gilroy's comment that in Britain "The symbolic restoration of greatness has been achieved in part through the actual expulsion of blacks and the fragmentation of their households" (Gilroy, 1992: 53). In the authoritarian polity, raising one's own collective status depends on lowering that of others defined as inferior. This cannot restore greatness, however, since there will be no resolution of the problem: the need to find a scapegoat will continue, and eventually there will be a search for 'enemies within' the group defined as native.

The need to find a scapegoat is characteristic of many 'messianic' belief systems. Adherents to the 'faith' are provided with the hope of redemption in some new political or spiritual order. The promise is of more just and equal relations between individuals and groups. In some versions of liberatory discourse, the state plays an important role in levelling opportunities for people, as in some varieties of political Islam (Ayubi, 1991). In others, the state appears as an institution of oppression to be dismantled. In France in recent years the nationalist 'resistance-liberation' discourse has come under attack, and liberation has increasingly come to be conceived as something which might operate at the sub-state or supra-state levels (Jenkins, 1992).

Questions of identity have implications for everyone who lives within the borders, or has family living within the borders, of the European Union. A growing emphasis on local-level, regional identities and sub-state forms of identity can appear radical if these are equated with internal colonies, fighting for their own liberation. But sharp local loyalties may also reinforce or create a reactionary form of parochialism. The normally sanguine *Economist* magazine comments, "Europe has to find a way of knitting together the many tribes within its borders. Working towards a common European citizenship will test how inclusive it is prepared to be" (*Economist*, 15.2.1992). The terms of such a citizenship will particularly affect non-white residents of the European Union.

Myths of revenge are used to legitimise racially exclusivist definitions of who can, or cannot, acquire citizenship, or even remain a citizen. There is a distinct danger in the current crisis of post-colonial identity in Western Europe that immigrants and asylum seekers from the third world can be seen as the scapegoat. Quasi-messianic beliefs that a 'new Europe' could lead to economic revival and cultural grandeur, and provide a way out of the painful long-term recession being experienced, are quite current. The hope is that a European Union could, somehow, plan for the future and bring about an end to unemployment, and a renewal of Western European political and economic life. By trying to gain security through a supra-state form of 'transferred nationalism', individuals seek what can also be achieved through scapegoating, namely "salvation without altering one's conduct" (Orwell, 1984: 312-3). As with any other form of messianic politics, there is the belief that life would be better were it not for the enemy within and without.

**Living Across Boundaries: Profiles**

Many voices speak for a sense of hybridity and post-colonial complexity. Not many are heard. They may be too confusing for the media, which prefers its news in easily digestible bites. Several such voices are listened to in this last section of the chapter. The poet John Figueroa is one such voice. Julia Kristeva is another. We also hear from David Upshal and Salim Muwakkil and from Grace Mera Molisa, a Vanuatan poet. Each has their own way of encapsulating and expressing some of the main concerns of this study.

**John Figueroa** is from Jamaica, and has worked in the Caribbean, in France and in Nigeria. For many years he has lived in the UK, writing, teaching and publishing. He described himself to me as an anti-independentist, not because he favoured colonialism, but because of how independence was engineered in the Caribbean. John recalls that those who opposed the nationalists in Jamaica accused them of making false promises. In particular, separation from Britain, it was promised, would lead to a sort of assimilation by replication, and Jamaica would come to resemble Britain (Figueroa, 1.5.1990). The Lewis model of development aimed to achieve this promised replication through a process of planning and technocratic intervention.

When the right to vote was introduced in Jamaica in the 1930s not even 1 per cent of the population was able to attend high school. The ideology of 'self-help' that was fostered in the run-up to independence obscured the fact that there was no referendum, and no self-determination process involved in the transfer of power to the national authorities. Colonial irresponsibility was thus dressed up as liberation. Moreover, much of the content of the new nationalism was inauthentic. John uses an analogy for this: "We should be eating potatoes, which are food from our part of the world. Instead our people are convinced that rice is more local, more ethnic", even though it is imported and was originally introduced as a staple food during the colonial period (Figueroa, 1.5.1990).

Not many anglophone West Indian scholars have been willing to risk disapproval by looking critically at independence. But there are some signs that this may be changing. In the 1990s, since the collapse of the Iron Curtain, the independence of the former colonies is no longer the sacred cow it once was. It has become possible for scholars openly to express their doubts about the equation between national independence and human liberation in the Caribbean. The theme of 'alternatives to independence' was treated in the 1993 conference of the Society for Caribbean Studies, for example. What might once have been condemned as inauthentic comes to be seen in a different light; like the unhappy potato, John Figueroa's poetry finally comes into its own.  This poem, taken from his collection, *The Chase*, seems a good example of Figueroa's own dictum "...fiction has its truths, which theory dreams not of" (Figueroa, 1982: xiii).

**Cosmopolitan Pig** (for George Lamming)

*Nihil alienum mihi humanum est* or "Man 'top yu 'tupiness"

*The minds of men are similar in their feelings and operations nor can anyone be actuated by any affection, of which all others are not, in some degree, susceptible.*
David Hume *Treatise*, 575-6.

A sculptured poem
Or long-lined church
Clean the line with rhymes
That chime but hardly show,
The poem in another language
From another time
The church at Brou
Geometry in stone
Or at Les Baux
Outcrop of bauxite soil
Before the earth became
Red mother of metal.

Irrelevant to those
Who hate to see
Beyond the dust beneath their feet
Who dare not look within
Lest they find their dreams
That stretch across the earth
Like air
Sympathies covering the globe
More urgent than missiles
Festering with hate.

The stone I break from Carib hills
To make a pot or build a church
Binds me to the Pyramids
And megaliths in Egypt and Peru
The church I love in Brou

Is part of that
Geometry of the sea
That rolls upon itself
In blues and greens
At Tower Isle
Or solidifes in whites
About the Crane

What is Barbados, or Peru
Provence or Rome
But places which Any Man
Can make their home?

Home is too human
Work, making, building
Too much part of us
To be particular.

No sharp stroke shaping stone
No bend of metal or curve
Of well-kept hill
No plotted field of cane
Or wheat or rice;
No garden by the railroad
Or formal as the French
No Ife bronze
Or illuminated sculpture
Is alien to me (Figueroa, 1992).

**Julia Kristeva**'s name is well-known to anyone working on questions of nationalism, psychoanalysis and critical theory.  She describes herself as a cosmopolitan "a rare species, perhaps even on the verge of extinction" (Kristeva, 1993: 15). Although she is not a lay person, Kristeva is now famous enough to write in a semi-autobiographical and informal style. In her most recent book she comments on the 'return to roots' that characterises people's search for identity in the present period in Western Europe (and elsewhere). "The cult of origin is a hate reaction," (Kristeva, 1993: 2). Antagonism is directed outwards at those defined as having different 'roots' from one's own, but also inwards, at oneself, and one's own powerlessness. People "run down their own freedoms whose preservation leaves so much to chance," and "...wounded souls may be seen to turn around and fight their neighbours who are just as hurt as they are" (ibid.: 3). Kristeva speaks in an extraordinarily compassionate way of the pain that causes scapegoating and racism, as well as the pain it provokes.

In *The Colour of Love*, one of the interviewees, Shyama Perera, makes a similar point about roots: "The problem is that when you become politicised you need an enemy, so you look for it outside and completely ignore the enemy within" (Alibhai-Brown & Montague, 1992: 119). Explaining her own position, as a cosmopolitan (literally a citizen of the universe), Kristeva says:

> I maintain that in the contemporary world, shaken up by national fundamentalism on the one hand, and the intensive demands of immigration on the other, the fact of belonging to a set is a matter of choice. (Kristeva, 1993: 15-16)

The criticism could easily be made that belonging is often not a matter of choice at all, since people may be restricted physically and socially. She recognises this, seeing the ability of people to choose which set they will belong to as a measure of their real freedom. The choice that she has been able to make, being relatively free, is cosmopolitanism. She explains, "...this means I have, against origins and starting from them, chosen a transnational or international position situated at the crossing of borders" (ibid.: 16).

Kristeva makes the case for a return to ancient and Christian forms of cosmopolitanism which she recommends updating (ibid.: 17-27). Universality, which is the basis of humanism, supports "a symbolic dignity for the whole of humankind" and is "a rampart against nationalist, regionalist and religious fragmentation" which Kristeva sees all around us (ibid.: 27).

She argues against what she calls the mystical concept of the nation, which claims to be rooted in blood and soil, rather than in law and politics (ibid.: 32), and envisages instead the possibility of a "polyvalent community...a world without foreigners", where everyone could feel at home in the neutral, public sphere (ibid.: 35-6). This is close to the utopian feminist vision of integration with respect for differences. Women, Kristeva argues "...have the luck and the responsibility of being boundary-subjects...more dramatically so than men" (ibid.: 35). They should be especially wary of falling into the trap of mystical, naturalising nationalist beliefs. Her own conclusion is that French political culture, as a model of a contractually based political order, offers hope for the rest of the world (ibid.: 39, 46).

In the end, what Julia Kristeva offers to "contemporary subjects: indomitable individuals; touchy citizens and potential cosmopolitans" is the French nation as a transitional object, akin to "...any child's indispensable fetish" (ibid.: 41-2). Kristeva's work is most interesting, but, as a psychoanalyst discussing politics, it seems that she too has fallen into the trap of equating the developmental psychology of the human being in relation to its parents with that of the body of the French population in relation to the French state.

**David Upshal** has the distinction of appearing twice in, *The Colour of Love*: once as a 'mixed race' person, and in the last section of the book, entitled 'An Eye to the Future'. The description of Upshal in this book informs us that he works for the BBC; that his mother was British and his father Nigerian; that he studied at Oxford and has worked as a freelance journalist. He informs us that he was raised by his white grandmother, and claims that this experience has given him an advantage over other Black people in understanding white racism. As he points out, "Malcolm X talks about this in his autobiography. He was adopted by a white family and went to school with white children" (Alibhai-Brown & Montague, 1992: 235). Malcolm X also claimed to have a deeper understanding of white racism for this reason. What is important in David Upshal's account is his ability to make the most of what others might regard as an impossible situation. He is clear that the difficulties he faces are not internally created, but externally imposed.

> What I'd say is strangest about being mixed race is to have been brought up so white and feel so Black. I pin that entirely on the way society treats non-white people. I don't believe you have a choice. I am half Black and half white, my upbringing was all white. Now if I go into a room full of white people and say 'Hi everyone, I'm white', they'll piss themselves laughing. If I go into a room full of Black people and say, 'Hi everybody, I'm Black', they'll say 'Come on in' and 'Yes, of course you are' I find that absolutely peculiar. (ibid.: 243-4)

Upshal does not accept this, and says that, although he does not feel accepted, the white society is "stuck with me and people like me, I'm not going anywhere and there's more of me every day" (ibid.: 234). Once it is recognised that most people are in fact 'mixed' in their ancestry and parentage, then the notion of mixed race will cease to make sense (Jardel, 1984: 227). As Yasmin Alibhai-Brown and Anne Montague observe, "[i]f we accept that there is no such thing as a hierarchical racial division, the very notion of mixed race becomes a racist concept" (Alibhai-Brown & Montague, 1992: 3). What comes through from David Upshal's account is his lack of illusions: recognising the depth and extent of white racism and prejudice, he nonetheless claims both sides of his upbringing: "I'm as proud of Oliver Cromwell being in my heritage as I am of Malcolm X or Shaka the Zulu...They're of equal importance, so that's where the balance lies for me. I've never disliked or hated what I am" (ibid.: 245).

It is this lack of self-hatred, and his understanding of others, that enables David Upshal to conclude that mixed marriages and relationships must be a matter for individuals. Although he himself expects that a black woman would understand him better than a white woman, he concludes, "I'm not going to reject anyone who's going to be good for me because of their colour" (ibid.: 281). As Mark Mathabane, a South African interviewed in Terkel's book asks, how can anyone who was at one time against apartheid and the Mixed Marriages Act, for example, also "say that a black person cannot befriend or marry a white person in the name of black pride" (Terkel, 1992: 324)? In finding the strength in himself to keep his self-respect, Upshal manages to achieve a kind of freedom from the categories that others may use to try and exclude or tie him down.

**Salim Muwakkil** is a journalist interviewed by Terkel in Chicago in 1990. He changed his name when he was stationed near maternal relatives who told him about his forebears, including a Guinea Sultan. He has been to Africa several times but acknowledges, "I know that I am peculiarly American. There is no getting around that" (Terkel, 1992: 170). He is against segregationist ideologies, seeing them as particularly dangerous for black Americans. "The Ku Klux Klan and the Aryan-movement people like Farrakhan because he's saying the same thing, essentially" (ibid.: 168). Dr Kenneth B. Clark, an Afro-American psychologist interviewed in the same volume, concurs: "I suspect the white supremacists would love the [black] separatists. My sense of irony might lead me to believe that black-separatist movements were anchored by white supremacists" (ibid.: 338).

But Salim Muwakkil's real concerns are with the tendency of the black American middle class to cut off from the majority of poor blacks, who suffer from poverty and from chronically high levels of homicide and drug abuse (ibid.: 168). While the white community has a responsibility and is steeped in denial of its own racism, the black middle class too has a responsibility to "connect with the underclass, who are drifting, falling off the edge into the abyss" (ibid.: 169).

Muwakkil formerly wrote for the *Nation of Islam* newspaper and was a member of the Black Panther Party. He was sceptical about "what I call its genetic theory, of black supremacy, of all that mysticism. If you're serious about human equality, freedom, you must reject any doctrine that condemns people because of their genetic makeup. Black people especially should be wary of any such doctrine" (ibid.: 167). Yet since he recognises that "black people needed some serious therapy to get us out of the situation we were in", and needed hope of "some kind of transformation", he suppressed his doubts about such beliefs for some time (ibid.). However, Salim eventually left these groups, as he found that they underestimated people's real resourcefulness in the face of oppression. What he calls "black people's ingenious adaptations to the situation" was dismissed by the "pseudo-Islamic" *Nation of Islam* as "a slave response" (ibid.).

Caryl Phillips, in his novel *Crossing the River*, describes "this really strange force called love", which created human bonds and possibilities for understanding between people who found themselves in the most unequal relationship possible: that between slaves and their 'owners'. Fromm describes non-possessive adult love as "...the spontaneous affirmation of others, as the union of the individual with others on the basis of the preservation of the individual self" (Fromm, 1960: 225). Once again, this expresses the ideal of integration without coercion or a 'melting' into the collective. It is the kind of love that gives one the capacity to act, as Muwakkil asks the black middle class to do.

**Grace Mera Molisa** is a leading Ni-Vanuatu political figure. Her work and its significance have been presented in detail by Margaret Jolly in a recent book chapter (Jolly, 1991). She is a powerful voice in favour of equating liberation with human liberation in general, rather than with 'national' liberation, which she sees as leading only to the freedom of men in the Vanuatan context. "Just as the tentacles of the colonisers are difficult to disentangle, so are those of men over women" (Jolly, 1991: 59). She argues, as many feminists have, that women's work is central to all life, to the reproduction of human society as well as the reproduction of human beings (ibid.: 65).

What is interesting in Grace Mera Molisa's outlook is that she sees both colonisation and decolonisation, in the form it took in Vanuatu, as mainly a male undertaking, "European imperial expansion and the conquest of other countries was a masculinist project" (ibid.: 66). She also argues that "...the politics of decolonisation and the construction of the nation of Vanuatu in resistance to whites was primarily a male enterprise" (ibid.: 71). Women were largely left out, having fewer opportunities for education or participation in politics and public affairs. Part of her poem presented in Jolly's article is reproduced here as well, and expresses well her critique of the notion of freedom as conceived in her country:

> Clear
> articulations
> of support
> for
> freedom fighters
> in East Timor
> West Papua
> French Polynesia
> and Kanaky
> Vanuatu
> Womenfolk
> half
> the population
> remain
> colonised by
> the Free men
> of Vanuatu (In Jolly, 1991: 63-4)

## Conclusion

It seems better to leave these five characters to speak for themselves rather than to identify what they exemplify about the discussion in the rest of this chapter. There are some parallels between their words, their views and the problematic themes that have been raised in this book. Some are obvious and some not so obvious, but it is hoped that this conclusion is a new departure and an expression of hope concerning the possibility of conceptualising a rounded and balanced form of liberation for human beings. Its implementation will always come up against the obstacles of states, sovereignty, prejudice and discrimination, but the conceptualisation matters nonetheless. Without it, there is no possibility of arguing against intolerance and exclusion with any real conviction. The consequences of these weaknesses may be deplored but at the same time there will be a tendency to sigh and say, "Oh well! That's life!" In exploring some unusual examples of post-colonial relations we have tried to challenge this sigh, which says that inequality internationally is inevitable and somehow normal.

Exclusivist and chauvinistic political ideas can be traced to a fear of vulnerability, and a dislike of the emotional insecurity that comes from tenderness, openness, change and adult love (Jagger, 1983: 127; Fromm, 1960; Memmi, 1991: 29). What we sometimes regard as the 'real world', as it is presented to us through television, newspapers and research, seems fraught with the forces of 'ethnic conflict', 'racial' attacks and the 'war of the sexes'. Yet these forces, which seem so real, may themselves be myths constructed out of fears and fantasies (Orwell, 1984: 313).

Sometimes 'idealists' have a better grasp of real, experienced problems in daily life than those who consider themselves hard-nosed and pragmatic. The 'realist' approach is often also a communitarian approach, based on "...a cultural analysis which accords metaphysical pre-existence to discursive unities such as races, peoples or to ethnic groups" (Cambridge & Feuchtwang, 1990: viii). This is its weakness analytically, but its strength politically, as it makes it appealing to scholars and to isolated and worried people generally. The communitarian approach tends to assume that people who 'come from the same communities' have more in common with each other in most significant respects, including politically, than they do with people from outside their 'community'. There simply is no clear evidence for this; indeed, since each community (however defined) will be split by differences of age, class, gender and possibly religion as well, cross-cutting connections between members of different communities are also very likely. As Bikhu Parekh has observed:

> gaps in mutual understanding obtain between classes, generations, religions and races (*sic*). Indeed, each individual is a world unto him or her self and carries areas of darkness which remain opaque not only to others but sometimes even to him or her self. (Parekh, 1994: 103)

It can be reasserted that what holds for the individual is likely to be even more true for communities. "People and actions do move in multiple directions at once", and any attempt to analyse human behaviour by linear models "will create dichotomies...disorientation and confusion in places where none exist" (Brown, 1989: 929). Those people who have been depicted in profile in the last section of this chapter all find themselves "at the intersection of two systems of signification" (Hargreaves, 1991: 118). But their disorientation, when they express it, seems to be overridden by their capacity for integration; for assimilation as an active rather than a passive process. For this reason, rather than in order to generalise about their experience as a post-colonial one, they have provided the conclusion(s) to this study.

# Notes

1. The words to the chorus of this song by Samantha Laval "L'Avenir est au Métissage" are as follows:

> Mon coeur a bu tous les sangs coulés
> Je suis la reine des sange mêlés
> Ma peau une jolie aquarelle
> C'est moi la mome, la mome arc-en-ciel
> L'avenir est au métissage
> Le racisme sera son hôtage
> Conservateur devenez donc plus sage
> Pour que ne tourne pas l'orage.

# Document and Cartoons

## Document 1

N.° 2262.

# DÉCRET

## DE LA

## CONVENTION NATIONALE,

282.ᵉ Envoi

Du 16 Pluviôse   an second de la République Française,
une & indivisible.

*Qui abolit l'Esclavage des Nègres dans les Colonies.*

LA CONVENTION NATIONALE déclare que l'esclavage
des Nègres dans toutes les Colonies est aboli ; en consequence elle décrète que tous les hommes, sans distinction de couleur, domiciliés dans les colonies, sont
citoyens Français, et jouiront de tous les droits assurés
par la constitution.

  Elle renvoie au comité de salut public, pour lui faire
incessamment un rapport sur les mesures à prendre pour
assurer l'exécution du présent décret.

*Visé par les l'inspecteurs.* Signé AUGER, CORDIER, & S. E. MONNEL.

  Collationné à l'original, par nous président & secrétaires
  de la Convention nationale. A Paris, le 22 Germinal,
  an second de la République une & indivisible. *Signé*
  AMAR , *président ;* A. M. BAUDOT, MONNOT ,
  CH. POTTIER & PEYSSARD, *secrétaires.*

AU NOM DE LA REPUBLIQUE , le Conseil

**Décret de la Convention Nationale.** Collection Bureau du Patrimoine.

**Cartoon 1**

**Source:** *Le Monde,* 27.2.1991

# Cartoon 2

**Source:** *Le Monde*, **16.12.1988**

## Cartoon 3

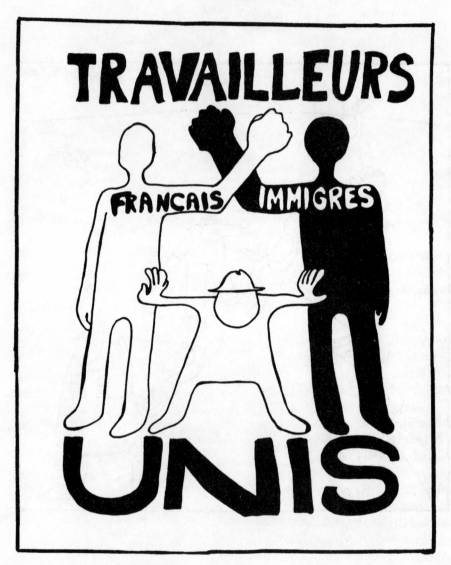

**Source:** *Le Monde*, 7.5.1988

# Bibliography

**Books, Reports and Articles**

Ait-Ahmed, H. 1980. *L'Afro-Fascisme Les Droits de l'Homme dans la Charte et la Pratique de l'Organisation de l'Unité Africaine*. L'Harmattan (Paris).

Akehurst, M. 1984. *A Modern Introduction to International Law*. 5th edition. George Allen & Unwin (London).

Albertini, J-M. 1965. "La Fausse Croissance". *Economie et Humanisme*. No. 163: 16-27.

Aldrich, R. & J. Connell. 1992. *France's Overseas Frontier: Départements et Territoires d'Outre-Mer*. Cambridge University Press (Cambridge).

Alibar, F. & P. Lembeye-Boy. 1981. *Le Couteau Seul Se kouto sel...La condition féminine aux Antilles*. Vol. 1, Editions Caribéennes (Paris).

Alibhai-Brown, Y. & A. Montague. 1992. *The Colour of Love: Mixed Race Relationships*. Virago (London).

Allen, M. 1979. "Sugar and Survival: the retention of economic power by white elites in Barbados and Martinique" in M. Cross & A. Marks (eds). *Peasants, Plantations and Rural Communities in the Caribbean*. Department of Sociology, University of Surrey: 220-62.

Amadiume, I. 1987. *Male Daughters, Female Husbands*. Zed Press (London-New Jersey).

Anderson, B. 1983. *Imagined Communities: Reflections on the Origin and Spread of Nationalism*. Verso (London).

Andrew, C. 1984. "Francophonie: a substitute Commonwealth" in H. Bull & A. Watson (eds). op. cit.: 335-44.

Anselin, A., 1994. "Les Antillais en France" in R. Burton & F. Reno (eds). op. cit.: 213-21.

Anthias, F. & N. Yuval-Davis (eds). 1991. *Woman Nation State*. Macmillan (London).

Anthias, F. & N. Yuval-Davis. 1992. *Racialized boundaries: Race, nation and gender, colour and class and the anti-racist struggle*. Routledge (London-New York).

Appleyard, R. (ed.) 1989. *The Impact of International Migration on Developing Countries*. OECD (Paris).

Armet, A. 1982. "Guadeloupe et Martinique: des sociétés krazé?" *Présence Africaine*. Nos. 121-2: 11-19.

Aron, R. 1960. *France Steadfast and Changing*. Harvard University Press (Cambridge, Mass.).

Aron, R. 1966. *Peace and War, a Theory of International Relations*. Weidenfeld & Nicolson (London).

Asad, T. (ed.) 1973. *Anthropology and the Colonial Encounter*. Ithaca Press (Ithaca-London).

Attfield , R. & B. Wilkins (eds). 1992. *International Justice and the Third World*. Routledge (London-New York).

Audige, M. 1985. "La desserte des bourgs isolés en Guyane Française". *Les Dossiers de 'Outre-Mer*. No. 82: 64-7.

Ayubi, N. 1991. *Political Islam: Religion and Politics in the Arab World*. Routledge (London).

Baca Zinn, M. 1989. "Family, Race and Poverty in the Eighties". *Signs*. Vol. 14. No. 4, Summer: 856-74.

Balibar, E. 1991. "Interview with Etienne Balibar" in M. Silverman (ed.) op. cit.: 71-83.

Barry, D. & R. Goodin (eds). 1992. *Free Movement: Ethical Issues in the transnational migration of people and of money*. Harvester Wheatsheaf (Hemel Hempstead).

Bayart, J-F. 1993. *The State in Africa: the Politics of the Belly*. Longman (London).

Beaujeu-Garnier, J. 1976. *La Population Française*. Librairie Armand Colin (Paris).

Belbahri, A. 1967. *Immigration et Situations Post-Coloniales*. L'Harmattan (Paris).

Belorgey, J-M. 1985. "Les Hmongs en Guyane". *Les Dossiers de l'Outre Mer*. No. 81, 4th quarter: 76-81.

Benoist, J. 1974. "Perspectives pour une connaissance des sociétés contemporaines des Mascareignes et des Seychelles". *Annuaire des Pays de l'Océan Indien*. Vol. I, (223-33).

Benoist, J. 1980. "Antilles et Mascareignes Contraintes et Variations des Archipels Créoles". *Espace Créole*. No. 4: 3-14.

Berger, J.(with J. Mohr) 1975. *A Seventh Man: The story of a migrant worker in Europe*. Penguin (Harmondsworth).

Berkhofer, R.F. 1978. *The White Man's India: Images of the American Indian from Columbus to the Present*. Vintage Press (New York).

Betts, R. 1961. *Assimilation and Association in French Colonial Theory 1890-1914*. Colombia University Press (New York-London).

Bevan, V. 1986. *The Development of British Immigration Law*. Croom Helm (London-Sydney-Dover, USA).

Bigo, D. 1991. "Menaces du Sud: Images et Réalité". *Cultures et Conflits*. No. 2, Spring: 2-8.

Bissol, B. 1980. *Aspects of the Link between France and the so-called 'French West Indies'*, paper presented to the annual conference of the Society of Caribbean Studies.

Blérald, A. 1984. "La Vie Politique et la Gestion du Statut aux Antilles Depuis Le 10 Mai 1981". *Archipelago*. No. 5: 68-83.

Bonilla, F. & R. Campos. 1981. "A Wealth of Poor: Puerto Ricans in the New Economic Order". *Daedelus*. Vol. 110, No. 2, Spring: 133-176.

Bottomley, G., M. De Lepervanche, & J. Martin (eds). 1991. *Intersexions: Gender/Class/Culture/Ethnicity*. Allen & Unwin (London-Sydney).

Boucher, J., D. Landis & K. Clark (eds). 1987. *Ethnic Conflict: International Perspectives*. Sage (London-New Delhi).

Bourgarel, S. 1990. "Les réfugiés surinamiens en Guyane". *Etudes Créoles*. Vol. 13. No. 2: 43-50.

Brandell, I. 1981. *Les Rapports Franco-Algériens Depuis 1962 Du Pétrole et des Hommes*. L'Harmattan (Paris).

Brasset, M. 1987. "L'exploitation de la forêt Guyanaise: difficultés et espoirs". *Antiane*. No. 4, September: 3-5.

Bréchon, P. 1991. "Le Front National en France: une montée inquiétante". *Economie et Humanisme*. No. 317, April-June: 61-78.

Brewer, R. 1988. "Black Women in Poverty". *Signs*. Vol. 13. No. 2, Winter: 331-9.

Brossat, A. & D. Maragnes. 1981. *Les Antilles dans l'Impasse?* Editions Caribéennes (Paris).

Brown, C. 1992. "Marxism and the transnational migration of people: Ethical issues" in B. Barry & R. Goodin (eds). op cit.: 127-44.

Brown, E.B. 1989. "African-American Women's Quilting". *Signs.* Vol. 14. No. 4, Summer: 921-9.

Brunschwig, H. 1964. *French Colonialism 1871-1914: Myths and Realities.* Pall Mall Press (London).

Buenor Hadjor, K. 1992. *Dictionary of Third World Terms.* Penguin (London).

Bull, H. & A. Watson (eds). 1984. *The Expansion of International Society.* Clarendon Press (Oxford).

Bullock, A. & O. Stallybrass (eds). 1977. *The Fontana Dictionary of Modern Thought.* Fontana (London).

Burac, M. 1994. "Les Antilles Françaises et le Reste de la Caraïbe" in R. Burton & F. Reno (eds). op. cit.: 223-54.

Burton, R. 1982. *Comment Peut-on Etre Martiniquais?* University of London Institute of Commonwealth Studies Collected Seminar Papers No. 29.

Burton, R. 1993. "*Maman-France Doudou*: Family Images in French West Indian Colonial Discourse". *Diacritics.* Vol. 23. No. 3, Fall: 69-90.

Burton, R. 1994. "Ki moun nou yé? La Question de la Différence dans la Pensée Antillaise Contemporaine" in R. Burton & F. Reno (eds) op. cit.: 123-51.

Burton, R. & F. Reno (eds). 1994. *Les Antilles-Guyane au Rendez-Vous de l'Europe: Le Grand Tournant?* Economica (Paris).

Calmont, R. 1981. "La Communauté Guyanaise en France". *Equinoxe Revue Guyanaise d'Histoire et de Géographie.* No. 14, October-December: 21-43.

Cambridge, A.X. & S. Feuchtwang (eds). 1990. *Antiracist Strategies.* Gower (Aldershot-Vermont).

Caporeal, L.R., R.M. Danes, J.M. Orbell & A.J.C. Van de Kragt. 1989. "Selfishness examined: co-operation in the absence of egotistic incentives". *Behavioural and Brain Sciences.* No. 12: 683-739.

Carchedi, G. 1983. *Problems in Class Analysis.* Routledge & Kegan Paul (London).

Carens, J. 1992. "Migration and morality: a liberal egalitarian perspective" in B. Barry & R. Goodin (eds). op. cit.: 25-47.

Carew, J. 1988. "Columbus and the origins of racism in the Americas, part 2". *Race and Class.* Vol. 30. No. 1, July-September: 33-57.

Castles, G. 1970. "Racial Prejudice in France". *Race Today*. Vol. 2. No. 1: 10-13.

Castles, S. *et al.* 1984. *Here for Good: Western Europe's New Ethnic Minorities*. Pluto Press (London).

Castles, S. & G. Kosack. 1973. *Immigrant Workers and Class Structure in Western Europe*. I.R.R/OUP (London).

Castles, S. & M.J. Miller 1993. *The Age of Migration: International Population Movements in the Modern World*. Macmillan (London).

Castor, E. & G. Othily. 1984. *La Guyane Les Grands Problèmes, les Solutions Possibles.* Editions Caribéennes, Paris.

Cels, J. 1989. "Refugee Policies of Western European Governments: a Human Rights Challenge on our Doorsteps" in D. Hill (ed.) op. cit.: 164-79.

Césaire, A. 1956. *Lettre à Maurice Thorès*. 24 October. Présence Africaine. (Paris).

Césaire, A. 1972. *Discourse on Colonialism*. Monthly Review Press (London-New York).

Chalifoux, J-J. 1990. "Créoles et Amérindiens en Guyane: la représentation des Amérindiens, perspectives du lycée". *Etudes Créoles*. Vol. 13. No. 2: 33-42.

Chane-Kune, S. 1991. "Le Chaudron Réunionnais". *Hérodote*. No. 62, September: 91-100.

Chane-Tune, R. 1987. "Des niveaux de vie assez élevés". *Les Dossiers de l'Outre-Mer*. No. 83: 103-10.

Charlton, Roger, R. Kaye & L. Farley. 1988. *Policing Refugees and Exiles: British Policy and Practice*. 12-14 April, Plymouth Polytechnic.

Cherubini, B. 1985. "L'Evolution des Rélations Inter-Ethniques et la Fermeture de la Société Guyanaise". *Les Dossiers de l'Outre-Mer*, No. 81: 95-103.

Cobban, A. 1945. *National Self-Determination*. Oxford University Press (London-New York-Toronto).

Cohen, R. 1987. *The New Helots: Migrants in the International Division of Labour*. Gower (Aldershot).

Cohen, R. 1989. "Citizens, Denizens and Helots: The Politics of International Migration Flows in the Post-War World". *Hitotsubashi Journal of Social Studies*. Vol. 21, No. 1, August: 153-65.

Collins, P. 1990. *Black Feminist Thought: Knowledge, Consciousness and the Politics of Empowerment*. Unwin Hyman (Boston-London-Sydney).

Comitas, L. & D. Lowenthal (eds). 1973. *Slaves, Free Men, Citizens*. Anchor Books-Doubleday (New York).

Constant, F. 1988. *La Retraite aux Flambeaux Société et Politique en Martinique*. Editions Caribéennes (Paris).

Constant, F. 1992. "Alternative Forms of Decolonisation in the East Caribbean: The Comparative Politics of the Non-Sovereign Islands" in H. Hintjens & M.M. Newitt (eds). op. cit.: 51-63.

Crowley, D. 1973. "Cultural Assimilation in a Multiracial Society" in L. Comitas & D. Lowenthal (eds). op. cit.: 277-85.

Dagenais, H. 1984. "L'Apport Méconnu des Femmes à la Vie Economique et Sociale aux Antilles: Le Cas de la Guadeloupe". *Anthropologie et Societés*. Vol. 8, No. 2: 179-87.

Daly, M. 1984. *Pure Lust Elemental Feminist Philosophy*. Women's Press (London).

Daniel, J. 1984. "Pouvoir Central, Pouvoir Local: Essai de Sociologie de l'Administration à la Martinique". *Revue Française d'Administration Publique*. No. 31, July-September: 71-88.

Daniel, J. n.d. *La Science Politique Antillaise entre Holisme, Individualisme Méthodologique et Hétérodoxie*. CRPLC mimeo. Université Antilles-Guyane Schoelcher (Martinique). c. 1989.

Davidson, B. 1992. *The Black Man's Burden: Africa and the Curse of the Nation State*. James Currey (London).

De Baleine, P. 1980, *Les Danseuses de la France*. Plon (Paris).

Debré, M. 1972. *Une Certaine Idée de la France*. Fayard (Paris).

Debré, M. 1976. *Une Politique pour la Réunion*. Plon (Paris).

Defos Du Rau, J. 1968. "La Réunion". *Revue Française d'Etudes Politiques Africaines*. No. 33: 58-79.

De Lépine, E. 1990. "Et si De Lépine avait raison?". *Antilla*. No. 375. 23-29 March: 1-11.

Deschamps, H. 1968. *Madagascar*. Que Sais-Je No. 529. Presses Universitaires Françaises (Paris).

Dietz, J.L. 1983. *An Economic History of Puerto Rico: Institutional Change and Capitalist Development*. Princeton University Press (Princeton).

Dijoud, P. 1976. "La France et les Immigrés". *Défense Nationale*. Vol. 32. No. 5, May: 11-17.

Donald, J. & A. Rattansi (eds). 1992. *'Race', Culture and Difference*. Sage with Open University (London).

Dowty, A. 1986. "Emigration and Expulsion in the Third World". *Third World Quarterly*. Vol. 8. No. 1, January: 151-76.

Dowty, A. 1987. *The Contemporary Assault on Freedom of Movement*. Yale University Press (London-New Haven).

Drekonja-Kornat, G. 1984. "On the Edge of Civilisation: Paris in the Jungle". *Caribbean Review*. Vol. XIII. No. 2: 26-7.

Drower, G. 1992. *Britain's Dependent Territories: A Fistful of Islands.* Dartmouth (Aldershot).

Dummett, A. 1992. "The transnational migration of people seen from within a natural law tradition" in B. Barry & R. Goodin (eds). op. cit.: 169-80.

Dummett, A. 1994. "Objectives for Future European Community Policy" in S. Spencer (ed.) op. cit.: 137-58.

Dummett, A. & A. Nicol. 1990. *Subjects, Citizens, Aliens and Others: Nationality and Immigration Law.* Weidenfeld & Nicolson (London).

Dupon, J-F. 1974. *Contraintes Insulaires et Fait Colonial aux Mascareignes et aux Seychelles.* Doctorat d'Etat (thesis) in Geography. Université Aix-Marseille III. Honoré Champion (Paris).

Dupont, L. 1988. *Les Départements Français d'Amérique, Guadeloupe, Guyana, Martinique face aux schémas d'intégration de la Caraïbe et de l'Amérique Latine.* L'Harmattan (Paris).

Eluther, J-P. 1981. "L'Evolution des Prestations Familiales dans les DOM". *Revue Juridique et Politique de la République Française.* Vol. 30. No. 3, July-September: 783-95.

Emerson, R. 1960. *From Empire to Nation: the Rise to Self-Assertion of Asian and African Peoples.* Harvard University Press (Cambridge, Mass.).

Eriksen, T.H. 1993. *Ethnicity and Nationalism: Anthropological Perspectives.* Pluto Press (London).

Etcherelli, C. 1967. *Elise ou la Vraie Vie.* Folio (Paris).

Etienne, B. 1989. *La France et l'Islam.* Hachette (Paris).

Faber, M. 1984. "Island Micro States: Problems of Viability". *The Round Table.* No. 292: 372-76.

Fanon, F. 1963. *The Wretched of the Earth.* Penguin (Harmondsworth).

Fanon, F. 1968. *Black Skin, White Masks.* Macgibbon & Kee (London).

Fanon, F. 1970a. *Les Damnés de la Terre.* François Maspero (Paris).

Fanon, F. 1970b. *A Dying Colonialism.* Pelican (Harmondsworth).

Fawzi El-Solh, C. 1993. "Be True to Your Culture: Gender tensions among Somali Muslims in Britain". *Immigrants and Minorities.* Vol. 12. No. 1, March: 21-47.

Festy, P. & C. Hamon. 1983. *Croissance et Révolution Démographique à la Réunion.* Travaux et Documents INED. No. 100. Presses Universitaires Françaises (Paris).

Feuchtwang, S. 1990. "Introduction" in A. Cambridge & S. Feuchtwang (eds). *Antiracist Strategies*, Gower (Aldershot-Vermont).

FIDH - Federation Internationale des Ligues des Droits de l'Homme. English release monthly newsletter. FIDH (London).

Figueroa, J. (ed.). 1982. *An Anthology of African and Caribbean Writing in English*. Heinemann, with Open University Press (Oxford-Kingston).

Figueroa, J. 1992. *The Chase*. Pepal Tree Press (Leeds).

Findlay, A. 1994. "An Economic Audit of Contemporary Immigration" in S. Spencer (ed.) op. cit.: 159-201.

Finn, G. 1989. "Natural Woman, Cultural Man: the Anthropology of Male Hysteria and Father Right". *Review of Feminist Research*. (Montreal). Vol. 18. No. 3: 24-7.

Freeman, G. 1987. "Caribbean Migration to Britain and France: from Assimilation to Selection" in B. Levine (ed.) op. cit.: 185-203.

Freeman, G.P. 1986. "Migration and the Political Economy of the Welfare State". *The Annals of the American Academy of Political and Social Science*. Vol. 485: 51-63.

Fromm, E. 1960. *The Fear of Freedom*. Routledge & Kegan Paul (London).

Galbraith, J.K. 1979. *The Nature of Mass Poverty*. Penguin (Harmondsworth).

Gardinier, D.E. 1982. "Decolonisation in French, Belgian and Portuguese Africa: a Bibliographic Essay" in P. Gifford & W.R. Louis (eds). *The Transfer of Power in Africa Decolonisation 1940-1960*. Yale University Press (London-New Haven).

Gaspard, F. & C. Servan-Schreiber. 1985. *La Fin des Immigrés*. Editions du Seuil (Paris).

Gautier, A. 1985. *Les Soeurs de la Solitude. La condition féminine dans l'esclavage aux Antilles du XVIème au XIXème siècle*. Editions Caribéennes (Paris).

Gautier, A. 1994. "Guadeloupéennes et Martiniquaises" in R. Burton & F. Reno (eds). op. cit.: 153-75.

Gellner, E. 1964. *Thought and Change*. Weidenfeld & Nicolson (London).

Gerbeau, H. 1992. "France: La Réunion". *Universalie*. Encyclopaedia Universalis (Paris): 264-7.

Gibran, K. 1991. *A Treasury of Kahlil Gibran*. Mandarin (London).

Gilroy, P. 1987. *There Ain't No Black in the Union Jack. The Cultural Politics of Race and Nation*. Hutchinson (London-Johannesburg-New Zealand).

Gilroy, P. 1992. "The end of antiracism" in J. Donal (ed.). *'Race', Culture and Difference*. Sage, with Open University. Press (London).

Girondin, K. 1986. "Les Tentatives de Peuplement de la Guyane de 1848 à 1918". *Equinoxe*. Vol. 10. No. 21, January: 1-37.

Goodin, R. 1992. "If people were money" in B. Barry & R. Goodin (eds). op. cit.: 6-22.

Gorgeon, C. 1985. "L'Immigration en Guyane". *Les Dossiers de l'Outre-Mer*. No. 81: 68-75.

Gosling, D. 1991. "Obligations of Affluent Nations to the Poor in the Situation of 'Radical Inequality'" in W. Twining (ed.) op. cit.: 49-70.

Gourdon, H. 1985. "Le Système Politique d'une Sócieté de Plantation? Le Cas Guadaloupéen". *Annales des Pays d'Amérique Centrale et des Caraïbes*. (Aix-Marseille III). No. 5: 93-106.

Grosser, A. 1984. *Affaires Extérieures: La Politique de la France 1944-1984*. Flammarion (Paris).

Grumet, M. 1989. "Knots: Feminist Theorizing in the Middle". *Review of Feminist Research*.(Montreal) Vol. 18. No. 3: 13-18.

Guillaumin, C. 1991. "'Race' and discourse" in M. Silverman (ed.) op. cit.: 5-13.

Guillebaud, J-C. 1976. *Les confettis de l'Empire*. Editions du Seuil (Paris).

Gurtov, M. 1991. "Open Borders: A Global-Humanist Approach to the Refugee Crisis". *World Development*. Vol. 19.No. 5: 485-96.

Hall, S. 1992. "Our Mongrel Selves". *New Statesman and Society*. Vol. 5, No. 207, 15 June: 6-8.

Hargreaves, A. 1990. Report on the Conference "L'Emigration Maghrebine en France" in Oran. *Modern and Contemporary France*. No. 40: 38-41.

Hargreaves, A. 1991. "Writing for others: authorship and authenticity in immigrant literature" in M. Silverman (ed.) op. cit.: 111-119.

Hargreaves, J. (ed.) 1969. *France and West Africa: An Anthology of Historical Documents*. Macmillan (London).

Harrison, C. 1983. "French Attitudes to Empire and the Algerian War". *African Affairs*. Vol. 82. No. 326, January: 75-95.

Hart, R. 1972. "Jamaica and Self-Determination 1660-1970". *Race*. Vol. XIII. No. 3: 271-97.

Hartz, L. (ed.). 1964. *The Founding of New Societies*. Harcourt, Brace & World (New York).

Hermann, C. 1981. "Women's space and time" in E. Marks & I. de Courtivron (eds). op. cit.: 168-73.

Hermant, D. & D. Bigo. 1986. "La Violence Politique en Guadeloupe-Martinique". *Etudes Polémologiques*. Vol. 37: 115-28.

Hill, D. (ed.). 1989. *Human Rights and Foreign Policy: Principles and Practice*. Macmillan (London).

Himberg, H.A. 1978. *Confronting Dependency: French-Algerian Relations in the Post-Colonial World*. PhD. Political Science, University of New York.

Hintjens, H. 1988. *Reunion, France and the EEC: the State in North-South Relations*, PhD. in Politics, University of Aberdeen.

Hintjens, H. 1989. "Reunion Island 'Closing Ranks': the Reassertion of Creole Identity". *Africa Contemporary Record*. Vol. XXI (1988-89): B439-45.

Hintjens, H. 1990. "Assimilation, Integration, Citizenship and Decolonisation". *Politics*. Vol. 10. No. 2: 15-19.

Hintjens, H. 1991a. "France in the Caribbean" in P. Sutton (ed.) *Europe and the Caribbean*. Macmillan (London): 37-69.

Hintjens, H. 1991b. "Regional Reform in the French Periphery: the Overseas Departments of Reunion, Martinique and Guadeloupe". *Regional Politics & Policy*. Vol. 1. No. 1: 51-73.

Hintjens, H. 1992a. "France's Love Children? The French Overseas Departments" in H.Hintjens & M. Newitt (eds). *The Political Economy of Small, Tropical Islands*. Exeter University Press (Exeter): 64-75.

Hintjens, H. 1992b. "Immigration and Citizenship Debates: Reflections on Ten Common Themes". *International Migration-Migrations Internationales*. Vol. XXX. No.1, March: 5-17.

Hintjens, H. 1994. "Evolution Politique et Constitutionnelle des Antilles Françaises Depuis 1946" in R. Burton & F. Reno (eds). op. cit.: 19-35.

Hoffman, S. 1965. *The State of War: Essays on the Theory and Practice of International Relations*. Pall Mall Press (London).

Holland, R. 1991. "Ends of Empire: Some Reflections on the Metropole". *The Round Table*. Vol. 317: 81-8.

Holmes, C. 1988. *John Bull's Island: Immigration and British Society 1871-1971*. Macmillan (London).

Houbert, J. 1980. "Décolonisation et Dépendance: Maurice et Réunion". *Annuaire des Pays de l'Océan Indien*. Vol. VIII: 103-23.

Houbert, J. 1986. "Reunion I: French Decolonisation in the Mascarenes". *Journal of Commonwealth and Comparative Politics*. Vol. XVII, No. 3, November: 145-71.

Houbert, J. 1992. "The Mascareignes, the Seychelles and the Chagos, Islands with a French Connection: Security in a Decolonised Indian Ocean" in H. Hintjens & M.M. Newitt (eds). 1992a. op. cit.: 93-111.

Houdaille, J. 1981. "Le Métissage dans les Anciennes Colonies Françaises". *Population*. INED. No. 2: 267-86.

House of Commons Home Affairs Committee 1986. *Bangladeshis in Britain*. Race Relations and Immigration Sub-Committee, Session 1985-89. Minutes of Evidence. Vol. XXVII. Paper No. 210.

House of Lords. 1992. *Community Policy on Migration*. Select Committee on the European Communities. Session 1992-93. 10th Report.

ILO. 1964. *Declaration concerning the policy of 'Apartheid' of the Republic of South Africa and ILO programme for the elimination of 'apartheid' in labour matters in the Republic of South Africa.* ILO (Geneva).

INSEE. 1988a. *Femmes en Chiffres Réunion.* Service Régional de l'INSEE (Sainte-Clothilde, Reunion).

INSEE. 1988b. *Femmes en Chiffres Guadeloupe.* Service Régional de l'INSEE (Basse Terre, Guadeloupe).

INSEE. 1988c. *Femmes en Chiffres Martinique.* Service Régional de l'INSEE (Schoelcher, Martinique).

INSEE. 1991. *Tableaux Economique de la Réunion.* Service Régional de l'INSEE (Sainte-Clothilde, Réunion).

Irigaray, L. 1981. "The Sex which is not one" in E. Marks & I. de Courtivron (eds). op. cit.: 99-106.

Jacquemart, S. 1983. *La Question Départementale Outre-Mer.* CNRS-Presses Universitaires Françaises (Paris).

Jaggar, A. 1983. *Feminist Politics and Human Nature,* Rowman & Allanheld-Harvester (Sussex).

James, C.L.R. 1963. *The Black Jacobins.* 2nd edition. Vintage Books (New York).

James, C.L.R. 1973. "The free coloured in a slave society" in L. Comitas & D. Lowenthal (eds). op. cit.: 95-103.

James, C.L.R. 1984. *C.L.R.James 80th birthday lectures.* Edited by M. Busby & D. Howe. Race Today (London).

Jardel, J-P. 1984. "Identités et Idéologies aux Antilles Françaises: Négrisme, Négritude et Antillanité". *Recherches Socologiques.* Vol. 15. No. 2-3: 209-231.

JCWI. 1992. *Immigration and Nationality Handbook.* Compiled by Sue Shutter. JCWI (London).

JCWI. 1993a. *Policy Review 1992-93.* JCWI (London).

JCWI. 1993b. *Annual Report 1992-93.* JCWI (London).

JCWI. 1994. *Towards Free Movement? Immigration Policy in the European Union after the Maastricht Treaty,* a one-day conference 26.5.1994, Westminster Cathedral Hall, London. Conference Report in *JCWI Bulletin.* Vol. 6, No. 6, Summer.

Jeffers, S. 1992. *Race and Community Involvement: When is Community a bad thing?* Paper presented to annual conference Society for Caribbean Studies, 8 July, Oxford.

Jenkins, B. 1992. *France and the decline of the nation-state.* Paper presented to the annual conference of the Association for the Study of Modern and Contemporary France, 11-13 September (University of Southampton).

Jolivet, M.-J. 1982. *La Question Créole: Essai de Sociologie sur la Guyane Française*. ORSTOM (Paris).

Jolivet, M.-J. 1987. "La construction d'une mémoire historique à la Martinique". *Cahiers d'Etudes Africaines*. Vol. XXVII. Nos. 3-4: 287-309.

Jolivet, M-J. 1990. "Entre autochtones et immigrants: diversité et logique des positions créoles guyanaises". *Etudes Créoles*. Vol. XIII. No. 2: 11-32.

Jolly, M. 1991. "The politics of difference: Feminism, colonialism and decolonisation in Vanuatu" in G. Bottomley *et al.* (eds). op. cit.: 52-74.

Jones, A.R. & P. Stallybrass. 1992. "Dismantling Irena: The Sexualizing of Ireland in Early Modern England" in A. Parker *et al.* (eds). op. cit.: 157-71.

Jones, B. 1989. *Problems of Identity in French Guianese Writing*. Paper presented to the Colloquium on The Three Guyanas. 3-5 May at the Centre for Caribbean Studies, University of Warwick.

Jones, B. & E. Stephenson. 1994. "Politique et Société à la Guyane" in R. Burton & F. Reno (eds). op.cit.: 101-21.

Jones, P. 1991. "Race, discourse and power in institutional housing: the case of immigrant hostels in Lyons" in M. Silverman (ed.) op. cit.: 55-65.

Jos, E. 1994. "La Déclaration du Traité de Maastricht sur les Régions Ultrapériphériques de La Communauté: Essai d'Appréciation" in R. Burton & F. Reno (eds). op. cit.: 255-68.

Kedourie, E. 1984. "A New International Disorder" in H. Bull & A. Watson (eds). op. cit.: 347-55.

Keenan, T. 1987. "The 'Paradox' of Knowledge and Power: Reading Foucault on a bias". *Political Theory*. Vol. 15. No. 1: 5-37.

Kesselman, M. 1985. "The French Communist Party" in P. Cerny & M. Schain (eds). *Socialism, the State and Public Policy in France*. Frances Pinter (London): 42-59.

King, R. 1986. *The State in Modern Society*. Macmillan (Basingstoke).

Kirkpatrick, F. 1985. "From Shackles to Liberation: Religion, the Grimke Sisters and Dissent" in E. Banks Findlay & Y. Hozbeck Haddad (eds). *Women, Religion and Social Change*. State University of New York Press (New York): 433-55.

Klein, H. 1986. *African Slavery in Latin America and the Caribbean*. Oxford University Press (Oxford-New York).

Klen, M. 1992. "Quel avenir pour Réunion?" *Défense Nationale*. Vol. 48. No. 7, July: 149-61.

Kobayashi, A. & L. Peake. 1994. "Unnatural Discourse: 'Race' and Gender in Geography". *Gender, Place and Culture*. Vol. 1. No. 2: 225-43.

Kofman, E. 1993. *When society was simple: the Far and New Right in France on gender and ethnic divisions*. Paper presented to the conference on "Gender, Sexuality and Identity: Commonalities and Differences", LSE, 20 February.

Kovats-Beaudoux, E. 1973. "A Dominant Minority: the White Creoles of Martinique" in L. Comitas & D. Lowenthal (eds). op. cit.: 241-75.

Kristeva, J. 1993. *Nations without Nationalism*. Columbia University Press (New York).

Lacoste, Y. 1991. "Les Territoires de la nation". *Hérodote*. No. 62, July-September: 3-21.

La Guerre, J. 1986. "The Social and Political thought of Aimé Césaire and C.L.R. James: Some Comparisons" in P. Sutton (ed.) op. cit.: 201-22.

Lahouari, A. 1994. *L'Algérie et la démocratie: pouvoir et crise de la politique dans l'Algérie contemporaine*. Editions de la Découverte (Paris).

Landes, D. 1969. *The Unbound Prometheus*. Cambridge University Press (London-New York).

Layton-Henry, Z. 1992. *The Politics of Immigration, 'Race' and 'Race' Relations in Post-War Britain*. Blackwell (Cambridge, Mass.-Oxford).

Leacock, E. 1981. *Myths of Male Dominance: Collected Articles on Women Cross-Culturally*. Monthly Review Press (New York).

Leclerc, A. 1981. "Woman's Word" in E. Marks & I. de Courtivron (eds). op. cit: 79-89.

Le Cointre, G. 1982. "La Population de la Réunion de 1975 à 1985". *L'Economie de la Réunion*. No. 2, June: 3-5.

Leméry, M. 1925. "Nos Vieilles Colonies". *Panorama* (Paris). No. 139, September: 1-34.

Levine, B. 1980. (ed.) *Benjy Lopez: A Picaresque Tale of Emigration and Return*. Basic Books (New York).

Levine, B. 1987. (ed.) *The Caribbean Exodus*. Praeger (London-New York).

Lewis, G. 1963. *Puerto Rico: Freedom and Power in the Caribbean*. Monthly Review Press (London-New York).

Lewis, G.K. 1972. *The Virgin Islands: a Caribbean Lilliput*. Northwestern University Press (Evanston).

Leymarie, P. 1981. *Océan Indien: Le Nouveau Coeur du Monde*. Karthala (Paris).

Lochon, C. 1992. "Le Tribalisme Planétaire". *Panoramique*. No. 5. Special Issue.

Loescher, G. 1993. *Beyond Charity: International Cooperation and the Global Refugee Crisis*. Oxford University Press (New York-Oxford).

Loughlin, J. 1989. *La Guerre d'Algérie et la République une et indivisible.* Paper presented at conference on "France and Algeria: Interacting Identities" 15-17 December, Loughborough.

Lowenthal, D. 1962. "Levels of West Indian Government". *Social and Economic Studies.* Vol. 11. No. 4, December: 363-91.

Lowenthal, D. 1972. *West Indian Societies.* Oxford University Press (London-New York-Toronto).

Lowenthal, D. & C.G. Clarke. 1980. "Island Orphans: Barbuda and the Rest". *The Journal of Commonwealth and Comparative Politics.* Vol. XVIII. No.3, November: 293-307.

Lüthy, H. 1955. *The State of France: a study of contemporary France.* Secker & Warburg (London).

Macartney, A. (ed.) 1984. *Islands of Europe.* Research Centre for Social Studies. University of Edinburgh (Edinburgh).

MacDonald, I. 1983. *Immigration Law and Practice in the United Kingdom.* Butterworths (London).

MacDonald, S. & A. Gastmann. 1984. "Mitterrand's Headache: the French Antilles in the 1980s". *Caribbean Review.* Vol. 13, Spring: 19-21.

McDougall, D. 1993. "The French Caribbean During the Mitterrand Era". *The Journal of Commonwealth and Comparative Politics.* Vol. 31. No. 3, November: 92-110.

MacMaster, N. 1991. "The 'seuil de tolérance'. The uses of a 'scientific' racist concept". in M. Silverman (ed.) op. cit.: 14-28.

McRae, K. 1964. "The structure of Canadian History" in L. Hartz (ed.) op. cit.: 219-34.

Madeley, J., 1982. *Diego Garcia: A Contrast to the Falklands.* Minority Rights Group Report No. 54. MRG (London).

Maestre, J-C. 1976. "L'Indivisibilité de la République Française et l'Exercice du Droit à l'Autodétermination. *Revue de Droit Public at de la Science Politique en France et à l'Etranger.* April-May: 431-61.

Mahmood, T. 1983. *Hand on the Sun.* Penguin (Harmondsworth).

Marks, E. & I. de Courtivron (eds). 1981. *New French Feminisms, an Anthology.* Harvester-Wheatsheaf (London-New York).

Marlow, D. 1992. "Constitutional Change, External Assistance and Economic Development in Small Islands: the Case of Montserrat" in H. Hintjens & M.M. Newitt (eds). op. cit.: 42-50.

Martinez, R.B. 1977. "Independence for Puerto Rico: the Only Solution". *Foreign Affairs.* April: 561-83.

Mason, P. 1970. *Patterns of Dominance.* Institute of Race Relations & Oxford University Press (London-New York-Toronto).

Massiah, J. 1989. "Women's Lives and Livelihoods: A View from the Commonwealth Caribbean". *World Development*. Vol. 17. No. 7: 965-77.

Mathieu, J-L. 1988. *Les DOM TOM*. Presses Universitaires Françaises (Paris).

Mazrui, A. 1981. "Exit Visa from the World System Dilemmas of Cultural and Economic Disengagement". *Third World Quarterly*. Vol. 3. No. 1, January: 62-76.

Mbou, C. 1979. *Le Théâtre d'Aimé Césaire*. Fernand Nathan (Paris).

Meissner D.M. *et al.* 1993. *International Migration Challenges in a New Era*. A Report to the Trilateral Commission. (New York-Paris-Tokyo).

Memmi, A. 1979. *La Dépendance: Esquisse pour un portrait du dépendant*. Gallimard (Paris).

Memmi, A. 1990. *The Coloniser and the Colonised*. Earthscan (London).

Memmi, A. 1991. "Mechanisms of Oppression-Interview with A. Memmi" in M. Silverman (ed.) op. cit.: 29-39.

Mendès-France, B. 1972. "La Réunion à travers ses comptes économiques". *Les Cahiers de la Réunion*. No. 1, November: 7-20.

Meyer, N. 1987. "De Passy à Barbès: Deux Visages du Vote Le Pen à Paris". *Revue Française de Science Politique*. Vol. 37. No. 6, December: 891-906.

Mies, M. 1989. "Self-Determination: the End of a Utopia?" *Review of Feminist Research* (Montreal). Vol. 18. No. 3: 51-5.

Mies, M., V. Bennholdt-Thomsen & C. Von Werlhof. 1988. *Women, the Last Colony*. Zed Press (London).

Miller, M. 1986. "Policy Ad Hocracy: The Paucity of Co-ordinated Perspectives and Policies". *Annals*. Vol. 485: 64-75.

Miras, C. 1987. "L'Economie Martiniquaise: Croissance ou Excroissance?". *Etudes Créoles*. Vol. 9. No. 2: 12-33.

Mishan, E.J. 1988. "What Future for a Multi-Racial Britain?" *The Salisbury Review*. June: 18-24.

Moore, R. & T. Wallace. 1975. *Slamming the Door: the Administration of Immigration Control in the UK*. Robertson (London).

Morisset. J. 1985. "La fin de l'Amérique Française et Saint Pierre-et-Miquelon". *Hérodote*. Nos. 2-3: 261-8.

Morse, R.M. 1964. "The Heritage of Latin America" in L. Hartz (ed.) op. cit.: 123-77.

Moutoussamy, E. 1988. *Les DOM-TOM: Enjeux Géopolitiques Economiques et Stratégiques*. L'Harmattan (Paris).

Mpumlwana, N.F.T. 1992. "On True Liberation". *Echoes*. No. 2: 18-20.

Munroe, T. 1972. *The Politics of Constitutional Decolonisation: Jamaica 1944-62*. Institute of Social and Economic Research, University of the West Indies (Jamaica).

Muntarbhom, V. 1989. "Current Challenges of Human Rights in Asia", in D. Hill (ed.) op. cit.: 180-200.

Muxel, A. 1988. "Les Attitudes Socio-Politiques des Femmes Issues de l'Immigration Maghrébine en Région Parisienne". *Revue Française de Science Politique*. Vol. 38. No. 6, December: 925-41.

Nabajoth, E. 1985. "Le Système Politique d'Une Société de Plantation? Le Cas Guadeloupéen". *Annuaire des Pays d'Amerique Centrale et des Caraïbes*. (Aix-Marseille III). No. 5: 141-55.

Najjar, O.A. 1992. "Between Nationalism and Feminism: the Palestinian Answer" in J. Bystydzienski (ed.) *Women Transforming Politics: Worldwide Strategies for Empowerment*. Indiana University Press (Bloomington).

Nicolas, N. 1973. *L'Opinion Publique Martiniquaise devant la loi d'Assimilation de 1946*. Mémoire de Maîtrise. Université Paris I.

Oakley, A. 1981. *Subject Women*. Martin Robertson (Oxford).

O'Neill, O. 1992. "Justice, gender and international boundaries" in R. Attfield & B. Wilkins (eds). op. cit.: 50-76.

Oraison, A. 1978. *Le Parti Communiste Réunionnais et l'Autonomie Démocratique et Populaire*. Centre Universitaire de la Réunion (St Denis, Reunion).

Oraison, A. & F. Miclo. 1978. "A Qui Appartient le Récif de Tromelin?" *Annuaire des Pays de l'Océan Indien*. Vol. 5: 263-272.

Orwell, G. 1984. *The Collected Essays of George Orwell. Volume 4: 1945-50*. Penguin (Harmondsworth).

O'Shaugnessy, M. 1993. "New and Old Racisms: the same old integration". *Modern and Contemporary France*. New series No. 1: 55-60.

Ousmane, S. 1986. *God's Bits of Wood*. Heinemann (London).

Owers, A. 1994. "The Age of Internal Controls" in S. Spencer (ed.) op. cit.: 264-81.

Parant, F. 1991. "Commercialisation et utilisation des Bois Guyanais". *Les Dossiers de l'Outre-Mer*. No. 81: 32-42.

Parekh, B. 1994. "Three theories of immigration" in S. Spencer (ed.) op. cit.: 91-110.

Parker, A. *et al.* (eds). 1992. *Nationalisms and Sexualities*. Routledge (London-New York).

Pasquet, C. & R. Squarzoni. 1988. *Les femmes à la Réunion: une évolution impressionnante, une situation ambigue*. Observatoire Economique de la Réunion. INSEE (Ste-Clothilde, Reunion).

Payne, A. 1984. *The International Crisis in the Caribbean*. Johns Hopkins Press (Baltimore).

Payne, A. & P. Sutton. 1993. *The Off-Limits Caribbean. The United States and the European Dependencies*. Paper presented to the Annual Conference, Society for Caribbean Studies, 6-8 July (Oxford).

Perinbaum, M. 1982. *Holy Violence: the Revolutionary Thought of Frantz Fanon*. Three Continents Press (Washington).

Petty, C. & N. Hodge. 1987. *Anguilla's Battle for Freedom, 1967*. Petnat Publishing (Anguilla).

Phillips, C. 1987. *The European Tribe*. Faber & Faber (London).

Philpott, S. 1973. *West Indian Migration: the Montserrat Case*. Athlone Press (London).

Plantey, A. "De Gaulle et la Décolonisation". *Revue Juridique et Politique*. Vol. 37. No. 3, June: 574-83.

Powell, E. 1968. *Still to Decide*. Elliot Right Way (Kingswood, Surrey).

Prager, E. 1992. *Eve's Tattoo*. Chatto & Windus (London).

Ram, K. 1991. "Moving in from the margins: Gender at the centre of cultural contestation of power relations in South India" in G. Bottomley *et al.* (eds). op. cit.: 1-13.

Randall, C. 1994. "An asylum policy for the UK" in S. Spencer (ed.) op. cit.: 202-31.

Rapaport, J. 1971. *Small States and Territories*. UNITAR-Arno Press (New York).

Reno, F. 1993. *Les départements français de la Caraïbe et l'Europe*. Paper presented to the Annual Conference, Society for Caribbean Studies, 6-8 July (Oxford).

Reno, F. 1994. "Politique et Société à la Martinique" in R. Burton & F. Reno (eds). op. cit.: 65-83.

Rex, J. & S. Tomlinson. 1979. *Colonial Immigrants in a British City*. Routledge & Kegan Paul (London).

Richardson, B. 1983. *Caribbean Migrants: Environment and Human Survival on St Kitts*. University of Tenessee Press (Knoxville).

Rivera-Ramos, E. 1991. "Self-Determination and Decolonisation in the Society of the Modern Welfare State" in W. Twining (ed.) op. cit.: 115-32.

Robinson, K. 1954. "Alternatives to Independence". *Political Studies*. Vol. 4. No. 3: 225-49.

Robinson, K. 1984. "Colonialism French style 1945-55: a Retrospective Overview". *Journal of Imperial and Commonwealth History*. Vol. XII. No. 2, January: 24-41.

Romose, M.B. 1991. "Self-Determination in Decolonisation" in W. Twining (ed.) op. cit.: 25-32.

Rose, H. & S. Rose. 1986. "Less than Human Nature: Biology and the New Right". *Race and Class*. Vol. 27. No. 3, Winter: 47-66.

Ross, G. 1987. "*Adieu vieilles idées*: the middle strata and the decline of Resistance-Liberation Left Discourse in France" in J. Howarth & G. Ross (eds). *Contemporary France. A Review of Interdisciplinary Studies*. Frances Pinter (London).

Royle, S. 1991. "The world's remaining colonies - tugging at the apron strings". *Geographical Magazine*. Vol. 63. No. 6: 14-16.

Rozario, S. 1991. "Ethno-religious communities and gender divisions in Bangladesh: women as boundary markers" in G. Bottomley *et al.* (eds). op. cit.: 14-32.

Sablé, V. 1955. *La Transformation des Iles d'Amérique en Départements Français*. Larose (Paris).

Sablé, V. 1972. *Les Antilles sans Complexes*. Maisonneuve & Larose (Paris).

Sachdeva, S. 1993. *The Primary Purpose Rule in British Immigration Law*. Trentham Books (London).

Sayers, J. 1982. *Biological Politics, Feminist and Anti-Feminist Perspectives*. Tavistock (London-New York).

Schain, M. 1986. *Racial Politics in France: the National Front and the Construction of Political Legitimacy*. Paper presented to the annual conference of the Political Studies Association, 8-10 April (Nottingham).

Scherm, G. 1987. "The Guyanan Countries". *Applied Geography and Development*. Vol. 29: 27-43.

Schwarzbeck, F. 1982. "La Guyane: un Département Français Comme Les Autres?" *Amérique Latine*. No. 12, December: 3-11.

Schwarzbeck, F. 1986. "Guyana, A Department like the Others?" in P. Sutton (ed.) op. cit.: 171-87.

Scruton, R. 1980. *The Meaning of Conservatism*. Penguin (Harmondsworth).

Seers, D. 1980. "Theoretical Aspects of Unequal Development at Different Spatial Levels" in D. Seers & C. Vaitsos (eds). *Integration and Unequal Development: the Experience of the EEC*. Macmillan (London).

Shiva, V. 1992. "Women, Ecology and Health: an Introduction". *Development Dialogue*. Nos. 1-2: 3-12.

Shivji, I. 1991. "The Right of Peoples to Self-Determination: an African Perspective" in W. Twining (ed.) op. cit.: 33-48.

Siedel, G. 1986. "Culture, Nation and 'Race' in the British and French New Right" in R. Levitas (ed.) *The Ideology of the New Right*. Basil Blackwell-Polity Press (Oxford).

Siedel, G. 1990. "The French National Front Family at Home to the Public". *Modern and Contemporary France*. No. 41, April: 39-42.

Silverman, M. (ed.) 1991. *Race, Discourse and Power in France*. Avebury Press (Aldershot).

Silverman, M. 1992. *Deconstructing the Nation: Immigration, Racism and Citizenship in Modern France*. Routledge (London-New York).

Smouts, M-C. 1983. "The External Policy of Francois Mitterrand". *International Affairs*. Vol. 59. No. 2, Spring: 155-67.

Souquet-Basiège, G. 1979. *Le Préjugé de Race aux Antilles Françaises; Etude Historique*. Désormeaux (Fort de France, Martinique).

Spencer, S. (ed.). 1994. *Strangers and Citizens, A Positive Approach to Migrants and Refugees*. IPPR-River Oram Press (London).

Spillman, G. 1981. *De l'Empire à l'Hexagone: Colonisation et Décolonisation*. Librairie Perrin (Paris).

St Helena. 1989a. A/AC.109/978. Report of United Nations Sub-Committee on Small Territories. 2 March.

St Helena. 1989b. A/AC.109/L1696. Report of United Nations Sub-Committee on Small Territories. 30 June.

Stagner, R. 1987. "Foreword" in J. Boucher *et al.* (eds). op. cit.: 7-16.

Stanyer, J. n.d. Lecture notes for course in Public Administration. Department of Politics. University of Exeter.

Stenhouse, T. 1990. "France and Algeria: Interacting Identities". *Modern and Contemporary France*. No. 41: 36-9.

Stephenson, E. 1978. "Déterminisme Historique et Cohésion Sociale. Une Approche de la Société Guyanaise". *Equinoxe*. No. 7, April-June: 23-37.

Storey, A. 1991. *Changing Eastern Europe: Implications for Third World Migrants and Refugees*. Paper presented to the annual Development Studies Associates Conference, 11-13 September (Swansea).

Storey, A. 1993. *An Outsider Looking In, an Insider Looking Out: Irish and EC Asylum Policy*. Paper presented to Trocaire seminar. Dublin, 5 March.

Storey, H. 1994. "International Law and Human Rights Obligations" in S. Spencer (ed.) op. cit.: 111-36.

Straubhaar, T. 1988. "International Labour Migration within a Common Market: some aspects of EC Experience". *Journal of Common Market Studies*. Vol. XXVII. No. 1, September: 45-62.

Sutton, P. (ed.). 1986. *Dual Legacies in the Contemporary Caribbean: Aspects of British and French Dominion*. Frank Cass (London).

Szondi, E. 1991. "Black Women and Europe 1992". *Feminist Review*. No.39, Winter: 189-92.

Taguieff, P-A. *et al.* 1991. *Face au Racisme*. La Découverte (Paris).

Tal, I. 1976. *Les Réunionnais en France*. Editions Entente (Paris).

Tarche, M. 1985. "L'Agriculture Guyanaise: Bilan et Perspectives". *Les Dossiers de l'Outre-Mer*. No. 81: 8-13.

Taylor, P. 1989. *The Narratives of Liberation Perspectives on Afro-Caribbean Literature, Popular Culture and Politics*. Cornell University Press (Ithaca-London).

Techer, A. 1983. *Le Bumidom et la Migration Réunionnaise*. Internal document, Agence Nationale du Travail, November (Paris).

Terkel, S. 1992. *Race*. Minerva (London).

*Third World Quarterly*. 1979. "South-South Dialogue: A Brief Report". Vol. 1. No. 2, April: 117-22.

Thorndike, T. 1987. "When small is not beautiful: the case of the Turks & Caicos Islands". *Corruption and Reform*. Vol. 2. No. 3: 259-65.

Thorndike, T. 1989. "The future of the British Caribbean Dependencies". *Journal of Interamerican Studies and World Affairs*. Vol. 31. No. 3, Autumn: 117-40.

Thornton, A. 1978. *Imperialism in the Twentieth Century*. University of Minnesota Press (Minneapolis).

Thürer, D. 1987. "The Right of Self-Determination of Peoples". *Law and State*. Vol. 35: 22-39.

Tinker, H. 1977. *Race, Conflict and the International Order*. Macmillan (London).

Trouillot, M-R. 1988. *Peasants and Capital. Dominica in the World Economy*. Johns Hopkins Press (Baltimore-London).

Turner, B. 1989. "From Orientalism to Global Sociology". *Sociology*. Vol. 23. No. 4, November: 629-38.

Turner, B. 1990. "Outline of a Theory of Citizenship". *Sociology*. Vol. 24: 189-217.

Turpin, I. 1979. *La Spécificité des Institutions Départementales d'Outre-Mer*. Mémoire in Law. Université Aix-Marseille III.

Twining, W. (ed.). 1991. *Issues of Self-Determination*. Aberdeen University Press (Aberdeen).

Van Den Berghe, P.L. 1981. *The Ethnic Phenomenon*. Elsevier Press (New York).

Verbunt, G. 1985. "France" in T. Hammar (ed.) *European Immigration Policy*. Cambridge University Press (Cambridge): 127-64.

Vié, E. 1978. *Faut-il abandonner les DOM?* Economica (Paris).

Wa Thiong'o, N. 1986. *Decolonising the Mind: The Politics of Language in African Literature.* James Currey (London).

Walker, I. 1986. *Zaffer Pe Sanze: Ethnic Identity and Social Change Among the Ilois in Mauritius.* KMLI (Port Louis, Mauritius).

Webster, R. 1987. *Scrapbook of Anguilla's Revolution.* Seabreakers Ltd. (Anguilla).

Westlake, D. 1972. *Under an English Heaven.* Hodder & Stoughton (London).

White, R. 1990. *Heroes through the Day.* New Beacon Books (Birmingham).

Williams, T. 1984. "The Message of the Bombs". *Caribbean & West Indies Chronicle.* No. 99, April-May: 6-7.

Winchester, S. 1985. *Outposts.* Hodder & Stoughton (Auckland-London-Sydney-Toronto).

Withol de Wenden, C. 1991. "North African Immigration and the French Political Imaginary" in M. Silverman (ed.) op. cit.: 95-108.

Wolf, E. 1988. "Inventing Society". *American Ethnologist.* Vol. 15. No. 4: 752-61.

Wolff, E. 1991. *Quartiers de Vie: Approche ethnologique des populations défavorisées de l'ile de la Réunion.* Meridien (Paris).

Women and Geography Study Group of the IBG. 1984. *Geography and Gender: An Introduction to feminist geography.* Hutchinson (London).

Young, R. 1994. "Post-colonial theory". *Wasafiri.* No. 20, Autumn: 77-8.

Zwerin, M. 1976. *A Case for the Balkanisation of Practically Everyone: the new nationalism.* Wildwood House (London).

## Main Magazines & Newspapers consulted

*Année Politique.* (Paris).

*Caribbean Insight.* (Paris-London).

*Combat Réunionnais.* (Paris).

*L'Economie de la Réunion.* (INSEE, Reunion).

*Economist.* (London).

*Le Figaro.* (Paris).

*Guardian.* (London-Manchester).

*Im'média.* Monthly newsletter, L'Agence de l'Immigration et des cultures urbaines, 164 rue St Maur, 75011 (Paris).

*Independent.* (London).

*Indian Ocean Newsletter (Lettre de l'Océan Indien)*. (Paris).
*JCWI Annual Report/Bulletins*. Joint Council for the Welfare of Immigrants, 110 Old Street, London EC4.
*JORFAN*. Journal Officiel de la République Française. Débats de l'Assemblée Nationale. National Assembly Debates. (Paris).
*Libération*. (Paris).
*Le Monde, Le Monde Diplomatique & Le Monde Hebdomadaire*. (Paris).
*Plein Droit*. Journal of GISTI (Groupement d'Information et de Soutien aux Travailleurs Immigrés, 30 rue des Petites Ecuries, Paris 75010.
*Le Point*. (Paris).
*Politis*. (Paris).
*Quotidien de la Réunion*. (Reunion).
*Témoignages*. Daily of the Reunionnese Communist Party (Reunion).
*The Times & Sunday Times*. (London).


**Interviews and Media**

Amrani, Fadila. 1993. Interview with representative of France Terre d'Asile. Paris, 14 April.
Bramble, Howard. 1990. Interview with local historian and politician. Montserrat, 21 March.
Canty, B.G.J. (OBE). 1990. Interview with Governor of Anguilla, 30 March.
Devacht, Michel. 1993. Interview with representative of CFDT Union on matters relating to Immigrant workers. Paris, 14 April.
Fergus, Howard (Dr) 1990. Interview with Acting Governor. Montserrat, 23 March.
Figueroa, John. 1990. Intervention in a conference on The Three Guyanas, Centre for Caribbean Studies. University of Warwick, 1 May.
GISTI. 1993. Inteviews with staff, including J-P Alaux, Patrick Mony, Claire Rodier. Paris, April.
Gumbs, Emile. Interview with Chief Minister of Anguilla, 30 March.
Harrigan, Atlin. 1990. Interview with local doctor. Anguilla, 31 March.
Harrigan, Carl. 1990. Interview with Official, Ministry of Finance. Anguilla, 30 March.
Henocque, Chantal. 1993. Interview with representative of parapublic Social Work Agency (SSAE). Paris, 16 April.
Hughes, Hubert. 1990. Interview with Leader of the Opposition. Anguilla, 30 March.

JCWI. 1992. Interviews with staff, including Don Flynn, Belayeth Hussain, Nirmala Rajasingham, Dawn Richards, Sue Shutter, August.

Jordan, Kenneth. 1989. Official with United Nations Committee for Decolonisation in New York. Intervention in conference on The Political Economy of Small, Tropical Islands. University of Exeter, September.

Kone, Aminata. 1993. Interview with representative of Confédération Syndicale des Familles. Paris, 15 April.

Legros, Auguste. 1988. Interview with mayor of St Denis. Reunion, 5 December.

Oraison, André. 1988. Interviews and discussions in Reunion island, November-December.

Patel, Krishna. 1988. Interview with Consul of India in Reunion island, 1 December.

Payet, Jean. 1988. Interview with representative of Chamber of Commerce and Industry of Reunion, 30 November.

South African Consul. 1988. Interview in Reunion island, 22 November.

Southey, Hugh. 1993. Interview with immigration advice lawyer. London, 19 February.

Tavernier, Bertrand, 1992. The Undeclared War. Video of testimony by French veterans of the Algerian war of independence. BBC2, 18 April. Also review in *Guardian*, 18 April.

Tual, Jacques. 1988. Interview with University lecturer, Reunion. 28 November.

Turner, Stephen. 1989. Interview with official from the Indian Ocean Islands Section, East Africa Department (FCO). London, 20 January.

Webster, Ronald. 1990. Interview with former Premier of Anguilla, 31 March.

Wijesinghe, Sarath. 1993. Interview with immigration advice lawyer. London, 18 February.

# Index